This space is
for the use of Public Libraries

THE
TRAMWAYS
OF
CROYDON

South Metropolitan No. 50 at the Low Level Station stop. Anerley Hill and the Crystal Palace loom large behind the car and the station is in the third turning on the right. Very little of this scene remains. (Photo C. H. Price

The Tramways of Croydon

By
G. E. BADDELEY, B.Com., M.C.I.T.

Published in London by
THE LIGHT RAIL TRANSIT ASSOCIATION
13A The Precinct, Broxbourne, Herts FN10 7HY

In conjunction with
THE TRAMWAY & LIGHT RAILWAY SOCIETY.

1983

Printed by W. J. Ray & Co. Ltd., Warewell Street,
Walsall, West Midlands WS1 2HQ.

ISBN: 0 900433 90 6

Single Deck horse car No. 8 at South Croydon. (London Transport

CONTENTS

Page

continued overleaf

BIBLIOGRAPHY

Annual reports of Croydon Corporation.

Annual reports of the South Metropolitan Electric Tramways & Lighting Company Limited.

Garcke's Manual of Electrical Undertakings.

Tramway & Railway World (later known as "Transport World").

Electric Tramway & Light Railway Journal (later known as "Passenger Transport")

Cassier's Magazine, New York.

Various Chief Inspecting Officer's Reports to the Board of Trade.

Applications to the Board of Trade for loans to construct tramways.

Five Decades of B.E.T., by Roger Fulford.

Modern Tramway.

Tramway Review.

"Penny Fare" (later known as "London Transport Magazine").

"Croydon Advertiser".

"Croydon Times".

Transports Publics à Londres, a thesis by Noel Monod, Paris 1934.

"The Herald", Carshalton.

"Southbound from Croydon" by J. T. King and A. G. Newman, London 1965.

London Transport Tramways Handbook, by D. W. Willoughby and E. R. Oakley, Dartford 1978.

"MetropolitaN" (Tramways (M.E.T.) Omnibus Co. Ltd.) G. J. Robbins, Omnibus Society, London 1977.

"The Great Days", Croydon Airport 1928-1939, by D. Cluett, J. Nash and R. Learmonth, London.

"Rails through the Clay" by A. A. Jackson and D. F. Croome, London 1962.

"A History of London Transport" by T. C. Barker and Michael Robbins, (Two Volumes), London 1963 & 1974.

6

INTRODUCTION TO THE FIRST EDITION

I have been asked to write an introductory chapter in this book, not an historical account, which will be found elsewhere, but just a few personal memories of the trams of the Croydon area as I knew them.

My very first recollection is of a visit we paid to friends at Purley, when I was still a small boy. We were living in Malden and the first part of the journey was simple enough, on an electric train of the London and South Western Railway to Wimbledon. Here we changed to the London, Brighton and South Coast train to West Croydon, a very different affair from the electric trains of today, running at regular intervals; the service at that time was rather infrequent and irregular—one had to look up the timetable and go to catch a particular train. The train consisted of three very ancient four-wheeled carriages and one more sumptuous vehicle (by comparison) on six wheels, almost exclusively reserved for the first class passengers—if any!

On reaching West Croydon, we boarded a Croydon Corporation tram for the last part of the journey, to the terminus at Purley. I had looked forward to a ride on the top deck, excellent for sight-seeing, but unfortunately, it was a wet day and we had to travel inside. (This was long before Croydon had any cars with covered top decks.) My recollections are, perhaps for this reason, somewhat more vivid than would otherwise be the case—with nothing much to look at in the way of scenery, I had more time to study the car itself. I remember the rather elaborate interior decoration, the ceiling of white lincrusta—an ancestor of the modern plastic styles and also the mirrors halfway up the stairs. These enabled passengers to see each other coming, so to speak and also helped the conductor to see when all had alighted. Such fittings are practically standard on all buses, but the trams pioneered them many years earlier.

The services to Purley were then two in number, from Norbury and from Thornton Heath alternately, giving a double service from Thornton Heath Pond, where the bus garage now stands (alas, like the trams, the pond is now no more), through Croydon to Purley. For our purposes, either car would do, but on subsequent visits on Bank Holidays or similar occasions, we found it better at Purley, to take a Thornton Heath car, as being less crowded than those for Norbury, which met the London County Council trams there.

Somewhat later in life, I received a camera for a birthday present, and some of my earliest efforts at tram photography, were at Purley terminus, to the great interest of the crew of the tram in question, who had never been photographed before! Subsequent exploration extended to the Addiscombe route, with a motorman posing himself and his car specially for me at the terminus.

My attention next turned to the other tramway undertaking in Croydon, a small system, which went far to atone for its lack of size, by what, I think, must have been the longest name ever inflicted on a British tramway system—"The South Metropolitan Electric Tramways and Lighting Company Limited". This mouthful required two full lines on the sides of the four-wheeled cars to accommodate it! I again approached the target area by train from Wimbledon, this time as far as Mitcham. A short walk brought me to the Cricket Green and the tram terminus there disused for some years, but I followed the rails to the Fair Green in time to see a car just leaving for Croydon. It was one of the original British Electric Traction Co.'s cars, rather like the London United ones, which served Malden and round-about, which also had two short, straight staircases in place of the more usual curved type. While the

7

London United cars were blue and cream, or later red and white, the S.M.E.T. cars of the type mentioned were chocolate brown and deep cream, rather like the London County Council cars. The rest of the fleet were in a green and yellow livery, except a few from a system at Gravesend, which were dark crimson and cream.

Returning to my visit to Mitcham, I caught the next car to Croydon, and after a brief look at the Croydon trams, I came back the same way, occupying the favourite seat of the tram enthusiast, the right-hand side front, inside, giving a fine view of the driver in action and the approaching scenery, other trams, etc. At one place the track was being relaid and the watchman with the approach of dusk, had just set out the usual array of red lamps. One of these it seemed was a bit too near the centre of things, for as my car sped by, there was a most satisfying crash and a tinkle of broken glass; the driver looked back, but apparently feeling that what's done is done, kept going, leaving the permanent way department short of one lamp.

Later on I tracked down, if that is the right expression, the Sutton terminus, which was in a side turning off the main street by the Grapes Hotel. The trolleybuses now come out here and continue to Bushey Road near the bus garage, there being no room for them to turn at the Grapes. The Sutton cars were of a type I had never seen before on four wheels, but longer than any others I knew, with a very long wheelbase and a very big square, impressive looking axleboxes, which were quite easy to see from the top deck if you leaned over the rail. There were a number of sharp curves on the Sutton route, at the top and bottom of Ringstead Road, in Wallington and so on, which seemed to suggest cars of a shorter wheelbase might have been better. However, they seemed to get on all right, although in the early days, a car overturned at Carlshalton. It was not one of the long cars as it happens and the reason was not very clear as to why it happened at all. The accident occurred on a hill, but only quite a gentle slope, there were much steeper hills, such as Ringstead Road, which seemed much more likely places for such an accident.

Then exploration took me to the last line, that to the Crystal Palace, which ended in the very long, steep climb up the hill to the Palace; the Crystal Palace itself was there then, not just a name as it is today. As a safety precaution, the cars went straight up the hill without a stop, at the foot of the steep climb there was a special stop marked "Last Stop before the Crystal Palace". On the descent, there were two compulsory stops fairly close together, to test the brakes and ensure that cars were always well under control and able to stop quickly, as a runaway on the hill might well have been a spectacular disaster. The nearest approach to such an accident, so far as I know, happened in the 1920's to a car climbing the hill. One of the steam driven road lorries, that were so common then, was climbing up to the Palace towing a trailer, when the coupling broke and the trailer ran back very fast and very much out of control. The tram driver, coming up the hill, saw this juggernaut racing straight down towards his tram and with great presence of mind reversed it and let it run back down the hill chased by the runaway. The conductor locked the door into the saloon to prevent the passengers from panicking and jumping off the speeding car. Fortunately there was not another car coming up the hill, the runaway was, of course, on the wrong track. At length the trailer hit the kerb and overturned. The tram resumed the climb and the passengers got quite a bit of extra travel, without extra charge. I think there was a presentation later on, to the two tram men, for their presence of mind, in averting what might have been a serious accident.

Earlier, I mentioned the derelict tram line from the Fair Green to the Cricket Green at Mitcham. This seems, when it was in use, to have been worked by a single tram, which just ran to and fro over a quarter of a mile, now forming the start of the 152 bus route among others. In the light of present-day conditions, this service seems quite useless and it was withdrawn in World War One, to save man-power. (It was, of course, part of a much larger project which never materialised). On one of my visits, I noticed that the disused tram standards were all being repainted with aluminium paint, a hopeful sign. Not very long afterwards, the London County Council trams began to run through from their former terminus at Tooting, to Mitcham Cricket Green. The SouthmeT trams for Croydon, now started from the junction at Fair Green, and this working continued until after the formation of the

London Passenger Transport Board, when the long through route from Willesden to West Croydon was instituted. For some time before the Board was formed, the SouthmeT fleet had been reinforced by a number of bogie covered top cars from my own system, the London United. (I mean that I had always lived on it, not that it belonged to me!) The arrival of the London United cars at West Croydon was an interesting development since, originally, the Tooting-Croydon line was to have been built by the L.U.T. They got as far as building a depot at Merton, near Colliers Wood tube station, and their line which ended at the London Boundary, would have continued on along Longley Road, Merton, to Tooting Junction, thence along the route as built and also on other lines to Sutton, etc., never constructed. The Longley Road line would have entailed very sharp curves at each end, especially at Tooting Junction. Anyhow, the L.U.T. cars did get to West Croydon, even if not on their own rails, and they also ran as well on the Sutton line from time to time, forming rather a sharp contrast to the long, open-top four-wheelers belonging to the company. An earlier group of visitors, though they became a permanency, were a few unusual looking trams belonging to the Gravesend & Northfleet Tramways Co., in Kent. They were too large for their home town, and found their way to other companies controlled by the B.E.T. Group, four coming to the SouthmeT. (Four others went to Swansea and two to Jarrow). Like the other SouthmeT bogie cars, they had reversed trucks, i.e. the small wheels were at the ends and the big ones in the centre, the opposite way round to the usual arrangement for bogie trams. They also had reversed stairs, curving outwards over the driver's head, an arrangement that was discarded in London at quite an early date, and five windows a side, instead of the more usual four or six.

In the later days of Croydon, before London Transport took over, the Corporation seemed to me to lose some of its original character; the Addiscombe line was closed, and the main line—Norbury to Purley—now formed part of long route to London, it was largely worked by London County Council cars and Croydon Corporation bought a new fleet of cars to go with them—almost the same to the average passenger, but the colour scheme was a little different and the expert could tell them at once by one or two other small features, but to the rest, the old uniqueness was gone. The Corporation's open-top bogie cars were still to be seen, running from Thornton Heath only as far as South Croydon, and even they were now a little different as the tops had been covered in and painted in a strange red and grey livery. With the coming of London Transport, changes were fast; the small Croydon cars disappeared, and the SouthmeT routes went over to trolleybuses. Only the big cars from London remained—the L.C.C. and the Croydon ones painted alike in the Board's livery. Now these too are gone, replaced not even by trolley-buses, but by seemingly small motor buses. So I feel I can end my recollections here, with the end of the trams. They may, I hope, recall the trams of Croydon to those who knew them, and give a slight idea of them to the others, who, because of their youth, or for other reasons, never saw them in the flesh as it were—or should it be on the rails.

George L. Gundry.

New Malden.
16th October, 1958.

9

INTRODUCTION TO SECOND EDITION

The first edition of this book "The Tramways of Croydon" appeared in 1960 and was the first of a series of books dealing with tramway systems in the London area. None of those involved had very much experience in researching and writing a book, but were greatly encouraged and assisted by the late J. W. Fowler, President of the Light Railway Transport League and himself a printer by profession.

Since that time, one of the original authors, Ron Harmer, who wrote the chapter about the Corporation Tramways has passed away, but Reginald Durrant, Richard Elliot and George Gundry have willingly co-operated in the preparation of this second edition. Unfortunately, others, although not named as authors, but who were closely associated with the production of the first edition, have also died, in particular Frank Merton Atkins, Walter Gratwicke, O. J. Morris, J. Pelham Maitland and G. D. Morgan of Croydon Corporation Tramways.

However, many others not named in the first edition, have since come forward with much additional information and pointed out to the authors, other sources not previously known to them. These include M. C. Beamish of London Transport Museum, L. C. Plowman, E. Dawes, H. Ellis, N. D. W. Elston, J. R. Falconer, J. B. Gent, R. F. Makewell, J. H. Meredith, R. J. Misson, E. R. Oakley, C. L. Withey and the members of the Publications Committees of the Light Rail Transit Association and the Tramway and Light Railway Society, especially G. B. Claydon and J. H. Price. J. C. Gillham must be thanked for updating his map used as an end paper and Brian Connelly for the remainder of the artwork.

Over the last few years, a great deal of additional information has come to light, largely from sources that were not available in 1960. For example, the Public Record Office which had a quite incomprehensible indexing system when at Chancery Lane, completely revised and rationalised the system on moving to Kew, resulting in many reports and inventories coming to light, whose existence had not been suspected before. The writers have also received much help from the British Library at Colindale and from Croydon Public Library, particularly from A. P. Glover and Mrs. D. J. R. Garrett. The present writer worked in the Chief Secretary's Office of London Transport during the last ten years, where he handled many deeds and other documents relating to acquired undertakings. He is grateful to A. G. Shaw, the Assistant Secretary for information about the London & Suburban Traction Co. Ltd. and to G. C. Hedge. In fact so much additional information has come to hand and so many more doors opened to us, that practically every fact quoted in this second edition has been verified from official documents. Miss J. Broughton of Sutton Public Library, D. W. K. Jones, F. P. Groves and L. S. Woolf must be thanked for some additional items.

A number of old South Metropolitan fare tables and other details were loaned to the authors, resulting in the chapter on Fares and Tickets being completely re-written by A. W. McCall, with the kind co-operation of R. J. Durrant. Rolling Stock details have been rechecked by R. Elliott and J. H. Price. We must also thank W. J. Ray & Co. Ltd., and their binders for the preparation of this book, and all those who have kindly loaned photographs for reproduction. Every effort has been made to give all credits correctly and the authors tender their humble apologies for any given wrongly or omitted.

Geoffrey E. Baddeley.

Croydon.
August, 1982.

10

CHAPTER ONE
THE PRE-ELECTRIFICATION ERA

Croydon, an old market town, lies on the edge of the North Downs, on the main London to Brighton road and its name is probably derived from the Anglo-Saxon word Crog-Daene meaning Crooked Valley, being applied to the valley extending southwards from Croydon, through Purley to Caterham and Godstone. The earliest reference to a hamlet on the site of Croydon dates from 962 A.D. For eight hundred years, the Archbishops of Canterbury had a palace in Croydon, but in 1758, they moved, finishing up at Addington. One of these Primates, Archbishop Whitgift, founded the Almshouse bearing his name in 1596, and this fine building still stands on the corner of North End and George Street in the centre of the town.

Throughout the tramway era, the well known school, also named after Archbishop Whitgift, stood back from North End, a short distance north of the Almshouses.

The nineteenth century centre of the town was made up of narrow cobbled streets, flanked on either side by overhanging timbered houses. Croydon has many public houses with quaint or picturesque names, those with nautical names relate to the Croydon Canal, which before the advent of the railways linked Croydon with London, branching off the Surrey Canal at New Cross Gate and extending to near the present West Croydon Station. One of the more quaintly named public houses, is the "Swan and Sugar Loaf" on the main road at South Croydon. It is said to have originally borne the name of a bishop, but as years went by, the sign outside became so faded that his outstretched arm and crook resembled a swan and his mitre a sugar loaf (a pile of caster sugar in the days when it was sold loose).

There was little public transport on the roads until the latter part of the nineteenth century, stage coaches served long distance traffic and carriers served local areas. On the other hand, private transport in the form of carriages and trader's own carts proliferated among those who could afford them. Few roads were paved and repaired by tipping loose stones into pot holes, these being broken up to a suitable size by the able bodied paupers in the workhouse.

Croydon was very early in the field of railed transport. The Surrey Iron Railway from Wandsworth to Croydon opened in 1803 and was extended to Merstham in 1805. However, neither this railway nor the canal was designed to carry passengers. Both carried freight only, with horses as the motive power. However, by the 1860s, when a need for local public transport began to be felt, Croydon was already well served by the main line railway companies, there being over a dozen stations within the Borough and no less than three hundred trains to London each day.

11

Croydon became a Borough in 1883 and a County Borough in 1888. With the revision of local authority boundaries in the London area in 1965*. Croydon, formerly in Surrey, became a London Borough within the area of the Greater London Council, its own boundaries being extended to include Purley at the same time. As a County Borough, Croydon had an area of 19.7 square miles and in 1959 a population of 249,500. Although physically a part of Greater London for many years before that title was adopted officially, Croydon still maintains much of the individuality of a separate town.

The first reference to a proposal for a tramway linking Croydon with London was recorded on 22 December 1868, but the first tramway to actually be built in London opened in 1870 and a Bill was placed before Parliament in 1872, entitled the London, Streatham and Croydon Tramways, which would have been an extension of the London to Brixton line of the London Tramways Co. (that opened in 1870). Unfortunately, the Croydon Bill was rejected by Parliament on 13 May 1873. Because of the steep gradient between Brixton and Streatham, the Brixton line was converted to cable operation from Kennington to the top of Brixton Hill in 1892 and then further extended to Streatham Library in December 1895, still leaving a gap of 1¼ miles to the Croydon boundary. The Croydon Local Board of Health (predecessor of the Corporation) had required a Mr. Webb, one of the sponsors of the Brixton-Croydon tramway to pay £200 a year for the privilege of running in their territory.

Nevertheless, various other interests more closely linked with Croydon were pressing for the construction of a local system of tramways to be worked by animal traction.

THE CROYDON TRAMWAYS COMPANY

In 1877, four local tradesmen, headed by Jabez Spencer Balfour, to encourage local trade, formed themselves into a company for the purpose of constructing a tramway system for Croydon. This received the approval of the Local Board on 8 January 1878.

A Bill was then placed before Parliament, requesting permission to build several lines of tramways, all within the boundaries of the area controlled by the Croydon Local Board. In the Croydon Tramways Bill, there were only five "Tramways". It would be tedious to set them out here but they may be found in Appendix B, with the names of the promoters.

Walter Webb, Solicitor and Parliamentary Agent piloted the Croydon Bill through Parliament and it received Royal Assent on 12 July 1878. The way was now clear to start constructional work on the ground and to emphasise this, the first ground was broken by J. Spencer Balfour, the first Chairman of the Company at a small ceremony on 6 May 1879. On the same day a plot of land just south of Thornton Heath Pond, was purchased by John Thrift from four sisters named Aspland for £1,650. Thrift was evidently a nominee of the Tramways Company and sold it to them the next day 7 May. He was a local grocer, Joshua Allder, the proprietor of a prosperous draper's shop in North End, Croydon, also had a financial interest in the tramways. (Allder's is now a large departmental store).

The land purchased, including a site formerly known as "Fern Cottage" was used for the construction of a depot and a manager's house. The signatories of the Conveyance from Thrift to the Company were Wm. Langley Smith, Wm. Pering Paige and Charles Selby the Secretary. Soon afterwards, another site was acquired, a little further south again, in Stanley Grove, opposite Mayday Hospital, on which to construct stables for the horses.

The roads, such as they were, were opened up and the rails laid to standard guage (4 ft. 8½ ins.). The rails themselves were of a lighter type than those laid later for electric tramways. The company was held responsible for paving the road across the space between the rails and for eighteen inches either side outside the rails, which was later found to constitute the provision of a free roadway for the tramways.

*—Under the Local Government Act of 1963.

rivals. The company would have preferred to lay the roadway with stone setts, which they found most durable, but on most roads in Croydon, the Local Board insisted on wood block paving. This was to prove to be the cause of much disagreement in later years.

Five cars were purchased from George Starbuck of Birkenhead, the leading tramcar manufacturer of the day. It is said that the company had hoped that each could be pulled by one horse, but in practise they required two, so must have been the earlier heavy design. They were single deckers with raised arched roofs.

Before a tramway could be opened for public service, it had to be inspected by an officer appointed by the Board of Trade (usually a Colonel or Major seconded from the Royal Engineers). A trial run took place on 25 September over part of the route in one of the cars and Major General C. S. Hutchinson made the official Board of Trade Inspection of the section of line from Thornton Heath Pond to North End at a point near Station Road, West Croydon on 3 October 1879.

One of the requirements insisted on by the Board of Trade, was that each Tramway company should draw up a set of Bye Laws, to be displayed on the cars, published in two reputable newspapers and a copy filed with them before the tramway could be permitted to open. The Croydon Bye Laws were published in the Croydon Times on 8 and 15 October and in the London Gazette on 10 October. It appears that the Croydon company were unsure what to do and on consulting the Board of Trade, were advised to take those of Great Yarmouth as a model, which they did. This done, the Inspecting Officer's certificate was duly received and the tramways commenced operation on 9 October, at first with only one car, on weekdays and two on Saturdays.

These Bye Laws were sent to the B.o.T. by N. H. Hebb, who was now the secretary of the company. They contained 25 separate numbered clauses the wording of some of which seems quaintly Victorian today, for example Clause No. 2 says "Every passenger shall enter or depart from the carriage by the hindermost or conductor's platform and not otherwise". Other clauses related to the prohibition of smoking, playing of noisesome musical instruments, swearing, offensive clothing, the carriage of dogs, travelling on the step, etc.

Work on the construction of the other lines continued and the next section was opened to the public on 1 January 1880. This included an extension of the original line along North End, from West Croydon Station to Crown Hill. To those who do not know Croydon, it should be mentioned that "Crown Hill" was the title chosen for the intersection where George Street/Crown Hill crossed North End/High Street at rightangles. All four roads were then very narrow and the Whitgift Alms Houses projected out into both North End and George Street (they still do). Crown Hill itself descends steeply to the old town and markets. There were also two branch lines, both of which started out along Oakfield Road, then a private road. At the far end of Oakfield Road, by Spurgeon's Tabernacle, they crossed a humped back bridge and then immediately separated. One line continued straight on along St. James' Road to Windmill Bridge over the main railway line. It was never extended and does not appear to have enjoyed a very long life in service. The other line bore left into Whitehorse Road and terminated at the "Gloster" public house. The tracks were single with one passing loop on each of the above mentioned sections. It appears that at this stage, still only five single deck cars were deployed over the system. Allowing for reliefs and sickness, the number of horses required was usually estimated at ten times the number of cars in stock; as unlike human crews, in the 19th century, horses were not required to work long hours! The length of route open then amounted to 2 miles, 11 chains.

At a General Meeting of the Company on 21 February 1880, it was suggested that "cars for outside riding" should be adopted. The early double deck horse cars in use at this time had back-to-back seats set along the clerestorey of the roof and were known as "Knifeboard seating". (In Victorian times, table knives used to be carried around in small narrow wooden trays, with a partition down the centre, which incorporated a carrying handle). However, some double deck cars must have been purchased after two more single deck cars had been acquired.

North End continues southward as the High Street, which at that time was too narrow for the trams. Consequently, the next section to be constructed was an isolated line, starting at the "Green Dragon" at the far end of the High Street and extending southwards along the Brighton Road, past the "Swan and Sugar Loaf" to the "Red Deer", South Croydon. To work this line, two more single deck cars, Nos. 6 and 7 were purchased from Starbuck. They had seven windows each side but were of a lighter type, which could be pulled by one horse. (Closely similar to Sheffield No. 15, now preserved at Crich).

A site for stables was acquired nearby in Crunden Road, but the cars were parked for the night in Davis' yard, behind the "Swan and Sugarloaf". There was no track connection into the yard, and the cars had to be pushed by hand over the stone setts. The South Croydon line was inspected on 10 May 1880 and opened on 14 May.

On 4 August, part of the plot of land adjoining Thornton Heath Depot was sold to a Mr. G. H. Holledge. It was not required as it was separated from the depot by a narrow strip of land in other hands. However, that strip was acquired from Edward Hopkins for £50 on 23 April 1884.

Early in 1880, under the Croydon Street Tramways (Extensions) Order 1880, Thomas Floyd, who was now acting as Parliamentary Agent for the Croydon Tramways Company, applied for permission to build two more lines as extensions of the existing system. These comprised:—

Tramway No. 1—1 mile, 5 furlongs, 9 chains (of which 11 chains double line).
Commencing at a junction with the existing tramway at the junction of London Road and Brigstock Road and extending along Brigstock Road, Colliers Water Lane, High Street, New Thornton Heath and Whitehorse Road to Selhurst Road.

Tramway No. 2—1 mile, 2 furlongs, 2 chains (of which 18 chains double line).
Commencing in St. James' Road East 30 links west of Clyde Road, along Cherry Orchard Road, Addiscombe Road and George Street, making a junction with the existing tramway in North End, 18 yards north of Crown Hill.

Horse cars 9 and 14 at Crown Hill, the same point as on the cover picture. No. 9 is a Starbuck single decker of 1880. (Courtesy J. B. Gent)

The above may not make sense to the present reader, as a number of street names were soon to be changed. At that time the area around Thornton Heath Pond was known as Thornton Heath and the High Street was known as New Thornton Heath. St. James' Road East is now known as Lower Addiscombe Road and Clyde Road is just beyond Addiscombe Station and opposite the "Alma" public house. Addiscombe Road commences at the centre of East Croydon Station Bridge so only a few yards of it was covered by the trams. Locals often call it "Upper Addiscombe Road" and this title was even used in one of the later Acts of Parliament. Both Addiscombe Road and Lower Addiscombe Road, with the side roads joining them were soon occupied by large mansions with imposing front gardens and were inhabited by business men, many of whom worked in the City of London.

Mr. Floyd wrote to the Board of Trade on 20 September 1880, enclosing a drawing and offering to pave the roadway, (a) with all granite setts, (b) with all wood-block paving or (c) with granite chips in tar macadam. He wrote again on 12 January 1881, requesting permission to include a passing loop opposite Holy Trinity Hospital in George Street (the back entrance to the Whitgift Alms House). It had not been authorized in the Order, but the local Road Authority approved of its inclusion.

On 6 April 1880, the Compressed Air Engines Co. asked the Company for permission to try compressed air locomotives for hauling cars on the isolated South Croydon section. This permission was freely granted, but the Roads Committee refused their permission, so the experiment came to nothing.

In the meantime, the Board of Trade were pressing Mr. Floyd to supply further details about the two proposed extensions and he submitted drawings on 20 September. On the Addiscombe Station route, these showed three passing places in George Street, double track on the bend in Cherry Orchard Road between Oval Road and Cross Road and a loop on the "Leslie Arms" corner where Cherry Orchard Road joins Morland Road and St. James' Road East, (Lower Addiscombe Road). Messers. Hall & Co., the large sand and aggregate merchants who had a yard on the left of Cherry Orchard Road, with railway connections and their own locomotive, objected to the tramway and insisted that the roadway passing their premises should be widened at the Tramway Company's expense. There were to be two tracks at the Clyde Road terminus.

The Thornton Heath extension was to be in the form of a loop, joining existing tramways at both ends. It was to branch off the existing line only a few yards short of the Thornton Heath Pond terminus, opposite the depot. It was to have two passing loops in Brigstock Road, two in Thornton Heath High Street and one at the point where the High Street met Whitehorse Road. It rejoined the existing tramway in Whitehorse Road at the "Gloster".

The next section of line ready to open, ran the length of George Street, Croydon's main business thoroughfare, as distinct from shopping, from the Whitgift Alms Houses to East Croydon Station. It was inspected by Major General C. S. Hutchinson and opened for traffic on 15 January 1881. The remainder of this line, from East Croydon to the "Alma" Addiscombe was inspected on 6 March, but was still the subject of objections from Hall & Co. Agreement could not be reached and the line was not permitted to open. The Board of Trade were asked to make a further inspection in November, but replied on 28, to the effect that the necessary documents were not yet to hand and they did not know who was the appropriate local authority which they should contact. In the correspondence which ensued, it was admitted that the roadway in front of Hall's premises was not sufficiently wide to leave a space of 9 ft. 6 in. between the outer rail and the footpath. Consequently the Major General stipulated that the cars must not be wider than 6 ft. 7 in. and must proceed at a walking pace past Hall's yard. Plans were sent to Mr. R. J. Cheesewright, Clerk to the Local Board and at the same time Mr. Floyd agreed to have the parts of the roadway for which the tram company were responsible, paved with Aberdeen Granite Setts.

These matters settled, Major General Hutchinson inspected the Thornton Heath line on 10 December in a special car and it opened on the 12th. He then inspected the Addiscombe line again on 18 February 1882, but instead of notifying the Company directly, he communicated his findings to the Town Clerk, on 20, and he submitted them to his Roads Committee at their next meeting before passing them on to the Tramway Company. Thus, the line from East Croydon to the "Alma" near Addiscombe Station did not open until 6 March 1882, over a year after the original inspection. The first double deck cars were delivered in 1883 and in that year the following services were provided:—

Crown Hill—Broad Green—Thornton Heath Pond. Dark green double deck cars.

Crown Hill—Whitehorse Road—Thornton Heath Pond. Blue single deck cars.

Crown Hill—East Croydon Station—Addiscombe (Alma). Red single deck cars.

High Street (Green Dragon)—Swan and Sugarloaf—Red Deer. Red single deck cars.

A contemporary photograph shows car No. 14, a double deck vehicle with back to back "Knifeboard" seats along the upper deck.

The horses were provided under contract by Thrale & Son, well known local equestrians (who still had a riding school at Addington in the 1950s). The system was built by Thomas Rigby, using rails supplied by Kerr Bros., Nelson & Co.

The line along St. James' Road attracted very little traffic and was given up after a short while. It did not cross Windmill Bridge to link up with the service in St. James' Road East (Lower Addiscombe Road). Except for the South Croydon route, separated by about a quarter of a mile from the others, the routes of the Croydon Tramways Co. served a compact built-up area and were reasonably profitable. As we shall see later, the company had every reason to wish that they had remained thus. They had no further extensions in mind for the time being.

It is reported that Joshua Allder, who was a director of the company, permitted a member of his staff to act as a part time inspector and from time to time, he would don his coat and hat, leave the draper's shop and ride on the trams to check the tickets.

J. Spencer Balfour, who cut the first ground for the tramway, became the first Mayor of Croydon, when it became a Borough on 9 June 1883. Mr. C. M. Elborough then became Town Clerk.

THE NORWOOD & DISTRICT TRAMWAYS COMPANY

The South Norwood area which occupies the north-east corner of Croydon was being developed in the 1880s and in view of the lack of interest in that area shown by the Croydon Tramways Co., others stepped in.

In the context of Croydon, the name "Norwood" may be taken to refer to South Norwood, which was separated by what became the Urban District of Penge, from Upper Norwood and West Norwood. Upper Norwood was partly in Croydon and partly in Lambeth. West Norwood was entirely in Lambeth; it was served by the London Southern Tramways and was the subject of a number of proposals over the years, for an extension to the Croydon area. Thus in later years the name "Norwood" was mentioned freely by both the Croydon and London Authorities, but meaning a different area in either case.

A consortium headed by P. Carnegy, R. Glasgow Kestin, and C. Phillips applied to Parliament in 1882, for powers to build eight Tramways, which added together formed two routes to South Norwood, each starting at an existing terminus of the Croydon Tramways Co's system. The Bill also requested powers to set up a company, the "Norwood & District Tramways Co." to work these lines. (Guaranteed by J. Spencer Balfour and A. T. Layton).

The Norwood & District Tramways Bill received Royal Assent on 24 July 1882 and the Tramways permitted are set out in Appendix B.

16

There were other extensions in the Bill, which were not authorized, apparently including one in Stroud Green Road, Woodside.

The last section in Portland Road, a connecting line, was on a steep gradient and passed under a low railway bridge; it does not appear to have been used in service. Cars terminated at the "Signal" public house.

The Act provided for these tramways to be worked by animal or mechanical traction and contained an appendix laying down conditions to be applied if steam were used. For example:—

Clause 39 refers to the use of animal, steam or other mechanical power.

Clause 40 refers to the penalties for using steam in a manner contrary to the Act.

Clause 46 says that where steam or other mechanical power is used, the contract with the road authority must be renewed annually.

Clause 54 states that the company may enter into agreements with the Croydon Tramways Company.

Clause 55 says either company may use steam traction for seven years from the date of receiving the consent of the Board of Trade Inspector.

The Appendix contains the following statements:—

1. The Break Power (sic) of the engines shall be such as the Board of Trade shall from time to time think fit.

2. Every engine shall be required to carry the following fittings:—

   (a) a number in a conspicuous position.
   (b) a speed indicator.
   (c) a fender to push aside obstructions.
   (d) a bell or whistle.
   (e) a seat at the front for the driver so that he can command the fullest possible view of the road before him.
   (f) every engine shall be free from noise, blast or clatter and all machinery concealed from view down to four inches above rail level.
   (g) the carriages shall be safe for the passengers.

The Act also contained a protective clause concerning a bridge under the London, Brighton and South Coast Railway. The tramway was to be laid to standard guage, was to be completed within two years of the passing of the Act. The company could lay temporary tramways while works were in progress and may purchase land for the provision of a depot, not exceeding five acres.

The Capital of the Company was to be £4800 in £10 shares, mortgages were permitted but debentures were not. There were to be five directors each of whom was to hold a minimum of thirty shares. Messrs., Patrick Carnegy, Reuben Glasgow Kestin, Charles Phillips, J. Pelton and D. B. Miller are said to have subscribed the required amounts. Deposits were to be paid only when the tramway was open to the public. These arrangements were approved by the Croydon Local Board of Health on 3 October and the plans submitted were also approved by them on 6 December. They showed the routes approved to be entirely single track with passing loops. The road Surveyor stated on 10 May 1883, that work had started on the Selhurst-Crystal Palace section!

Early in 1883, Alderman A. T. Layton broke the ground for the first laying of track in South Norwood High Street. This was followed by a luncheon in South Norwood Public Hall in Station Road (later a warehouse—demolished August 1981). However, although the directors of the company were able to raise sufficient capital to pay for the Act of Parliament and to satisfy the requirements specified therein, they were evidently unable to raise enough to pay for the actual construction of the proposed tramways. The outcome was that this company, after much discussion persuaded the Croydon Tramways Company to agree to an amalgamation. This necessitated a further Act of Parliament, the Croydon and Norwood

Tramways Act 1883, which as well as authorizing the amalgamation, authorized a number of additional tramways, amounting to about three miles in all, none of which was ever constructed.

The amalgamation took effect on 2 August 1883 and the combined undertaking took the title "Croydon and Norwood Tramways Company".

THE CROYDON & NORWOOD TRAMWAYS COMPANY

The amalgamation having made the necessary capital available, work was quickly put in hand on building the two lines to South Norwood and the short connecting line in Clifton Road, using a heavier type of rail than that employed by the original company. A depot was built behind St. Luke's Church at the south end of Portland Road, with an open ballasted track fan leading out into Spring Lane, Woodside. (The depot building was demolished and a small housing estate built on the site in 1972).

In the meantime, the combined undertaking was leased to the Steam Tramways Traction Co., with the intention of experimenting with steam on the South Norwood lines. This company was registered on 2 July 1883, with 800 £10 shares, of which 400 were held by the City of London Contract Corporation of 20 Bucklersbury, London E.C. and others by H. O. O'Hagan and T. O'Hagan. The only local director was William Elborough of Albert Road, South Norwood. The registered office is described as Croydon Tramways Depot, Thornton Heath, Croydon. In the published version of "The History of the Steam Tram", Charles E. Lee says "Part of the odium incurred by urban steam trams in Great Britain may be attributed to the fact that their introduction was associated with some of the more dubious methods of an early wave of company promotion. Henry Osborne O'Hagan (1853-1930) the principal promoter concerned, gave lurid details in his two volume autobiography "Leaves from my Life" (1929) of bribery of local officials to secure concessions, at very high promotion expenses, and of what is usually regarded as "watered capital". The City of London Contract Corporation, of which he was the main shareholder, built many of the lines he promoted at prices which were not subject to competitive tender!''.

The new lines when completed were inspected by Major General Hutchinson on 3 December, when he walked from Addiscombe Station to the "Prince George" in Grange Road, Thornton Heath, covering the length of both new lines. He made his report the next day and said rather grudgingly, "The tramways appear to be fit for public traffic. They propose to use steam power but the engines are not yet ready". The locomotives had not yet been delivered, and possibly not even ordered at that date. He continued by saying "should the lines come under steam regulations now or when the engines come into use? If we give them full authority now, they will not be bound to give us notice when they do introduce steam". Thus, the lines were authorized for animal traction only.

The completed lines to South Norwood, via Selhurst and via Woodside and Portland Road were opened to the public on 15 December 1883 and worked with horse trams as extensions of the existing Croydon Tramways Company's lines. A 20 minute service was provided on each line and the journey time was 25 minutes. There is no mention of any service on the Clifton Road route, but there is one report that a one-man single deck car provided a shuttle service for a time, "but the low boys used to throw stones at it from the clay pit" (presumably where the Crystal Palace Football Ground is now located).

The lessees were still interested in trying steam traction, but not in the usually accepted form. While searching through the records of German locomotive manufacturers in connection with another book, the writer discovered the fact that the Hohenzollern company of Dusseldorf supplied thirty fireless enclosed locomotives to a tramway in Java, (Batavia—Meester Cornelius), followed by an order for six similar machines for "Norwood-Croydon" in 1884. The works numbers were 319—324 of 1884. Those for Java are known to have been enclosed with four coupled wheels and could be driven from either end.

18

Fireless locomotives appear to have been invented around 1870 and first used for shunting around industrial establishments, where a fire on the engine would have constituted a hazard (munitions and paper factories etc.). They were adapted for use on tramways by Dr. Lamm of New Orleans. In 1875, Monsieur Leon Francq of the Cail engineering works in France, improved on the design and some of his locomotives were put into service on the Rueil—Marly tramway near Paris. Later versions were used in Paris itself also at Lyon, Marseille, Lille and other French cities. Francq set up his own works for building fireless locomotives for tramways, but it is believed that the majority were in fact rebuilds of existing live steam locomotives. Nevertheless, they ran successfully for many years. This type of machine had a number of obvious advantages for tramway work, since they were silent and did not give off offensive smoke, only a little steam when actually running. They did not have to carry supplies of fuel and water around with them. Their main disadvantage was that they could not operate at any great distance from their depot, to which they had to return at intervals to be recharged by compressors from a static boiler.

Locomotives built to the Lamm & Francq principal had the underframes, wheels, cylinders and motion (Stephenson's link motion) of an ordinary four coupled locomotive, but a large heavily lagged reservoir (sometimes known as a thermos flask) instead of a boiler. The particular feature for which Lamm & Francq claimed credit, was that this container was filled with water and when recharging, steam was forced into it under pressure through a perforated pipe near the bottom. This appeared to allow a larger quantity of steam to be held in suspension in the water, than otherwise. More steam was released as the pressure fell and it was collected in a very large dome on top of the container and passed to the cylinders through a stop valve, which could be operated from either end of the locomotive. Naturally, the efficiency of the machine gradually deteriorated as it used up the volume of steam supplied at each recharging and it then had to be returned to the depôt to be charged again.

Equipment found in the Spring Lane depôt many years later when it was in use as a factory, has been described as supporting the theory that compressed air locomotives were once tried. With the above information in mind, the present writer is of the opinion that this must have been the steam compressors, essential to the Lamm & Francq system.

Messrs. Hohenzollern, who probably already had experience in building fireless locomotives for industry, obtained a concession to build fireless locomotives to the Lamm & Francq design, but with Joy's valve gear, for use in countries other than France; hence those for Java & Croydon.

A letter which appeared in the "Norwood News" for 19 January 1884 asked why the line between the Signal Hotel and the High Street was not used. "Norwood News" for 2 February 1884 gives a list of times of cars from South Norwood, but with no mention of the Clifton Road line, while on 5 August, a report on repair of roads, quoting nine sections of tramway, gives Clifton Road as No. 8.

In the meantime, the Company notified the Town Clerk on 5 February that they intended to introduce steam traction on the Portland Road line in April, but the "Croydon Advertiser" for 22 August published a letter complaining that the promised steam operation had not yet materialised. Similar letters appeared during 1885 and 1886. Thus, there is no firm evidence that the locomotives ever ran. In the 1960's, certain old Croydonians, (particularly L. E. Brailsford and J. T. Fitch) claimed to have seen them standing in the depôt yard, and one undergoing trials on Selhurst Hill, with a large double deck bogie car offering first and second class accommodation, which it appeared to be unable to pull up the hill. This hill normally required a trace horse, with the horse cars and perhaps the locomotive had come too far from the depôt in Spring Lane and was already "winded". Apart from possibly this one occasion, the connecting curve at South Norwood was not used. In service, cars on the one route terminated outside the "Signal" in Portland Road and on the other service, outside

19

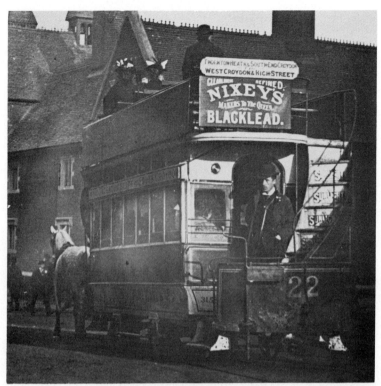

Large Stephenson horse car No. 22 at Crown Hill. This car appears to have had the upper deck converted from knifeboard to the "garden seat" arrangement. (Courtesy J. B. Gent

Birmingham built knifeboard horse car No. 13 in George Street. (Courtesy J. B. Gent

20

the small fire station in the High St. just beyond the "Albion" Hotel. The fire station was entered through a small arch between shops. The arch still exists (1982) but the fire station did not survive the horse-drawn era.

In November 1884, it was decided not to run a service on Sunday mornings and on 20 December 1884, proposals were put forward for a cable tramway between Anerley Station, Crystal Palace and Gipsy Hill, all on steep gradients, but the Croydon Council and the Metropolitan Board of Works viewed the scheme with disfavour, and it was dropped.

To emphasise the fact that no success had been achieved with steam, the Steam Tramways Traction Co. pulled out and the owning company took over operation on 31 December 1884. They continued to operate the tramways with horses.

In 1886, the "Railway & Tramway Express" says the Directors have not accepted the fireless locomotives and the contractors, The City of London Contract Corporation, are taking the matter up with the manufacturers. Presumably they returned to Germany.

During 1885 there was a great argument about the paving of the track in Selhurst Road, because the company had paved the road with granite setts, when the Council had stipulated wood blocks. The Corporation wished to hold the company to its obligations and the company were willing to repair the track with macadam. On 6 August, it was agreed that Joseph Kincaid, a Civil Engineer, should act as referee and the Town Clerk consulted the Board of Trade, but they were not interested. The decision reached eventually went against the Corporation.

Evidently operation of the new extensions to South Norwood turned out to be an embarrassment rather than an asset, particularly the Portland Road line. It met built up areas at Addiscombe, Woodside and in Portland Road and there was Croydon Race Course in Long Lane, off the route near Woodside, but much of the route ran through undeveloped country. The company got into financial difficulties in 1887 and on 7 January, Edmund Dean presented a petition to the Board of Trade on behalf of John Tidy, requesting the winding up of the company and on 25, the Town Clerk, Mr. Elborough wrote to Durnford & Co., Parliamentary Agents of 38 Parliament Street, Westminster, evidently in reply to a letter from them: He stated "The Council consider that the construction of the tramways authorized but not yet completed, would be of no public advantage, therefore the Council would not oppose the abandonment of the tramways. This information was passed on to the Board of Trade on 2 February. In the letter, reference was made to the Croydon & Norwood Tramways Bill of 1887 and described the amalgamation of the two companies and asked for the release of the sum of £1466 in Consols, deposited against the construction of certain additional tramways. The union between the two companies had proved unfortunate for the Croydon Tramways Co., whose lines lie more in the centre of the town and could have been successful if they had remained separate from the Norwood company's tramways, on some of which there was no traffic and no return to shareholders. The population although large was well served by the railways, as it consisted largely of business men engaged in the City of London, to which there was an adequate train service from the several stations in the area.

E. A. Dean, of Elborough & Dean, Solicitors to the C.&N.T.Co., wrote to the Board of Trade on behalf of the company on 7 April, explaining the purpose of the Bill, which was to enable the company to divest itself of the liabilities of the Norwood undertaking, recover the deposit and revert to the title "Croydon Tramways Company". Some of the directors of the original company wished to turn the clock back and carry on as though the Norwood Company had never existed. Mr. Dean was told that the Bill could not be passed until the company had disproved the presumption of insolvency. Nevertheless, the Croydon & Norwood Tramways Co. did fail financially on 25 October 1887 and Edwin Waterhouse of 44 Gresham Street in the City of London, was appointed as liquidator, in which capacity he continued to work the tramway undertaking.

While these moves were afoot to salvage the viable parts of the system there was a great deal of argument about lifting those sections of the track which would no longer be required and the poor condition of the roads on which they were laid, particularly Portland Road. Major General Hutchinson was called upon to arbitrate in the dispute between the liquidator and the Corporation over this matter. As a result the Corporation obtained an injunction against the company in 1889, to enforce the removal of the rails and to reinstate the roadway to their satisfaction. Subsequently there were complaints about the condition in which the roads had been left after the rails were lifted.

The roads over which trams were no longer running were quoted as Lower Addiscombe Road (Ashburton Road to Woodside), the "Gloster" to Thornton Heath and Clifton Road to Thornton Heath; they were said to have become a danger to the public.

The Act of Parliament permitting a new company to be set up, but reviving the old name "Croydon Tramways Company" received Royal Assent on 26 August 1889. It set out which tramways of the previous Acts the company was entitled to work.

The new company acquired the properties, rolling stock (14 cars and 95 horses) and chatels from the liquidator on 1 January 1980. The Deed of Conveyance was signed by Edwin Waterhouse for the one part and by W. Pering Paige and J. G. Elliot, for the other.

With regard to the lines added by the "Norwood" company, the new owners operated the line via Selhurst as far as South Norwood, possibly only to the Clock Tower, but the Addiscombe line only had a regular service as far as the "Alma". The company stated that it could not create traffic on Lower Addiscombe Road between Ashburton Road and the "Black Horse". Nevertheless, it was decided in 1891, that so long as Croydon Race Course remained in use, the track could remain in position as far as the "Black Horse". Even this left nearly half a mile to walk to the Race Course in Long Lane. (The Race Course was later removed to Gatwick and the Long Lane site became allotments—it was built over as recently as 1980).

Although the old company's experiments with steam had been a failure, this was not to be the end of trials with mechanical traction on Croydon's tramways. A Council Minute records that on 20 October 1888, they had been approached by the Electric Tramcar Syndicate for permission to carry out trials with an electric car. The Council were quite agreeable so long as the Board of Trade were consulted first. Consequently, in 1891, a Mr. Jarman, assisted by the Rev. J. M. Braithwaite, persuaded Alderman Miller, who was Chairman of the Croydon Tramways Co. at the time, to permit him to carry out trials with a battery electric car on the Crown Hill—Thornton Heath Pond section of the tramway. It was a converted horse car painted in a light colour, with eight small windows each side and "knifeboard" back to back seating on the upper deck. The title "Jarman's Electric Car" appeared on the cantrail. There were lifeguards like American "Cowcatchers" under the platforms. A primitive electric motor drove one of the two axles, deriving power from acid accumulators placed under the saloon seats. It was to be seen on several nights running trials up and down North End. In 1892, Mr. Jarman tried a slightly heavier car, with only seven side windows and reversible "garden" seats on the upper deck; it was painted in a dark colour and lettered on the cantrail, "Crown Hill—Broad Green—Thornton Heath" above "Electric Tramcar Syndicate Ltd.—Jarman's System". On 12 January 1892, the Board of Trade sanctioned the use of electric power over 2½ miles of Croydon tramways, but the car ceased running on 5 March.

The main difficulty seems to have been that the accumulators emitted evil smelling fumes and if the acid spilled out it burned passengers' clothing. The two cars used for these experiments are said to have been adaptations of existing horse cars of the London Tramways Company. Mr. Jarman also conducted experi-

Hohenzollern fireless locomotive for Java. Those tried in Croydon are thought to have been similar. (Courtesy J. H. Price

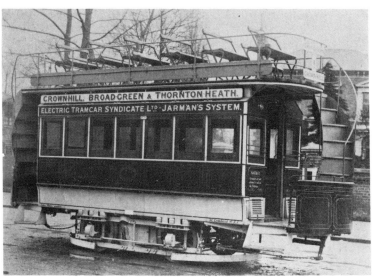

The Jarman accumulator car at Thornton Heath. This was the second car to be tried by Jarman. (Courtesy late Walter Gratwicke

ments with electric traction on the North Metropolitan Tramways at Canning Town in 1883 and with improved equipment and more lasting success in Birmingham.

A Croydon double deck horse car was decorated and toured the system in connection with a fund in aid of the dependants of men killed in the Boer War.

There were yet further experiments in order to discover a more economical and efficient means of traction in Croydon. The Connelly Oil motored car ran in Croydon on 1 July 1893 for the benefit of an inspection by members of the Tramways Institute. It was tried on the same route as the Jarman car and remained in Croydon until December. It comprised a single deck horse car body mounted on a strengthened underframe, but without platforms. The motor was inside the saloon and the driver stood in front of it, viewing the road ahead through the bulkhead windows. It did not carry passengers, but was used as a tractor to tow an ordinary horse car. Its regular use was sanctioned by the Board of Trade on 17 October. It had a 13 horse power two cylinder water cooled engine.

A Croydon tram driver was kicked to death by one of his horses on 7 September, but there is no mention of what had happened to bring this about.

On 2 October, the Traction Syndicate Ltd., who had acquired the rights in the Lührig gas motored tram car, wrote to the Board of Trade requesting an inspection of a car on the Croydon Tramways. The Board replied that such a request should have come from the tram company, but nevertheless, Major General Hutchinson would inspect the car at Thornton Heath Depôt on 21 October. The inventor was German and his car had been tried in Dresden and Dessau, but he had died before conclusive results had been obtained and his designs were taken over by the Traction Syndicate Ltd. of London and Dresden. The fuel was coal gas carried compressed in a large cylinder under the seat on one side of the car. The motor was a pair of counter-opposed cylinders under the other seat, driving a large flywheel between the inner and outer panelling, with large access doors on the outside. A technical description in Cassier's Magazine says "The engine is kept in continuous motion when the car is standing. The supply of gas is almost turned off and one cylinder is fired every eighth revolution, but the engine is kept in continuous motion by the four feet diameter flywheel and is ignited by an electric battery. When the car is stationary, the lever on the platform is in an upright position, if inclined over to the left, the gas supply is turned half on and a friction clutch engaged, which drives one pair of road wheels through a train of gears at a speed of 4½ miles per hour. When the lever is inclined to the right, the gas is turned full on and a larger friction clutch engaged, which drives the road wheels at 9 miles per hour. There is also a reversing lever and the usual hand brake staff".

Having made his inspection on 21 October, General Hutchinson reported, "I have inspected the Lührig car. It is made to carry 14 passengers inside and six on each platform, but none on the roof". He referred to the flywheel and gearing and said that the gas pressure was not to exceed twelve atmospheres and the gas was sufficient for twelve miles. Commenting on the vehicle he said, 1. The steps must not project more than 11 inches beyond the outside of the wheels, 2. The car must be fitted with life protectors at each end, 3. The brakes must be much more effective, 4. The Governor pedal on the platform at the rear end must be locked up to prevent it from being tampered with by passengers and 5. The brake wheel should have an arrow marked on it to show in which direction to turn to apply the brake. The car was not to be used until these defects had been corrected.

On 1 May 1894, Major General Hutchinson was asked to inspect an improved Lührig gas car. On 15 May he reported "The car resembles the one which I inspected on 21 October last in all essential features, but is lighter and carries 28 passengers. It is slightly over the permitted width, but not sufficiently serious to prohibit operation. The car ran very smoothly and regularly on test but lacked power to ascend gradients and the clutches were not properly adjusted". He permitted the car to run for a period of six months on the same route as the Connelly car.

As it was unable to climb gradients, the car was to run in service from the foot of the bridge at Thornton Heath Station to Crown Hill. The Corporation was represented at the inspection and rather splitting hairs, Mr. Elborough the Town Clerk said subsequently in correspondence with the Board of Trade, although the Corporation had not raised any objection at the inspection, they had not agreed either, to the running of the car. They did not agree to the car running along North End beyond Poplar Walk and wished to be able to give 21 days notice to terminate the arrangement. "We think is very undesirable that Croydon Tramways should be used as an experimental ground in the matter of tramway construction". Mr. Carruthers Wain replied for the Company, stating that experiments were for the good of the inhabitants of Croydon as well as themselves. At the same time the Board of Trade inferred that the Corporation had left it too late to object.

In the meantime, things were not going too well for Jabez Spencer Balfour§, Chairman of the original Croydon Tramways Company and first Mayor of Croydon. In connection with the crash of the Liberator Building Society in which he was also involved, a receiving order for Bankruptcy was made against him on 12 January 1893, but he had already fled the country and was arrested in Argentina on 21 January. At his trial on 28 November, he was sentenced to 14 years hard labour. Soon afterwards, Mr. E. Mawdesley was appointed Town Clerk on the death of C. M. Elborough.

Late in 1893, the former Croydon & Norwood Tramway's depôt in Spring Lane, Woodside, was sold to the Scientific Boiler Fluid Co., who no doubt were able to make use of the existing static boilers. The fate of the locomotives and why the scheme was not a success, have never been established, but experience in France and Java tended to show that at least twenty locomotives in regular service were necessary to get economic use out of the fixed equipment.

The Company applied to the Board of Trade on 27 June 1895 for permission to introduce new Bye Laws, but they objected to one clause which said "A passenger must pay a new fare if he gets off one car and boards another". There were changes in management around this time, when W. J. Carruthers Wain, President of the Tramways Institute and Chairman of Swan & Edgars Ltd., became Chairman of the Croydon Tramways Co. Also, T. E. Polden replaced Mr. Woolley on the Board of Directors. In 1896, J. W. Newton became the Company's Engineer.

In 1894, the Croydon Tramways Co. obtained the Croydon Tramways (Extensions) Order, enabling them to build a tramway 1 mile 3 furlongs in length connecting the existing terminus at Thornton Heath with the London Tramways Co.'s terminus in Streatham High Road. However, the Company were unable to raise the necessary capital and applied for extensions of time on 27 June 1895 and again in 1896 and 1897, still without success.

Henry Albert Durke was appointed Manager on a three year contract on 16 March 1897. Several additional cars (probably eight) were purchased on 1 May and were of the type with reversible "garden" seats on the upper deck. The original single deck cars were disposed of at the same time. In the hope that he might be in a more influential position to raise capital, Major General T. Kyffin Kaye replaced Carruthers Wain, as Chairman of the Company on 12 May 1898. In the meantime, in connection with a street widening programme, the Corporation obtained powers to extend the isolated South Croydon line to Crown Hill, to join up with the rest of the system. When completed, they leased the line to the Company (see Chapter 2 for details).

§ J. S. Balfour is believed to have had no connection with the Balfour, Beatty Organization, who had interests in tramways at Dartford, Luton and other places and are still trading.

The British Electric Traction Co., a powerful tramway owning group, also interested itself in the Croydon Tramways Co., with a view to electrification and on 11 January 1898, Major General Kaye found it necessary to take out an injunction against the B.E.T. to prevent them from taking over the Croydon Tramways against the wishes of the shareholders. However, in August 1898 the Corporation stated that with the growing traffic in Croydon, it was becoming impossible to provide an adequate service within the limitations of horse trams, so they must take over, extend and electrify the system, when the lease expired, which it was soon to do.

The final organization of the Company was as follows:—Capital £21,000 in 5% Debentures, £14,343 in 6% Preference Shares and £27,000 in Ordinary Shares. The registered address was 22 Queen Victoria Street, London. Chairman—Major General T. K. Kaye, Directors—W. L. Smith, T. K. Freeman, C. J. Baker and W. Pering Paige, Secretary—Charles Selby, Manager—H. A. Durke, Engineer—J. W. Newton. (Smith, Paige and Selby had held office in the original company.)

An inventory of all chattels and equipment handed over to the Corporation including every item down to brushes, spades, buckets, curry combs, harness, etc., was signed by Mr. Selby for the Company and Mr. Mawdesley, the Town Clerk, for the Corporation.

The horse cars shown on the inventory were Nos. 12, 13 and 14, knifeboard open top cars built in Birmingham*, Nos. 15, 16, 17 and 18, built at the Falcon Works, Loughborough. No. 19 is described as "Birmingham Pattern", Nos. 22 and 23 large cars built by John Stephenson, with seven side windows and evidently converted at some time from knifeboard to two and two garden seats upstairs. Nos. 24-31, again built by Falcon Car Works, with five side windows with two and two garden seats upstairs. 24-31 were probably the additional cars purchased when the single deck cars were disposed of in May 1897. There was no mention of cars 1-11, 20 and 21 in the inventory. In addition to the tramcars there was one phaeton (an open carriage) and four pairs of rail cleaners on hire from Harry Penn & Co. on a contract dated 24 September 1895. Cars Nos. 15, 19 and 23 were shedded at Davis Yard behind the "Swan and Sugarloaf", South Croydon and the rest at Thornton Heath. There were stables and granaries at Green Lane off Stanley Grove near Thornton Heath and Crunden Road, South Croydon.

Included in the inventory were the title deeds of Thornton Heath Depôt, leases of Stanley Grove stables dated 26 January 1893 for £20 per annum and Crunden Road stables leased from Alfred Bullock, dated 14 September 1898, for £160 per annum. (These leases probably replaced earlier leases for these two properties.) Other documents included the three year agreement with Mr. Durke, one with Richard A. Thrale, Veterinary Surgeon, dated 16 May 1898 and one with the Ticket Punch & Register Co. Ltd., for the hire of punches for three years, dated 1 April 1897.

There were references to Half Moon depôt and Napier Road stables. These are not clear, but Napier Road is the next turning beyond Crunden Road and could have been a back entrance to the stables. (The site between Crunden Road and Napier Road is now occupied by Croydon Bus Garage, built 1916). The "Half Moon" public house is on the corner of Dennett Road between Broad Green and Mayday Road.

There were 175 horses, but no mention as to how they were allocated to the two stables.

The actual take-over by the Corporation is described in the next chapter, but when that had been done, the Company went into voluntary liquidation in 1900.

* Probably the Birmingham Railway Carriage & Wagon Co. Ltd.

The Connelly oil motored locomotive tried at Croydon and Stratford. (Unknown photographer

Horse car No. 27 by Williamson's shop in South Norwood High Street, where the Clock Tower now stands.   (Photo courtesy L. S. Woolf

27

Croydon Corporation No. 18 and horse car, probably No. 27, opposite Selhurst Station, 24 January 1902. (Courtesy J. B. Gent

Croydon Corporation car No. 3 at Norbury terminus, Hermitage Bridge sometime between 1909 and 1912. Note the large number of people transferring from the L.C.C. car in the background and framed list of places served on traction post. (Courtesy A. D. Packer

CHAPTER TWO
THE CORPORATION TAKES OVER

The first participation into the tramway business by the Corporation of Croydon, was on a very modest scale. In 1893 the Corporation decided to embark upon, what in those days must have been regarded as a major redevelopment scheme in the town centre. The principal feature was that the High Street was to be widened and a number of important buildings demolished and replaced elsewhere in the process. It occurred to them that once the High Street was of a reasonable width, there would be no objection to linking up the two separate parts of the existing horse tramway system. The new tracks could be provided as an integral part of the development scheme.

The old Town Hall was demolished during 1893 and replaced by a new one of imposing appearance and dimension in Katharine Street, on the site of the former short lived Croydon Central Station. The offices of the "Croydon Advertiser" newspaper were also rehoused.

In October 1893, application was made to Parliament for a Provisional Order to permit the construction of a tram track from North End to South End, passing through the widened High Street. On 9 April 1895, Croydon Corporation entered into a contract with the British Thomson-Houston organization, to light the streets of Croydon by electricity and thus, were very early in this field. (This connection with B.T-H. must have had an effect on their subsequent tramway plans) (lighting was switched on, on 6 November 1896).

However, by the end of 1896, little progress had been made on the tramway side and the Corporation were evidently beginning to realise their lack of experience in this particular type of work. The Town Clerk wrote to the Board of Trade, in rather stilted language, enquiring whether having built the tramway, it would be in order for them to lease it away, i.e. to the existing company. The Board of Trade replied on 23 December to the effect that it had no objection.

Evidently still not satisfied that they had done the right thing the Corporation then submitted a copy of the proposed lease to the Board on 11 May 1897. The terse reply came back that there was nothing unusual in the terms of this lease, on which the Board would wish to comment. A copy of the formal Application appeared in the "Croydon Times" on 20 and 27 January and in the "London Gazette" on 5 February, Only then did the Corporation enter into negotiations with the Croydon Tramways Company over the lease of this few yards of tramway when completed. In the meantime, the Company had asked the Board of Trade on 27 June 1896, for a copy of the estimate of the cost of this tramway as submitted by the Borough Engineer. The reply was that they had "No claim to this information"—in other words, the Company were told to mind their own business.

The Act under which this tramway was constructed, specified two numbered "Tramways".

These were:—

Tramway No. 1.—1 Furlong, 3 Chains, commencing at a junction with an existing tramway authorized by the 1878 Act, in the High Street at Mint Walk, extending along Croydon High Street and terminating in North End at a junction with another tramway constructed under the 1878 Act.

Tramway No. 2.—1 Chain only, commencing in the High Street by a junction with Tramway No. 1, and terminating in George Street by a junction with a tramway constructed under the 1878 Act.

Both were to be laid as single track except for the one passing loop already mentioned in connection with the Approved Plan. The Corporation arranged with the Croydon Tramways Company, that the line should be leased to them and worked as part of their system when completed.

Work soon started on laying Tramway No. 1, but Tramway No. 2, which was only an additional connecting curve from George Street, southwards, was not constructed. It was reported in the "Croydon Times" that the line was inspected on 1 June 1897 by Major Mandarin (sic). The certificate, permitting the line to open, was duly received, dated 3 June and signed by Major F. A. Marindin, R.E., C.M.G., Inspecting Officer for the Board of Trade. Thus, the connecting line in the High Street was opened on Sunday 6 June and was henceforth worked as a through service from Thornton Heath High Street to the "Red Deer", South Croydon, requiring nine cars. The rest of the system was then combined into another through service, from South Norwood to Addiscombe, via West Croydon and George Street. This also required nine cars. Both routes ran over common track between West Croydon Station and Crown Hill.

In a statement made by the Corporation it was said, "Traffic is increasing and it is impossible to improve the service with the present horse cars". They pointed out that the lease had nearly expired and they were therefore thinking of taking over the undertaking. Their view was confirmed at a meeting held in the Public Hall in October, where there was a conclusive vote in favour of municipalization. Thereupon the Corporation appointed a Tramways Committee from among the Aldermen and Councillors, charged with the task of formulating a plan for the acquisition and electrification of the Croydon tramways system. However, one of their first responsibilities was to oppose a Bill for a proposed Crystal Palace Light Railway, which evidently impinged on their own plans.

On 19 June 1899, the Tramways Committee gave their official support to the proposal to acquire the system and recommended the adoption of the overhead wire system of electric traction. This was followed in July, by the Corporation making a resolution to purchase the Croydon Tramways Co.'s undertaking at an agreed price of £50,000.

In October, Mr. E. W. Monkhouse, a Consulting Engineer, made a report on the prospects of electrifying the system. At that time, the only tramways in the greater London area, in course of electrification were so far the London United at Hammersmith and East Ham, neither of which was as yet completed or open.* Evidently happy with the recent installation of electric lighting in the borough by the British Thomson-Houston organization and mindful of the interest recently shown by the British Electric Traction Co. the Corporation now favoured a scheme whereby the B.T-H. would construct an electric tramway system for them, which would be leased to the B.E.T. for day to day operation for 21 years, but which could be terminated after five years if either party was dissatisfied with the way it worked out. In view of the Corporation's inexperience, this was a sensible arrangement and the B.T-H. and B.E.T. were quite happy to work together on the project.

* There had been a short private line at Alexandra Park.

Therefore, the Corporation reached a firm decision to purchase the horse tramways and on 16 October 1899 decided to lease them to the British Electric Traction Co. Ltd. Of the alternatives which Mr. Monkhouse put forward, that costing £139,370 for 17.51 miles of track was approved, the B.E.T. were to pay 6% of the capital cost plus £100 per route mile. The Corporation paid a Parliamentary Deposit of £388 - 14 - 0d and a Guarantee Bond of £30,000.

There were to be a number of extensions beyond the termini of the existing horse tramways and Oakfield Road, now used in both directions, was to be used by electric cars, inward bound only, it would meet the outward bound track on Spurgeon's Bridge and that would proceed to West Croydon Station via Wellesley Road and Station Road. In December, there was a protest from residents of Wellesley Road.

The contract between the Corporation and the old Company was signed 22 January 1900, the signatories for the company being Wm. Langley-Smith, Wm. Pering Paige and Charles Selby and for the Corporation, F. T. Edridge (Mayor), N. Page and E. Mawdesley (Town Clerk). The tramways were now theirs for £50,000 and the agreement with the B.E.T. was signed in March, at their office, Donnington House, Norfolk Street, Strand, London (for B.E.T. John S. Raworth, E. Garcke, Charles H. Dade and for Corporation Fred. T. Edridge, N. Page, E. Mawdesley). In the same month the London County Council made a number of applications to build several new tramways, including one which was to serve the Urban District of Penge, which adjoined South Norwood, already served by Croydon trams. (Penge Vestry had made an application to be incorporated in Croydon on 24 March 1890, but the Government refused.)

While all this was going on, Messrs. Birstall & Monkhouse, electrical advisers to the Corporation, who appear to have acted as Parliamentary Agents as well, were busy preparing a Bill to place before Parliament, to authorize the reconstruction and electrification of the system. It was intended that the main line on the London—Brighton Road should be extended to the borough boundary at both ends, the Selhurst route to Oliver Grove, South Norwood (the Clock Tower and Norwood Junction Station Road), the Addiscombe route to the railway bridge at Bingham Road Halt (this bridge at 14 feet clearance was just too low for double deck electric trams).

Mention has been made elsewhere of the practice in horse tram days, of dividing a proposed system up into a great many short "Tramways" for the purpose of presenting it to Parliament. This was done again with the CROYDON TRAMWAYS BILL 1900, on which although the main line was almost covered in two "Tramways", it took 35 "Tramways" to describe the whole lot! Most were exactly three chains in length. (See Appendix B).

The reason for this apparently peculiar behaviour was that the existence of the horse tram lines was taken for granted and they did not require further authorization, but any deviation from them did. Thus, the main line outside the central area and including the new extensions to the Borough boundaries was to be laid entirely with double track and could be accommodated on two "Tramways". On the other hand, the track in the town centre and on the branches was to be laid single or interlaced with passing loops in different places to those of the horse tramways. Hence, each loop had to be shown as a separate "Tramway". As far as possible, these loops were laid symmetrical to the centre of the road, just allowing the prescribed space between the outer rail and the edge of the pavement. However, in some places, this was not possible, particularly in Northcote Road and South Norwood High Street. In such cases, the outward bound track remained in the centre of the road and the loop was made on the inward track, at the mouth of a side turning, where there was no pavement against which the prescribed distance could be measured. In all cases turnouts were laid with sprung movable tongues in both rails.

The B.T-H. took over the construction and the B.E.T. began preparations for the working of Croydon's electric tramways on 1 January 1900. The depôt at Thornton Heath had to be enlarged, by an extension built behind and at right-angles to the original building and the adjoining house became the Head Office of the undertaking. Equipment in the workshop was driven by a gas engine, formerly used to work the machine that cut up the horses' fodder. Another depôt was to be built at Purley, some distance short of the terminus. Purley itself was not part of Croydon and the municipal boundary ran close to the road.

Nevertheless, the Corporation did not hand over every detail of construction and on 22 February, appointed a Tramways Sub-Committee to visit other tramways already electrified and report back. They visited Liverpool, Sheffield, Leeds and Hull. On their return, they recommended that 35 cars similar to those at Liverpool be built by the British Electrical Engineering Co. (sic). (It is thought that *Brush* was intended by this title) and that the traction posts should be like those at Hull. As it turned out, the order for 35 cars was eventually given to George F. Milnes & Co., while although the design of traction post and its scroll work as used by Leeds, became very widely used throughout the country, that adopted by Hull and Croydon, which was slightly more ornate, was to be peculiar to those two towns.

In April, the same month as this report was made, the B.T-H. detailed Tender for the reconstruction was accepted. This included the provision of additional dynamos and other equipment in the power station which already existed to supply current for the lighting of Croydon. It was located in Factory Lane off Mitcham Road and the additional equipment enabled it to supply the trams as well. The contract included feeder cables from the power station to two points on the tramway system and the necessary opening up of roads to lay them. As the power station was a little distance from any point on the then proposed tramways, the cables were run down unimportant side turnings, so as to cause a minimum of interference. The tendered prices were:—

(a) B.T-H. Car equipments (including trucks)   £13,052
(b) Feeder cables and road works   £12,963
(c) Overhead wiring and traction posts   £20,045
(d) 35 car bodies from G. F. Milnes & Co.   £9,680

Croydon Corporation Nos. 31 and 9 near the "Mitre", Croydon Road, Anerley. Note, the scrollwork and finials not yet fitted on traction posts. Corporation cars were the first to run on South Metropolitan tracks.　　　　　　　"Scienco" postcard. (Courtesy "Len's of Sutton"

Double track was laid beyond the "Swan & Sugar Loaf" on the strong recommendation of Mr. Monkhouse, who pointed out that three additional cars would be needed for single track, even if single track were laid on one side of the road, with the passing loops on the other, so that they could be joined later when double track really became necessary. The Corporation did not accept Mr. Monkhouse's other proposal, that traction posts should be planted on both sides of the road, with span wires between them. Certainly, there were posts on both sides between Norbury and West Croydon, but the "open sky" system was adopted. The wires for either direction were attached to very short bracket arms, with in places, the wires almost hidden in the trees. The trolley poles on the cars had to reach out far to one side to make contact with the wires. The rest of the system, including the Purley section, was equipped for ordinary side bracket suspension with the posts on one side of the road only.

The Corporation purchased a plot of land in Brighton Road on the corner of Purley Downs Road on 12 December 1900, from C. Pearce for a depôt. Pearce had recently acquired it from the Croydon Land Investment Co. A tender for the construction of this depôt was accepted from E. J. Saunders and one from J. Smith and Sons, for rebuilding Thornton Heath Depôt, both in March 1900. In the same month, the Corporation submitted drawings of the type of rails and methods of track laying to the Board of Trade and copies of the proposed Statutory Rules & Orders were submitted in April. Mr. Monkhouse notified the B.o.T. that construction work on the ground was to commence on Monday 26 November. In acknowledging this letter it was pointed out that part of the Borough of Croydon was within ten miles of Kew Observatory and operation of the trams could affect the instruments there; special insulation precautions might be required. The Town Clerk replied to this on 17 January 1901 "The nearest point on the tramways is at such a tremendous distance from Kew Observatory that no damage could arise and the whole installation would be carried out under Board of Trade regulations. There will be no risk whatever". In March, after consulting the H.M. Office of Works, the B.o.T. accepted.

Thirty five cars, to be the property of the Corporation, were ordered from G. F. Milnes & Co. of Birkenhead, (successors of Starbuck who built the original horse cars). The bodies were to agree in every detail with the drawings submitted to the Board of Trade for approval in September 1901. A drawing of a large "Providence" type lifeguard to be hung on the front dash of the car and described as the "Dover" lifeguard (as used at Dover), was submitted at the same time. Sixteen of these cars were to be mounted on Peckham Cantilever trucks and nineteen on Brill 21E trucks. All were to be provided with B.T-H. electrical equipment. As they were to resemble the cars seen by the Sub-Committee at Liverpool, they were to have three side windows and reversed stairs.

On 20 April 1901, Birstall & Monkhouse announced that a portion of the track was now completed. It had been necessary to discontinue the horse car service while work was in progress and they now asked for an inspection so that horse traction could be resumed until the electric cars and equipment were ready. The length of line to be inspected was 2 miles 3.55 chains of new track, including extensions not formerly worked by horses. These were Tramways Nos. 26 and 27, Croydon High Street at Mint Walk to Purley Fountain. The scissors crossover for Purley terminus had not yet been delivered and a temporary crossover costing £95 had been installed for the time being.

The Board of Trade was asked to carry out an inspection of the line so that a public service could be resumed over the section reconstructed. This inspection was carried out on 26 April by Colonel von Donop and his certificate was dated The following day. It stated clearly that the line from Friends Road* to Purley terminus was approved for horse traction only. It seems that the Corporation had hoped for an open ended certificate, which would have enabled them to

* Friends Road has now disappeared under the Croydon Flyover.

change over to electric traction as soon as the new cars were delivered and the various electrical installations completed, without further formality. This was much at variance with the B.o.T's practices and of course they insisted on an inspection for electric traction at an appropriate time.

A horse car service was reinstated on the South Croydon line, plus the new Purley extension on 2 May 1901. Then the same procedure had to be repeated for the Norbury—Crown Hill section, which opened for horse cars on 3 August. The erection of traction posts, overhead wires and other electrical equipment continued in the meantime and the B.o.T. were notified at the beginning of September that five miles of track were now ready for inspection.

While this work was in progress, 23 car bodies were delivered by Milnes in April. Neither depôt was yet ready to receive them and as they were without trucks or electrical equipment, they were stored for the time being in the yard of Pitlake Power Station. When the work on Thornton Heath depôt was sufficiently advanced, the remaining twelve bodies, with all the trucks and electrical equipment, were delivered there, to be fitted out ready to start running and testing. To make room for them 10 horse cars and 100 horses no longer required were sold.

At last, on 20 September, Col. von Donop inspected the track and cars for the through Norbury—Croydon—Purley route and Mr. A. P. Trotter inspected the electrical equipment and installations, which he found much to his satisfaction. On the other hand, the Colonel was not too happy about the "Dover" lifeguards, but was prepared to let them stay on the cars for a trial period. He also took note of the fact that the almost new horse tram rails had been retained in the High Street, but did not object.

The public opening with electric traction took place on Thursday 26 September after a number of trial runs. First Alderman Miller, Chairman of the Lighting Committee, escorted the Mayoress to Pitlake Power Station to switch on the current, then a procession of 20 cars toured the system, led by the Mayor and the Home Secretary, Rt. Hon. C. T. Ritchie and his wife. This was followed by a banquet in the Town Hall and the system was declared open to the public. The new chocolate and ivory cars each seated 52 and seemed very large compared with the horse cars. They ran from Norbury Station to Purley Fountain, the southern boundary of the borough. The short section from Norbury Station to the northern boundary at Hermitage Bridge could not be opened, as at a late stage it had been found that the station bridge was too low for electric cars and the lowering of the road under it was not yet completed. The temporary crossover was still in use at Purley. Nevertheless, for the first few days, every car was crowded, particularly on the Sunday, when passengers had to be asked to queue for seats on the cars (in 1901!).

In December, in correspondence with Mr. Jeckyll of the Board of Trade, Mr. Monkhouse asked for more lines to be inspected. The inspection took place on 3 January 1902 after some delays because Mr. Trotter had been on leave. The Crown Hill—Addiscombe route commenced running the next day, on the Colonel's verbal assurance that all was well and a certificate would be in the post as soon as possible. The section in Brigstock Road from Thornton Heath Pond to Thornton Heath Station opened on 10 January but further progress had to await the completion of widening the station bridge. The remaining four horse cars were transferred to the Selhurst route, where reconstruction had reached the stage of lowering the road under the twin bridges at Selhurst Station to take double deck cars.

At each inspection, the Inspecting Officer prescribed a number of speed limits at places where there was thought to be particular danger. As each line was opened individually, the Corporation became rather put out at the fact that it was expected to produce a revised Rule Book each time, pointing out any new speed restrictions and compulsory stops required and deposit a copy with the B.o.T.

Also, some concern was being expressed in official circles about telephone and telegraph wires which crossed the road above tram wires. If one of these wires broke, it could touch the tram wire and pick up the 500 volts which it was carrying with disastrous results. The Corporation discovered that automatic cut-outs at the sub-stations could cost £3,050. A representative of the Post Office attended most inspections and insisted that guard wires were fixed above the tram running wires at all places where this danger existed.

In the meantime, the British Electric Traction Co. had been setting up a local organization, through which to run the Croydon tramways. It was that group's usual practice to set up a subsidiary company, to which were left all the day to day details of running the system, but in the case of Croydon, because of the terms of the Corporation's lease, this might have been rather difficult and they made an exception by running the system themselves. True, they used the trading name "Croydon & District Tramways" and wished to have the cars lettered "The Croydon Tramways" but in fact the cars were lettered "Croydon Corporation Tramways" in the usual style on the rocker panels, with "The British Electric Traction Company Limited, Lessees" in very small letters underneath and there was the municipal coat of arms on the waist panel. H. A. Durke of the horse tramways remained as Traffic Manager and from January 1902, Arthur Lea Barber acted as Secretary.

In February, T. B. Goodyer of Edinburgh, who had been a roving Traffic Superintendent for the B.E.T., was appointed General Manager at Croydon. (See Appendix C for biography). The Tramways Committee appointed by the Mayor of Croydon, Sir Frederick T. Edridge, comprised Councillor T. Rigby, as Chairman, with Alderman G. C. Allen, and Councillors D. B. Miller, M. Taylor and B. M. Johnston to act on behalf of the Corporation.

The section from West Croydon to Selhurst Station was opened on 24 January 1902, but the line beyond to Norwood Junction was not yet ready and continued to be worked by a horse car, usually No. 27. There was some difficulty with frontagers in South Norwood High Street, where it was intended to lay a passing or terminal loop very close to the kerb.

The section from Selhurst Station to South Norwood was inspected on 7 March 1902 by Major Pringle. He noted that there was one steep gradient of 1 in 18 (Selhurst Hill) but did not think it warranted the use of track brakes, he also noted several 40 ft. radius curves. A representative of the G.P.O. was present at this inspection and noted that guard wires would be required at several points. This section of route was opened on 14 March and cars ran a little beyond the Clock Tower to Portland Road, the old horse tram terminus. The final passing loop just before the Portland Road/South Norwood Hill intersection was tucked into the opening of Grosvenor Road. It was this loop about which complaints were made and local traders affirmed that a tram standing on the loop would prevent their vans from unloading and customers' carriages from access to their shops.

Major Pringle followed up Col. von Donop's remarks about "Dover" life-guards and said they were not satisfactory. Soon 35 sets were offered for sale and replaced on Croydon cars by other types. It was found that more cars would be required and agreed that the next batch should be the property of the B.E.T., who ordered 10 cars of a later type from Milnes late in 1901. They were mounted on Milnes' own German designed trucks. They were delivered early in 1902 and were usually to be seen running on the main line. They were in the same livery as the other cars. As traffic grew, it was considered that the main line would be better served by large capacity bogie cars and ten were ordered for the Corporation fleet in February 1902. Later five more were ordered for the B.E.T. fleet. Although built by Brush instead of Milnes, the bodies were almost identical to the ten Corporation cars but the trucks were quite different. As it turned out, the Corporation had the better bargain. (See Chapter 7 for technical details of Rolling Stock). The 10 were delivered in October 1902 and worked both on the main line and the Thornton Heath branch, alternate cars from Purley running through to Norbury or Thornton Heath High Street. The remaining horse cars and horses were sold by auction on 17 February 1902, by Messrs. Hooker & Webb.

On 15 July 1902, Mr. Monkhouse told the Board of Trade that the last section of tramway under the 1900 Act was now ready for inspection. Owing to the large number of tramways presently under construction, both Col. von Donop and Mr. Monkhouse were very busy men and it took some time to fix a date for this inspection and the Certificate for the section from Norbury Station Bridge to Hermitage Bridge boundary was eventually issued on 17 November. 1 furlong 6 chains was involved. Even so, the scissors crossover at Purley terminus was not installed until June 1903 and cost £445 15s. 9d.

On 18 June the Post Office informed the Board of Trade that they now required double guard wires to be fixed above tram wires, wherever they passed under their own telephone wires. The Corporation strongly objected to the expense and indiscreetly asked whether the requirement applied retrospectively. The Post Office replied that it did and on 7 April 1904 complained that they still had not been installed as required — the reply came back that the Borough Electrical Engineer had left and gone to Hong Kong!

The five B.E.T. bogie cars were delivered in March 1903 and put into service on the Thornton Heath route. A Brush street watering car was delivered for the B.E.T. in April. To house 15 additional cars, £3,500 was borrowed for enlarging Purley depôt and an extension was completed in August, in spite of some difficulty caused by the sudden death of Mr. Mawdesley, the Town Clerk, when his deputy, Mr. Samuel Jacobs, was unaware of what had been discussed at a meeting with the Board of Trade.

While the Corporation tramway system was being developed, it became clear that the B.E.T. was interesting itself in other tramway schemes just outside the borough boundaries, such as the Mitcham Light Railway Order of 1901 and schemes for tramways to Wallington and Sutton on one side of Croydon and in the Urban District of Penge on the other side, all promoted under the Croydon & District Tramways Acts of 1902 and 1903. There would be connecting lines to link these new tramways with the existing system and entering Croydon territory. This much alarmed Croydon Corporation, who envisaged the B.E.T. building up a vast empire of tramways around them, largely at their expense, but from which they would not profit. On the other hand, the B.E.T. tried to reassure the Corporation that they would gain considerable benefit from the traffic and trade which would be generated from a wider area.

The disagreement came to a head when the Corporation learned that Tramway No. 20 of the 1902 Bill,* a connecting line between the existing South Norwood terminus and the Penge boundary at Selby Road, would be entirely within the Borough and other connecting lines would be largely within it. Naturally, the Corporation opposed the Bill and asked for protective clauses even though at the time, there was some public outcry against municipalities who thought all electric tramways should end at their boundaries. Therefore, the clause introduced to pacify Croydon Corporation said in effect, "You have the prior right to construct this tramway yourself, but if you do not do so by the time the Company are ready to start work on their Penge lines, then the B.E.T. may step in and construct this line at their own expense". This made the Corporation feel that a pistol was being held to their head to extend a line which now terminated at a useful objective, South Norwood shopping centre to an arbitrary point which was of no use to them. The B.E.T. insisted that Tramway No. 20 be laid entirely with double track, like their Penge area system. This involved widening Goat House

* By a coincidence, this tramway met Tramway No. 20 of the Corporation's Act of 1900.

Bridge, which crossed five railway tracks and replacing the low brick arch railway bridge just before Selby Road by a girder bridge on brick pillars. The Corporation objected strongly to the additional expense of double track.

Loans to municipal tramways always required authorization by the Board of Trade and on 14 July, the Borough Accountant requested permission to borrow £10,000 for the construction of tramways, including £7,164 for the bogie cars. He also wished to borrow £2,000 for a depôt site. The site was acquired in 1905 in Morland Road, Addiscombe, near the school and Blackhorse Lane, but the depôt was never built. At the time, Thornton Heath Depôt housed 9 bogie cars and 18 four-wheelers, while Purley housed 6 bogie cars and 27 four-wheelers.

It will be recalled that either party, the Corporation or the B.E.T., had the right to terminate the lease of the tramways after five years, if not satisfied with the way it had worked out. The Corporation became very upset about the arrangements being made by the B.E.T. and decided on 29 May 1905 to terminate the lease at the end of its first 5 years. This was put into writing to the Company on 9 August and the date of termination named as 1 June 1906. The B.E.T. came back with a proposal to increase the rent paid to £4,000 per year—to no avail.

The Corporation began building Tramway No. 20 late in 1905, for completion by November. It was constructed by direct labour under the supervision of Mr. E. F. Morgan, the Borough Surveyor. The B.E.T. had to contribute towards the rebuilding of Goat House and Selby Road bridges. Nevertheless, the line was laid with single track, except for an extended loop on Goat House Bridge and one other loop, even though Selby Road Bridge was rebuilt to take double track under it. The Selby Road boundary now became a real frontier and there was no communication between either party on each side.

When Tramway No. 20 was completed, the Corporation wrote to the B.E.T. who were still lessees of the track and cars, for the use of a car with which the Board of Trade could carry out an inspection. They received the following reply, addressed to F. C. Lloyd, the new Town Clerk:—

"We understand you have asked for the loan of one of our cars to run over the new line, which you state you have laid down under powers of our Act of 1902. On referring to the Act, we find that the line was to be laid as double line, subject to certain conditions and that it has to be laid in accordance with certain specifications to the reasonable approval of our Engineer. We are informed that the line has not been laid with double line, but as single line with passing places. Moreover, you have altogether ignored our request for a copy of the specification, without which it is impossible for our Engineer to see whether the line that has been constructed, has been constructed within the terms of the Act.

We understand that you asked for the use of a car for the purpose of the Board of Trade inspection, but it appears to us that it would be a waste of time to ask the Board of Trade to inspect what clearly has not been carried out within the terms of the Act. We suggest therefore that any test of the line you have laid down, be postponed until these matters have been disposed of.

We are sending a copy of this letter to the Board of Trade. Subject and without prejudice to the above, you can of course have the use of one of our spare cars at any time and on the usual terms."

Neither Croydon Corporation nor the Board of Trade were disposed to postpone the inspection and Mr. Lloyd replied to the effect that the Corporation had received no request from the B.E.T. for specifications of Tramway No. 20, nor had the B.E.T. notified them that they were starting work on Tramway No. 21. Thereupon, as the B.E.T. were not prepared to make a car available, Croydon Corporation took the unusual step of asking the newly opened West Ham Corporation Tramways to let them have the use of a car similar to their own, to be used for inspection. West Ham No. 66 was despatched

West Ham Corporation No. 66 in South Norwood High Street, just beyond Portland Road, with Col. von Donop on the step. This photo was taken by Mr. Norton Collins, who had a photographic studio near the Clock Tower, and was known by the author.

(Courtesy Croydon Public Library. Photo E. Norton Collins

on a flat wagon towed by a steam traction engine and placed on the track in South Norwood High Street, by the South Norwood Hill inter-section. Col. von Donop carried out the inspection on 5 November and forwarded a certificate the next day. The line opened to traffic on 14 December and the West Ham car was returned to its owners in the same manner by which it came. In spite of the discord, the extension to Selby Road was worked as a continuation of the South Norwood route, using Corporation cars, from the 1-35 series. As far as possible, the Brill trucked cars were used on the South Norwood route and the Peckham trucked cars on the Addiscombe route. Cars running to Selby Road continued to show "Norwood" as the destination.

In the meantime, the B.E.T. had set up a subsidiary company, the South Metropolitan Electric Tramways & Lighting Co. Ltd., to take over and work their lines when the Corporation withdrew their lease. This new company set about building the proposed new lines without delay. The first to be tackled was Tramway No. 21, the extension of the South Norwood line beyond Selby Road to Penge, the section as far as the "Pawleyne Arms" on the corner of Penge High Street, being completed and inspected on 13 February 1906 and opened without ceremony soon afterwards. As the B.E.T's lease still had a few months to run, the Penge section was worked as a further extension of the South Norwood line, using the same cars, as a through service, West Croydon—Penge. This must have annoyed the Corporation, but there was little they could do about it. However, as soon as the lease expired on 1 June, the Corporation at once cut their service back to Selby Road and left the South Metropolitan Company to make their own arrangements on the other side.

To emphasise the point, the Corporation informed the B.E.T. that they must remove immediately, the 15 cars which were their property. The Corporation saw these cars as less satisfactory than the 45 cars they owned themselves and at once ordered fifteen new cars to take their place. The Corporation were then able to say that the space the B.E.T. cars occupied in the depôts, was required. We will not dwell further here on the Penge service, as the South Metropolitan Company is the subject of another chapter.

A semaphore signal arm was attached to the traction post on the corner of George Street and inscribed along its length "Addiscombe Car Waiting". Cars waiting at the terminus in George Street were not visible from the stop in the main road and the signal was pulled to a horizontal position by the regulator, whenever an Addiscombe car appeared. At night it was replaced by a lamp held by a point boy.

It will be recalled that in horse tram days, cars had run from the centre of Croydon to Thornton Heath High Street, either via Thornton Heath Pond and Brigstock Road, or more directly, via West Croydon, the "Gloster" and Whitehorse Road. The two routes met end-on and a loop service could be worked. The Brigstock Road route was included in the original powers for electrification and completed with the rest, but Whitehorse Road route was not, owing to the lack of development along that thoroughfare.

There was now pressure for a quicker and more direct route to Thornton Heath High Street and a Bill comprising five "Tramways" was put before Parliament in 1905. The Bill also included the proposed extension from the "Leslie Arms" at the corner of Cherry Orchard Road and Lower Addiscombe Road, along Morland Road to Woodside and Norwood Junction.

Tramways Nos. 1, 4 and 5 were approved on 13 February 1906. No. 1 was the Morland Road line, while 4 and 5 were Whitehorse Road on which there were to be four passing loops. There is no indication as to the nature of Tramways 2 and 3, which were thrown out. The Corporation had powers to build any tramway shown as single on the Deposited Plans, as double provided that necessary road widening was carried out. It was decided to invoke these powers in this case in spite of many protests from frontagers and the route was duly built with double track, the revised plan being submitted on 16 October.

Col. von Donop inspected Whitehorse Road and issued his certificate on 3 November. The route opened on 9 November, with a circular service to Thornton Heath, in either direction via Whitehorse Road and Brigstock Road. No more was heard of the Morland Road route, although included in the powers obtained. The Thornton Heath service became a victim of delays caused by traffic congestion, which because of the circular working could become cumulative and on 15 January 1908, it was split up, Whitehorse Road then being worked by a separate shuttle service, West Croydon—Thornton Heath High Street, but on 4 July the service on Whitehorse Road was discontinued.

The 15 new cars were built by Brush later in 1906 as Milnes had now gone out of business. At the Corporation's special request, they had a Brush version of Milnes' "Exhibition" stairs. They also had destination boxes on tall stanchions above the ends of the top deck, a feature which now became standard on Croydon cars. They took the numbers 36-45 and 56-60 of the B.E.T. cars which were taken and dumped on a site which the new South Metropolitan Company had acquired near West Croydon Cemetery, for a depôt. An embarrassing complication was that some cars, probably eight, which the new company had on order, were then delivered to Thornton Heath depôt and remained there for some weeks, while the company pleaded that they had nowhere to put them. However, it was agreed that while awaiting the arrival of their own new cars, the Corporation could use them in service, with the B.E.T. insignia covered over. They are believed to have run on the main line. When the Corporation's new cars arrived they cost £10,000 in all.

With their 15 cars, the B.E.T. took away the street watering car and the Corporation ordered another one in July; it was delivered during 1907, by the United Electric Car Co. of Preston and cost £619 10s.

One sign of the change in management, was that the staff were all fitted out with new uniforms, with brass cap badges designed by Mr. Goodyer (a coat of arms within a wreath). The actual handover took place at midnight on 31 May 1906, when Mr. Goodyer ceremonially handed over the keys of Thornton Heath depôt to the Mayor, Alderman Lillico. T. B. Goodyer, A.M.Inst.E.E., H. B. Harris, A.M.Inst.M.E., A.M.Inst.E.E., the Engineer, C. G. Foster the Traffic Superintendent, F. J. Reavey the Chief Clerk, and most of the staff numbering 286, were invited to remain with the Corporation. The only staff who did not remain were some half dozen who lived outside the Borough. There were 60 cars and 10.7 route miles or 17.13 miles of track on the system. In May 1907, it was stated that since the Corporation took over, 1,207,157 additional passengers had been carried, but there had been one regrettable accident; a Mrs. Suhr, aged 63, had fallen from the top deck of a car on 8 April and had died later in hospital.* Ten more cars like those of 1906 were purchased in 1907, to meet increasing traffic and were numbered 61-70.

Eventually, after relations between the Corporation and the South Metropolitan Company had improved, Alderman Trumble and Mr. Goodyer visited Newcastle to study through running arrangements and an agreement was reached between Croydon Corporation and the Company for through running across the Selby Road boundary at 3 pence per car mile in each case, on 14 April 1907. Through working commenced on 24 June, when Corporation cars were permitted to take over the Penge service and work right through to the Thicket Road terminus from West Croydon and in return, South Metropolitan cars from the Crystal Palace were permitted to run through to West Croydon. Each undertaking was to provide a ten minute service with eight cars. Only South Metropolitan cars were equipped with the necessary track brakes demanded on Anerley Hill. This arrangement always worked quite well. The Company's other two services started from Tamworth Road, opposite West Croydon Station, but the Corporation were not prepared to extend the hand of friendship further and permit the Tamworth Road terminus to be connected with their own system.

In September, Corporation staff holidays were put on a firm basis and fixed at 2 days after one year's service, 4 days after two years and a maximum of six days after three years for platform staff. Crews were to be paid one-and-a-half rate for working on Christmas Day.

In December, new proposals for tramways were put forward, under the title "Croydon & Southern District Tramways" when it was decided to set up an undertaking to construct tramways starting from Croydon's southern boundary at Purley, with four lines extending to Coulsdon and Whyteleafe. However, when Coulsdon electors were asked to support the scheme, they voted 288 in favour and 375 against. A Bill was rejected by the Lords on 13 March 1908.

At a meeting early in 1908, it was stated that the Corporation's Power Station was supplying electric current to the tramways at 2 pence per unit. Alderman Trumble made a report at the end of the first year's working by the Corporation, and speaking as Chairman of the Tramways Committee, said the charge for electricity was too high and the £3,850 profit on the Electrical Department should really have gone to the tramways. In June it was decided to renew the Quin trolley wire cut-out apparatus, which was installed in the sub-stations to cut off the current if a trolley wire broke. This would cost £483. Alderman Trumble also said that the results of the first year's working were disappointing because of bad weather and trade. The surplus was £3,000 but should have been around £9,000. There was competition with the new South Metropolitan Company for country ride traffic on Saturdays and Sundays. The Corporation carried heavy weekend traffic on the Purley route, for people wishing to walk and picnic on Riddlesdown and in the country beyond Purley.

* Evidently misinformed—Mrs. W. Suhr died in the Carshalton accident on the South Metropolitan Tramways.

On Wednesday 22 July 1908, a tramcar decorated with hundreds of coloured lamps and floral decorations toured the system as part of a National Lifeboat Day procession. The crew were suitably attired in blue jerseys, red woollen caps and cork jackets, while other members of the staff similarly attired, walked alongside the car with collecting boxes.

Until now, the nearest London County Council tramway service had terminated at Streatham Library 1¼ miles north of Croydon Corporation's Norbury terminus, but on 31 July, an extension of the L.C.C. tramway was opened, bringing their tracks within six inches of Croydon tracks! The rails were not joined, but the L.C.C. did use overhead wires on most of this extension and these were strained off to the Croydon wires and separated by insulators. The L.C.C. used large bogie cars with covered top decks, from the outset on this line. In October, Mr. Goodyer reported that through bookings had been introduced, and brought a considerable increase in receipts, which in December amounted to £4,500. He added that in spite of passengers having to change at Norbury, the new service had caused motor bus competition to disappear. Croydon cars were soon fitted with boards attached to the upper deck, proclaiming the through bookings provided.

In March 1910, the Corporation decided to withdraw £16,815 from the Tramways & Electricity Account, to be put to the relief of rates. In the same month, they learned of a L.C.C. proposal to extend one of their routes to the Crystal Palace via Forest Hill. Five new four wheeled cars were ordered in September 1910, to meet still increasing traffic. Built by Brush, they were identical to Nos. 61-70 and delivered early in 1911. They must have been the last new open top cars to be purchased by a London area tramway, but open toppers were necessary as they might be required to work on the Penge route, which had low bridges at Selhurst, Selby Road and Penge West Station. The new cars were numbered 71-75.

In November 1910, the Town Clerk F. C. Lloyd, applied to the Board of Trade for permission to extend the passing loop on East Croydon Station bridge, to join that leading round the corner into Cherry Orchard Road, making a short section of double track. The Solicitor for the London, Brighton & South Coast Railway objected on the grounds that if cars stood on the loop, they would obstruct the entrance to the Parcels Office. The Board of Trade agreed, however, provided that cars did not remain on this new section of track and the loop was extended early in 1911. The Thornton Heath service was extended to the "Gloster" on 28 July serving Whitehorse Road again.

A report made in June 1912 said that the low current consumption, for which Croydon cars were noted, was entirely due to the use of meters. The tramways again contributed £8,000 to relief of the rates in that year and in December a covered top L.C.C. car was pushed across the gap at Hermitage Bridge, Norbury, to be tested on Croydon track, but it would not pass under the bridge at Norbury Station, which had been lowered only for open top cars.

In July 1912, the Tramways Committee recommended that powers be sought to operate feeder bus services, to combat the competition from private bus companies. For a number of reasons, bus operating powers were never granted to London area municipal tramways and Croydon Corporation evidently became aware of this and dropped the plan. Therefore, Mr. Goodyer lobbied Members of Parliament in August 1913, to persuade them to pass legislation which would put bus operators on the same basis as tram operators and make them accept the same obligations. He gave detailed statistics to support his views.

In March 1913, the Tramways Committee recommended the extension of the Addiscombe route over the old horse tram line to Norwood Junction as they considered it would pay and add to the rateable value of the district. It was admitted that there was already heavy bus competition, but a tram cost six pence per car mile to run and a bus cost 7 pence. On the other hand, there was a constant loss on the Whitehorse Road route and in April, the Council accepted the Manager's recommendation that it be closed. It closed on 8 March, this time for good. There were still complaints of overcrowding on other routes.

In May, a presentation was made to H. B. Harris, the Tramways Engineer, on his retirement. "Tramways Engineer" was a title inherited from the B.E.T. administration and Gordon V. Stanley was now appointed Assistant Engineer (Tramways) in charge of rolling stock and overhead lines. He was regarded as an assistant to the Borough Engineer who directly controlled the track as part of the road surface.

Mr. Goodyer's salary was increased from £500 to £550 in March 1914 and later Mr. Stanley's, to £185. In May one of the four-wheeled cars was fitted with longitudinal cushioned seats.

A Mr. Hefford sued the Corporation when his car was smashed up by a tram. In August, automatic points were installed at Thornton Heath Pond and at Norbury terminus. There were floods on the Norbury route on 14 June 1914.

The outbreak of war in August 1914 necessitated the dropping of plans to straighten the road by Hall's works and double the track in Cherry Orchard Road. By September, 40 employees, including 10 motormen and 24 conductors, were serving with the colours. The street-watering car was decorated with over 150 lamps and covered with patriotic posters in connection with a recruitment campaign. The main streamer read "Young men desirous of joining HIS MAJESTY'S ARMY should apply to the nearest Post Office".

In spite of the war, £2,550 was voted for doubling the track on the short length between Selhurst Station and Prince Road, by joining two passing loops. This was done in 1915 to serve the Crystal Palace Football Club, which was then established at "The Nest", opposite Selhurst Station, on the site now occupied by British Railways' Electric Train Works. A loan of £1,272 was approved for an auxilliary cable on the Norwood route.

In 1915, when many British Tramways decided to employ women conductors, Mr. Goodyer was very doubtful whether it would be possible to get them out by 4.00 a.m. or keep them up for late nights, but the final decision rested with the police. However, so many men were called up by October, that it was necessary to take on women. On 2 June 1916, the male staff came out on strike against the proposed employment of women drivers. Some of them were suspended and then summoned for retaining their uniforms! Women conductors received the same wages as the men. The strike was settled in five weeks.

Croydon Corporation No. 20 approaching the "Gloster" from Whitehorse Road. The South Norwood route diverges to the right.
(Courtesy J. B. Gent.
(Commercial postcard "Card House"

Also in 1916, it became necessary to apply various air-raid precautions. On the cars, the headlamps were masked and side lamps were fitted. The opening lights were given a wash of blue paint. Route letters were cut in stencil form on the headlamp masks—N for Norbury, P for Purley, TH for Thornton Heath and a few cars had G for George Street on the Addiscombe route. A hooded air-raid warning sign was fixed on a traction post outside Thornton Heath depôt. One car was fitted with a searchlight and taken each night by military personnel to Purley terminus. It was kept locked up and Corporation staff were not allowed to touch it. Nos. 25 and 34 were modifed for this use.

There was a regrettable accident on 10 January 1917, when the points were set wrongly at Crown Hill and a car on the main line turned into George Street at speed. It knocked down and killed Inspector J. W. Chandler who was supervising the Addiscombe route. Owing to the shortage of motormen, Councillor Wood-Roberts, a solicitor, drove a tram during 1917.

T. B. Goodyer was appointed Vice-President of the Municipal Tramways Association in October 1917. Late in 1917, Croydon Corporation built a new battery driven tower wagon, to replace a horse drawn vehicle. It cost £921.

Owing to the shortage of coal for power stations, Sunday morning tram services were withdrawn on 17 May 1918, but restored in August.

Because so many of the engineering staff were called up in the forces as well as drivers and conductors, maintenance could not be carried out to pre-war standards and several cars had to be withdrawn from service, because of mechanical defects, for which replacement parts could not be obtained. The 1-35 class cars suffered worst, but Mr. Goodyer and Mr. Stanley did their very best to keep as many cars on the road as possible. Cars, overhead equipment and track were all in urgent need of repair, but thanks to the very high standards previously maintained, Croydon tramways came through the war in a very much better state than most of their neighbours. The war eventually came to an end on 11 November 1918.

Male staff began returning from the forces and all women conductors had been replaced by men by May 1919. The foundations beneath the track on the Addiscombe route was now in such a bad state that it had to be replaced urgently in July 1919. The work was undertaken by the British Reinforced Concrete Co. Ltd.

The hard work put in by Thomas B. Goodyer was recognized when he was elected President of the Municipal Tramways Association for the period 1918/1919. He was subsequently made an O.B.E. for his war efforts. He used his influence to see that tramways attained their rightful place in the country's transport network and were not put at a disadvantage against the many motor bus services which soon sprung up throughout the London area and did not have to pay for upkeep of the roads over which they ran ran, like the trams did.

The Penge route had been cut back to the "Pawleyne Arms" on the corner of Penge High Street, for the "duration", but in 1919, most journeys were reinstated to the Thicket Road terminus. Some journeys continued to turn short.

On 30 September 1919, the two houses adjoining Thornton Heath depôt were purchased by the Corporation for use as offices for the Tramways Department and were known as "Brigstock Villa". Later a memorial tablet was fixed on the outer wall. It named war casualties.

Air Raid alarm.

(Courtesy "Tramway & Railway World"

Corporation No. 25 (new numbering) with top cover, in short-lived red and ivory livery at Thornton Heath terminus. (Richard Elliott

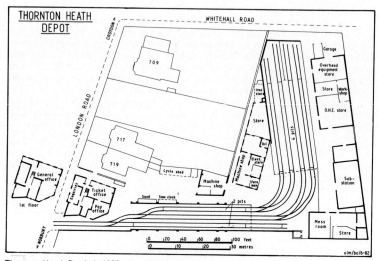

Thornton Heath Depôt in 1933, showing awkward layout.

(B. Connelly from official drawing

CHAPTER THREE

THE POST-WAR REORGANIZATION

Most tramways in the London area, and indeed those throughout the country, came through the 1914-1918 war with their fleets of cars and other assets in a very depleted condition. In the meantime, recovery was not helped by the fact that in March 1919, £14,000 was taken from the tramway profits to help relieve the rates, instead of putting it towards repairing the cars. In February 1920, the Corporation recommended the compulsory purchase of the two short sections of South Metropolitan track within the Borough of Croydon. This was a political move which would have brought no actual benefit to the Croydon Corporation Tramways, because under the powers granted by their Act of Parliament, the company would still have had to be granted full through running powers. Fortunately no action was taken.

On the other hand, motorbus competition soon reasserted itself and Thomas Tilling Ltd. came to an agreement with the London General Omnibus Co. who handed over a newly built garage near the "Red Deer", South Croydon and permitted Tilling to operate the majority of bus services in the Croydon area. (Particularly routes 12A London to South Croydon via Penge and 75F Woolwich & Caterham via Penge). While a few of their services could be said to be feeders to the trams, the majority were in direct competition with them. The Petrol-Electric buses which Tilling used were said to be too complicated to have been requisitioned during the war, but in the early 1920s, "pirate" bus services were establishing themselves, small operators in many cases using new bus bodies mounted on ex-Army lorry chassis, which could be obtained cheaply in 1919/20. Many broke down on the tram tracks obstructing the service.

The need to repair both cars and track as soon as possible was vital. The most urgent task, that of repairing the track on the main line at Broad Green, was undertaken in 1919 and cost £2,500. It was followed in 1920 by the track in North End from West Croydon Station to the High Street, at a cost of £11,283 in 1920. At the same time, it was found necessary to alter and extend the workshops in Thornton Heath depôt, including extensions to the maintenance pits, so that the best use could be made of the facilities available when the cars were overhauled. Croydon was always very tight for depôt accommodation, but an extension to Purley depôt which would have cost £11,400 was turned down by the Council in October 1920.

The actual costs of the work done at this stage have been quoted as follows:—

Alterations to pits in Thornton Heath depôt		£468
New Wheel Lathe in Thornton Heath depôt		£980
New motor for lathe		£70
Extension of terminal loop at Addiscombe		£1,850
Crossover at Haling Park Road		£250
New feeder cables "Gloster" to Tennison Road		£2,000
	Total	£5,168

These were to be charged to the reserve fund.

In January 1921, the "Sandberg" rail hardening process was used on 1½ miles of the main line under the direction of the Borough Surveyor.

Work was soon put in hand on the reconstruction of cars and many required complete rebuilding, in particular Nos. 13, 25, 34 and 35. The first was rebuilt in exactly the same style as before, but the other three had their reversed stairs exchanged for the normal half-turn type like the newer cars. In all, 45 cars were rebuilt to a greater or lesser extent in the works.

In February 1921, a communication was received from the newly formed Ministry of Transport, asking for future tramway policy to be formulated and mentioning that it would be desirable to establish through running from London to Purley over London County Council and Croydon Corporation tracks. In March, a special sub-committee was formed, as it was thought that £289,000 would soon have to be spent on the renewal of track on the main line. Two oil burning boilers for the power station were purchased in June.

Negotiations commenced in 1922 between the London County Council and Croydon Corporation and in correspondence between their respective managers, it soon became evident that the L.C.C. was prepared to consider an arrangement whereby a through joint service could be provided, using cars belonging to both authorities. Cars of the L.C.C's standard type were larger and heavier than any that Croydon possessed and all were top covered. Consequently substantial alterations would have to be made to the track layout of Croydon's main line. As the L.C.C. used a trailing trolley rope, they demanded centre running overhead wires. There was insufficient clearance for a covered top car under Norbury Station Bridge and the road would have to be lowered. Emphasising the urgency of improvements, the L.B.S.C. Railway announced that they would be electrifying their line to West Croydon in August.

On the other hand, in response to a number of demands that the trams be abandoned, Mr. Dalrymple of Glasgow and R. J. Howley of the B.E.T. were called on to make a report on the prospects of Croydon Corporation Tramways. In July, they made it clear that they were completely opposed to scrapping. At the same time, Councillor Thomson appealed to the Chamber of Commerce to support the trams. He said there was no reason why Croydon should not pay as well as the L.C.C., with through running. On Monday 30 October 1922, it was voted by 24 to 15 to reconstruct the main line. It would cost £132,460 if undertaken by direct labour, which might be cheaper than by contract and application was made to the Ministry of Transport for a loan, so that work could start at once. During 1922, H. E. Smith, the Chief Clerk, died suddenly and G. D. Morgan from Aberdare Corporation Tramways, was appointed in his place.

In April, the Ministry sanctioned a loan of £5,893, repayable in twenty years, so that the track could be relaid with heavier rails and doubled wherever possible; the bracket overhead suspension would be replaced by span wires. Work had started on the Brighton Road as it was in extreme disrepair!

Nevertheless, this was not the only improvement which the Corporation had in mind, since Councillor Thomson, Chairman of the Tramways Committee submitted a report on 23 April, suggesting that the Addiscombe route be converted to railless car operation (trolleybuses) and that it be extended to Woodside. He said he had already led a deputation to Birmingham and inspected the "Railless" vehicles working on the Nechells route and had returned much impressed. A certain amount of road widening would be necessary and turning facilities would have to be provided. A Bill was prepared to be put before Parliament in 1924, asking for powers in a number of municipal activities, including the proposed trolleybus route. The Act when approved, said "The Corporation may provide, maintain and equip, but shall not manufacture trolley vehicles". There were clauses protecting the interests of the South Metropolitan Company. There were also proposals for a loop working via Morland Road to Woodside, with a depôt on a site already owned by the Corporation, in Morland Road. The scheme would cost £110,000. The 14 vehicles were to be like those at Birmingham.

In the meantime, it was considered that work on the main line would take eight months and was proving difficult because the existing wood blocks had sunk. However, the Council considered that once this was completed, work on the remainder of the system should be suspended until they had thoroughly considered Councillor Thomson's report. A poll of ratepayers in the Woodside and Addiscombe area early in January 1924, produced the result 8,168 votes in favour and 7,219 against the trolleybus proposals, but a subsequent poll of the whole Borough defeated the scheme by a big majority.

As one can imagine, while all this discussion of a side issue was going on in Council, there was a continuous flow of correspondence between T. B. Goodyer, the Croydon Manager and J. K. Bruce, Traffic Manager of the L.C.C. Tramways. One of the letters concerned has come to light. It is from Mr. Goodyer, dated 26th October 1923 and evidently a reply to a lengthy questionnaire from Mr. Bruce. In it he goes into great detail, describing all stopping places, special instructions, permitted speeds, the training of drivers and conductors, fare structure, who was entitled to free travel, rules and documentation. In other words it gave Mr. Bruce a complete picture of how the Croydon tramways undertaking was worked. It evidently guided him when suggesting what alterations should be made in Croydon practices to make them compatible with the L.C.C. (one example was bell signals—Croydon used two bells for stop and one for go, opposite to the L.C.C.). One proposal made by Mr. Goodyer, which evidently impressed Mr. Bruce, was that before through running commenced, Croydon motormen should each be permitted to attend a course of instruction at the L.C.C. Driving School to learn the intricacies of driving larger cars in London traffic and of the conduit system. The L.C.C. prepared a draft Agreement on 6 November 1923.

One problem which beset those tramway undertakings which sought through running agreements with the London County Council, was the fact that nearly ninety percent of its route mileage used the slot conduit system for current collection instead of overhead wires. True the L.C.C. alone had to bear the cost of installation and maintenance of this rather expensive system, but for any of the other tramways who dared venture more than a short distance onto L.C.C. tracks, it required special fittings on the cars and special driving techniques. This was to have an effect on the tramway systems of West Ham, East Ham, Walthamstow, Croydon and the Metropolitan Company. Hence Mr. Goodyer's concern about making sure that his staff were properly trained to drive cars on conduit equipped track.

The conduit consisted of a concrete tube containing two live current rails, positive and negative, buried about a foot below the road surface and connected with the outside world by a continuous slot, the top part of which was protected by two inverted "L" shaped rails 1 inch apart. The current collector, known as a plough, comprised a flat lamina of metal and insulating materials, hung from special brackets on the car. There were sprung shoes either side near the bottom, which picked up the current from the positive and negative rails within the slot. Although the slot had to be continuous, through all junctions and crossings, the live rails were not and were broken for a few feet at junctions, crossings and feeder points. It was knowing where to cut off current and make the car coast at these breaks in the current rails that was the principal factor of the special driving techniques. A complicated junction such as at the Elephant & Castle would entail several breaks in quick succession. The plough carrier comprised special steel channels which supported the head of the plough, had to run the full width of the car, as in London the slot was not always exactly central between the tracks and the plough passed out to one side at changeover points.

Croydon cars on passing over the L.C.C. boundary at Hermitage Bridge, continued to run under overhead wires for about half a mile to Streatham, where there was a changeover point. The tracks were splayed slightly for a small traffic island between them, onto which the two conduit slots from the up and down tracks were directed in a "Y" formation. When a car approached from Croydon, it would pass the island very slowly, while an L.C.C. official fed a plough which had been held at the tail of the Y, into the plough-carrier of the car, with a large pitch-fork. The car would then stop while the conductor pulled down the trolley and the driver changed over the electrical circuits with a large switch under the stairs. (Croydon cars had these switches at both ends, some L.C.C. cars had them at one end only). The overhead wires overlapped the conduit by a short distance. On returning with a car towards Croydon, the conductor placed the trolley on the overhead wire and the driver operated the changeover switch; the deflection of the current rail across the running rail automatically disengaged the plough from the carrier on the car and the "Ploughman" caught it on a sort of roller-skate as it fell away. He then dragged it to join other ploughs held in readiness at the end of the Y.

Although there were other similar conduit systems abroad, the method of changeover was unique to the L.C.C. The changeover switch was necessary because the overhead wire system used an earthed return and the conduit had positive and negative current rails—different circuits were necessary on the car, each of which had four master current breaker switches, one for conduit and one for overhead at each end of the car.

The work on the main line was undertaken by direct labour. The road was lowered under Norbury Station Bridge, so that L.C.C. covered top cars could pass under it. While the Thornton Heath Pond—Norbury section was being relaid, temporary track was laid as required and all motor bus services were diverted by Norbury Crescent and Melfort Road to Thornton Heath and Brigstock Road. This probably annoyed the bus companies at the time, but in the long run, the joke was on them as they found that there was a genuine demand for a service in Melfort Road and when the main road was clear again, one service continued to go that way. By 30 April 1924, 263 men were being employed on reconstructing the main line and 1,500 tons of new rails had been ordered at £10 7s. 6d. per ton, together with new traction posts and three concrete mixers. Modern road-making techniques had not yet been invented, hence the large number of men employed and the most complicated piece of equipment was the Corporation steamroller.

When the turn came for the last section of the Purley line to be relaid, by Purley High Street, the down track was relaid first and cars ran one at a time to Purley terminus on the old up track and returned that way, before the next car could proceed. The work was completed by May 1924, but two more years of continued discussion were to pass before more progress on a through service to London was achieved.

While all this was going on, the condition of the track on the other routes was continuing to deteriorate at an increasing rate and the decision to relay the Thornton Heath and Penge routes and lift Whitehorse Road was taken on 28 April.

So that cars waiting at the terminus should not impede the work, the Penge route was extended southward to the "Greyhound" in Croydon High Street from January to October 1924. Evidently it would have upset the through running agreement, if the South Metropolitan cars had been similarly extended and they continued to terminate at West Croydon Station. No alterations to the track layout of the Penge

L.C.C. 1762 in Croydon High Street. The "Greyhound" public house is on the right, but the cars from Thornton Heath actually ran a little further. (Courtesy "Len's of Sutton"

New Croydon Corporation bogie car No. 48 on the Victoria Embankment on route 18, at the end of its journey to London. (Photo Dr. H. A. Whitcombe 60185 (Courtesy Science Museum, London

route were made immediately and few were possible owing to the narrowness of the streets traversed. During October, November and December 1924, the Thornton Heath branch line was relaid and the opportunity was taken to lay a proper double track junction from the main line into Brigstock Road, with a separate track connection into the depôt. (Previously there had been a single track connection and crossover on the main line for Thornton Heath cars. Another single track connection crossed the main line from Brigstock Road into the depôt.) Further down Brigstock Road, the sections of single and interlaced track beyond Frant Road had to remain as the road thereon to Melfort Road was too narrow for double track, but the track in Thornton Heath High Street was doubled.

The Thornton Heath—Purley service was cut back to the "Red Deer" on 3 November 1924.

So that the service could continue uninterrupted while these improvements were going on, temporary passing loops were laid with special flat rails on a bed of cinders. The writer recalls one outside the "Ship" at the foot of Goat House Bridge, when walking to school in South Norwood. The Norwood route was relaid between September 1924 and January 1925.

At the same time other improvements to the tramway system were in hand. In June the Council approved the Tramways Committee's proposal to spend £30,000 on improving Purley Depôt, and extending the workshops at Thornton Heath. £36,000 was to be spent on new feeder cables suitable for the higher current consumption of the L.C.C. cars when they ran through and the reconstruction of the track on the Norwood and Thornton Heath routes cost £75,779. A plea was made that the Council should borrow £7,090 towards this work. Bogie car No. 55 was fitted with air brakes acting on the wheels and track in August 1924.

However, at the Council meeting of 15 December, the picture did not look quite so bright and it was stated that the trams were losing £900 each week. Now that the reconstruction of the main route was complete, the bus operators benefited as well as the tramways and it was in this atmosphere that the Corporation turned down an offer by the London General Omnibus Co. to take over and work the Addiscombe route. In fact, in his capacity as a former President of the Municipal Tramways Association, Mr. Goodyer took a large part in pressing for the Restricted Streets Order which followed the Road Traffic Act of 1924. Under this Order, a very large number of streets in the Greater London area were named and from then on each bus company had to submit copies of its time schedules to the authorities and the number of bus journeys they were permitted to operate on these streets were restricted. In December 1924, the Minister of Transport obtained powers to insist on through running between adjoining tramway systems.

With regard to the Addiscombe route, Alderman Thomson reminded the Council that powers had already been obtained to work trolleybuses and negotiations with the L.G.O.C. would doom the proposal.

No work was done on the Addiscombe track which continued to deteriorate rapidly under the heavy traffic which it now carried. After considering briefly a through service from Addiscombe to Thornton Heath, further thought was given to the provision of a loop trolleybus service to Woodside Station both via Addiscombe and Morland Road.

At the same time as the track was relaid on the main line, the bracket overhead suspension was replaced with span wire, with posts on both sides of the road. In addition to the new posts thus required, many old ones required replacing.

A gloomy picture was also painted at the Council's meeting in March 1925, when it was stated that the loss for 1924 had been £61,000 and discussions with the L.C.C. it became apparent to Mr. Goodyer, that if an agreement was to be reached on through running, then Croydon Corporation would be required to supply a quota of cars which matched up to the L.C.C. standards in all respects. The number of such cars required could be as many as thirty.

This added expense horrified the Council, who estimated that they could cost £79,320. The proposal was referred back by 24 votes against 23. The Council were quite convinced that ten cars would be sufficient and that the ten existing 1902 bogie cars could be modernized to bring them into line with L.C.C. practices.

It will be recalled that cars on the Penge and Crystal Palace routes partook in one-way working in the centre of Croydon, inwards via Oakfield Road and returning via Wellesley Road and Station Road. This necessitated running along a short section of the southbound track of the main line. Where the cars turned off into Station Road, the up and down tracks were so near together that the rear platform of a car turning could foul a car passing northbound on the main line and strict instructions were issued that a northbound car must wait while a Penge car turned. This was mentioned among the restrictions in Mr. Goodyer's report of 26 October 1923, to Mr. Bruce of the L.C.C. and he must have commented on it, as in July, the decision was taken to do away with the one-way working and use Station Road in both directions. The necessary alterations to the track layout would cost £13,437. The Ministry of Transport sanctioned a loan of £5,893 repayable in twenty years.

As a preliminary, a temporary loop was laid in Oakfield Road, which was for the time being used in both directions, while Wellesley Road and Station Road were closed for reconstruction and the installation of loops. As the former was very narrow, bays had to be cut into the pavement at one point to make room for a passing loop. Another loop was arranged on the corner between Wellesley Road and Station Road and two more in Station Road itself, the second of which was to be used as a terminal. The connecting curve from Station Road towards Purley was removed, but that towards Thornton Heath had to be retained for depôt working. Station Road was almost as narrow as Wellesley Road, but had to be shared as a terminal with a number of country bus routes of the East Surrey Traction Co. Their buses stood in front of the then station building.

In the meantime, there were changes on the L.C.C. which affected the prospects of through running. Mr. A. L. C. Fell, the General Manager, resigned on health grounds at the end of December 1924 and his place was taken by J. K. Bruce, who as Traffic Manager was already in negotiation with Croydon Corporation. This put him in a stronger position and he showed a more progressive attitude towards running the tramways than Mr. Fell had done; for example, Mr. Fell had maintained to the last that the L.C.C. "Standard" car was not suitable in basic design for the fitting of transverse seats in the lower saloon. Mr. Bruce lost no time in showing how this could be done and meanwhile purchased 400 new more powerful motors for fitting to South London cars and speeding up the services. Croydon were still thinking in terms of refurbishing the ten existing bogie cars for through running and rather tactfully Mr. Bruce told them that these cars were unsuitable because of their lower seating capacity than the L.C.C. cars, omitting to mention the many other ways in which they fell short of L.C.C. standards.

In March 1925, arrangements were made with the Post Office for the fixing of letter posting boxes on cars leaving certain points in the evenings. The boxes would be provided by the G.P.O. who would fix and remove them from cars as necessary (see page 190). The writer recalls seeing a Penge car one evening with a red posting box hung on the outside of the dash and padlocked to the corner handrail near the hand brake staff. There was a black card in the nearside bulkhead window with the letters "Postal Car" cut out and filled behind with red celluloid. The boxes were cleared as each car returned to the central point at about 10.30 p.m. Several other London area municipal tramways had a similar arrangement, including Ilford and Bexley.

Early in April 1925, the London County Council put a firm proposal to Croydon Corporation, setting down clearly, the terms on which they were prepared to arrange a through service to Purley for a trial period of six months. It was

51

basically the Agreement already approved by the L.C.C. on 6 November 1923, which provided that the L.C.C. should make available 35 cars and Croydon 25 cars on a joint through service. The Croydon cars were to be similar to those of the L.C.C., but as the Corporation were still unable to make up their minds about the purchase of new cars, the L.C.C. were willing to lend them twenty cars, for the period of this agreement only, under the following terms:—

(1). Croydon Corporation was to pay the L.C.C. a sum for each car-mile operated within the Croydon area ascertained by the Corporation and Council from Operating Expenses, including wages of drivers and conductors, repair of cars and debt charges on the car-shed space occupied by those cars earmarked for loan to Croydon. This was expected to amount to 9.13 pence per car mile. The cars would be housed in a L.C.C. depôt.

(2). As the L.C.C. at that time had cars to spare, but not crews to operate them, all suitable Croydon drivers and conductors, were to be instructed by and loaned to the L.C.C., to work the Croydon portion of the through service. They were to return to Croydon employment at the end of the period.

(3). Receipts were not to be apportioned in accordance with the mileage in each area, but in accordance with the earnings in each area, which was to be ascertained from the results of a test week in each quarter.

(4). The Agreement was to be extended beyond six months, only if by mutual consent. Each undertaking was to make its own arrangements for the supply of electric current and tickets.

Croydon Corporation indicated in May that such an agreement would be acceptable. Each authority would fix the fares in its own area, with through fares mutually agreed.

A short distance north of Norbury Station, at a slight bend in the road, Croydon tram tracks terminated at the south side of Hermitage Bridge, an insignificant bridge across the River Graveney, which the through passenger could easily pass unnoticed. Here there was a six inch gap in the rails, between the Croydon and L.C.C. termini! This gap was finally closed early in September 1925 and at long last, through running commenced on Sunday 7 February 1926, with 20 Croydon crews reporting daily to Telford Avenue Depôt and taking out such L.C.C. cars as were allocated to them. The drivers chosen were those which had attended the course of instruction at the L.C.C. Driving School at Clapham Depôt. Mr. Morgan once told the writer that the L.C.C. staff used to laugh at what they regarded as quaint uniforms of the Croydon crews, with their plaited straw topped hats and the motormen's leather aprons.

As the frequent service with larger L.C.C. cars was ample for the section from South Croydon to Purley, the Thornton Heath service was now curtailed at the "Greyhound" reversing on the short section of single track just past Mint Walk. One morning and one afternoon school journey continued to run as far as the "Red Deer".

Nevertheless, Croydon Corporation was still thinking in terms of modernizing its existing rolling stock and in November, four-wheeled car No. 39 appeared fitted with two and one-cushioned transverse seats for 18 passengers in the saloon and other improvements to the internal decor. In the New Year, bogie car No. 48 was similarly treated and in March the Corporation accepted the B.T.-H. tender for 12 car sets of electrical equipment, to be fitted to the ten bogie cars and two four-wheelers.

However, the L.C.C. were not prepared to continue lending Croydon 20 cars indefinitely and made it quite clear that unless a complement of cars in every way up to their standards had been ordered by the time this short term agreement ran out, they would not renew it. Croydon Corporation pleaded that they needed time to assess the benefits of through running, particularly as the arrangement had started in the winter, when takings were at their lowest anyway.

The Minutes of the Meeting of the full Council of Croydon Corporation, held on 11 and 12 June 1926, were considered so important that they were distributed in the form of a pink covered booklet, which set out in detail the terms of the Agreement with the London County Council for through running. All aspects of the expenditure involved and the receipts obtained over the experimental period from 7 February to 3 May, the first three months, were analysed, but some items such as the additional electricity consumed, could not be isolated to the main route alone. It was said that if thirty new cars were to be required, they would cost approximately £80,000. It had already been necessary to hire Converters and Switchgear for the new sub-stations at Thornton Heath Depôt and at South Croydon and these would have to be replaced by permanent equipment if through running was to continue. Converters would cost £9,024 and Switchgear would cost £5,271. Hire charges had amounted to £2,365. In connection with these, new feeders would also be required, costing £14,550. It was also estimated that the capacity of Purley Depôt would have to be increased and overhaul facilities at Thornton Heath improved. The Ministry of Transport was prepared to sanction a loan of £30,000.

It was estimated that if the 30 new cars were purchased and an Agreement entered into with the L.C.C. for an extended period, the receipts would be increased by 2.79 pence per car mile and the running costs reduced by 2 pence per car mile. The net receipts would be increased by £25,000 a year, before deducting capital charges.

Each authority was to continue to supply the electric current for operation within its own area and the service to be so organized that the mileage operated by Croydon cars in London would be as nearly as possible equivalent to the mileage operated by London cars in Croydon. Each authority was to retain the receipts earned by its own cars, subject to certain adjustments, ascertained from a quarterly check.

The booklet also contains a report from the Finance Committee disputing the Capital Expenditure on new cars, reminding the Tramways Committee that provision had already been made to fit the existing bogie cars with new motors, covered tops and air brakes, so that they would be suitable for through running to London.

New Trucks for 10 bogie carsat £315 each pair	£3,150
New controllers 10 bogie cars at £102 each pair	£1,020
Top covers for 10 bogie cars at £600 each	£6,000

The new trucks were considered necessary, as it was thought that the Brill 22E bogies with which these cars were fitted, would be unsuitable for the fitting of conduit plough carriers which would be necessary if the cars were to be able to proceed north of Streatham Common, from which point the L.C.C. used the centre slot conduit system of current collection. Of course, the L.C.C. did not bother to point out that at that date, they still had a few cars of their own on Brill 22E bogies! Nor did they favour air brakes at that date.

It was stated that for the three months since through working had commenced net receipts had increased by £346.

The cars which the L.C.C. provided,including those loaned to Croydon were of their standard E/1 type, 78 seat bogie cars with totally enclosed top decks, but the Metropolitan Police still did not permit glass wind screens round the driver's platforms. As yet they still had wooden seats, longitudinal inside and two and two transverse upstairs. Telford Avenue Depôt, on which they were based, was one of the L.C.C's larger ones and located on the east of the road between Streatham and Brixton. Some of the L.C.C's own complement of cars came from the nearby Brixton Hill Depôt. The two services extended to Croydon and Purley were numbered 16 and 18. At the London end, both made a loop round the Victoria Embankment. No. 16 ran clockwise via Westminster Bridge—Embankment—Blackfriars, while No. 18 ran anti-clockwise Blackfriars—Embankment—Westminster. Unlike some tramway networks in the north of England, crews worked right through and there was a complicated system of through tickets (explained in another booklet) but at first some of the L.C.C. crews objected to issuing tickets with odd half-penny values, only current in Croydon.

When the time came to renew the through running agreement, the L.C.C. again made it quite clear that its renewal on a longer standing basis depended on Croydon producing a firm order for suitable new cars. In September 1926, the Corporation Tramways Committee considered a report on the first six months of through running ending 7 August. The first three months had been disappointing, but the other three months were better. There had been an increase in receipts of £2,522 of which £2,176 could be written off to expenses, so no real comparison was possible. Thirty new cars would cost £80,000 and if the cost of the new switchgear and converters was added, the figure would be £120,645. It was stated that the procrastination over the purchase of new cars had lost precious time. However, a vote showed 28 to 15 in favour of new cars.

In the meantime, Mr. Bruce of the L.C.C., had found the solution to the problem of fitting two and one turn-over cushioned seats in his cars and a number were already in service on the Wimbledon line. Very soon some were to be allocated to Telford Avenue Depôt and appeared as part of the L.C.C. complement on the Croydon/Purley line. Those cars so modernized were painted in a new red livery and by April 1927, there were 100 of them in service.

Although most of the track of the main line had been doubled before through running commenced, there were still a few sections of single line in the centre of the town, which caused delays. Demolition of old properties and widening enabled some sections in the High Street and South End to be doubled. £2,500 was voted for this purpose in July, but the work was not completed until 1929. In the meantime, the L.C.C. raised the question of through running again and said they would be prepared to extend the Agreement until 30 September, only if the Corporation took a firm decision at their meeting on 27 September—fortunately they did and as the L.C.C. were willing to permit their drawings to be used, Croydon played safe and ordered ten cars of the L.C.C. "E/1" type from Hurst Nelson & Co., of Motherwell, Scotland, who had already supplied a large number of these cars to the L.C.C.

Croydon Corporation Tramways now enjoyed through running agreements with the London County Council on one hand and with a member of the UndergrounD Group on the other hand. It might be remarked that the practices and terminology employed by these two powerful bodies varied considerably. Even certain words had different meanings and pronunciation between the two. The clearest example was "Route". On the UndergrounD Group it was synonymous with "service" and was pronounced as today with a soft "u". A route number was the plate on the front of a car indicating where it was going. With the L.C.C., the word "Route" was pronounced "Rowt" and a "Route Number" was the small blue plate with a white number, hung on a window pillar, which indicated the particular set of journeys in the Time Schedule, that this car was expected to perform. Croydon were advised to have 50 of these plates made. The L.C.C. had "Inspectors" and "Regulators" each with different duties, the latter only being concerned with time-keeping. The UndergrounD Group had Inspectors in senior and junior grades, but the differences in their duties were not so clearly defined.

While the Corporation were busy coping with the different character which the main line had now taken on, with a large fast L.C.C. car every few minutes, the track of the Addiscombe line was deteriorating at an ever-increasing rate, but at the Council Meeting held on 29 March 1926, it was decided by 30 votes to 17, to reconsider the proposal to close the route. Nevertheless, information had just come to hand that Cherry Orchard Road, used only by the trams, was to be widened. (Buses used the parallel Canning Road, which came out opposite Addiscombe Station.) The Ministry of Transport (which took over the control of Public Transport from the Board of Trade in 1919) was insisting that the track in Cherry Orchard Road be doubled and presumably, when widened it would be used by trams and buses alike. (Canning Road was not very wide and entirely residential.)

The position now was that so much money had been committed to improving the main line, that there was insufficient available to improve the Addiscombe line as well or to purchase a trolleybus installation. The matter was considered again in Council and early in February 1927, the decision was taken by 24 votes to 20 to abandon the Addiscombe route. Offers to provide a replacement service were received from the London General Omnibus Co., the City Motor Omnibus Co. and other smaller independent operators. Sir Henry Maybury of the Ministry of Transport was consulted and his opinion was that only the proposals of the L.G.O.C. came completely within the law. The trams would cease running by 31 March, as it was considered that it would cost at least £50,000 to renew the track which was now dangerous, but the Corporation were concerned about the fate of at least sixty tramwaymen rendered redundant.

Agreement was reached when the L.G.O.C. decided to accept 60 tramway staff suitable for training as bus crews. The few remaining were to be transferred to other departments of the Corporation. The last tram ran to Addiscombe on 28 March 1927 and a new bus service numbered 178 began running the next day. It was in effect a short working on Tilling's Route 12A, but was worked by "General" open top NS type buses and ran from a loop working George St./Katharine Street to the "Black Horse" Addiscombe. The tram terminus at Bingham Road Station Bridge had been just at the beginning of the shopping centre, but the bus service extended to the "Black Horse" served all the shops. The buses carried a different service number to 12A, as the Croydon Corporation fare structure applied on them. Although Bingham Road bridge was too low for the trams, the L.G.O.C. soon began fitting top covers on their NS buses and these could still just get under the 14ft. bridge.

Another new bus service, numbered 197, like 178, worked by L.G.O.C. NS type buses, ran via the "Leslie Arms" and Morland Road to Woodside and Norwood Junction Station (rear entrance off Portland Road). This completed the other arm of the proposed trolleybus service. The site in Morland Road intended for a depôt was subsequently sold. These bus services and 12A continued to run via Canning Road until the works in Cherry Orchard Road were completed and were then diverted to that thoroughfare.

An event in no way connected with the modernization of the system, occurred in the form of a remarkable, but not serious accident, when early in March 1927, one of the cars on the Penge route was passing Selhurst Station, where the four railway tracks cross the road on two bridges a few feet apart. As the car passed under the first of these bridges, its trolley dewired, and was held either by the troughing or the other wire, but on reaching the gap between the two bridges, it was released and flew up so hard that the head was parted from the pole and disappeared. It could not be found until a complaint was received from the Southern Railway that a trolley wheel had broken the window of an empty compartment of one of their electric trains! Mr. Morgan was sent to Victoria Station to make the necessary apologies, and collect the head. No doubt he had a suitable mixed metaphor ready for the occasion.

With the closure of the Addiscombe route and the Norbury—Purley main line worked by L.C.C. cars, Croydon had a lot of cars to spare and the space they occupied would soon be required for the new cars when they arrived; they were to be allocated to Purley depôt, which had to be emptied and the gateway widened, for these larger cars. The Greyhound—Thornton Heath route required the ten existing bogie cars, with two four wheelers stood by for emergencies. The Penge route was normally worked by eight or nine four wheelers. It was decided therefore to retain only the twenty best four wheelers and dispose of the rest. They were offered for sale, and of those available, the South Metropolitan took the first pick, purchasing twelve with spare parts at the bargain price of £700 the lot. They intended to use them to replace those cars which had been the original Corporation (B.E.T.) Nos. 36-45. In May 25 cars were sold to T. W. Ward & Co., the scrap merchants, for £560. (The fate of the other 8 is not known.)

In July, following the trials with bogie car No. 55 with air brakes acting on the wheels and track, all ten bogie cars were fitted with air brakes on the wheels only. There was a valve and pressure gauge alongside the brake staff on each platform. They were retained for the life of the cars.

While these developments were taking place in Croydon itself, work was proceeding in Motherwell, Scotland, on the construction of the ten new bogie cars, intended for the through running. In due course, each was delivered in three parts (upper saloon, lower saloon and trucks) to East Croydon goods yard in September, whence they were taken on lorry trailers to Purley depôt for assembly and testing. The new cars generally resembled their L.C.C. brethren, but seated 69 in slightly greater comfort. They incorporated all the improvements recently made on L.C.C. cars of the E/1 class now operating in the area, plus a few more yet to be adopted by the L.C.C., such as large route number stencils and fog lamps. As the modernized L.C.C. cars with two and one cushioned seats were painted red, so the new Croydon cars were also red, a deeper carmine red and ivory. The first went into service on 15 December and the others soon followed.

However, the L.C.C. lost no time in reminding the Corporation that ten new cars were only part of Croydon's commitment, but although they had originally demanded thirty cars, in the light of operating experience they would be prepared to accept 25 cars from Croydon, 21 scheduled for service each day and four spares to cover maintenance and repairs. The purchase of fifteen more cars was approved by the Corporation on 18 October and the L.C.C. was promised that the order would be placed by 1 January 1928. Again, they were to be built by Hurst Nelson and identical to those already going into service.

The fifteen additional cars were delivered during the summer of 1928. They differed only from the first ten in being painted carmine and grey instead of carmine and ivory. From now on, this was adopted as the livery for the whole fleet. Croydon was now able to fulfil its commitments on the whole through joint service. As their motormen had been trained in the L.C.C. school to drive the larger cars and they had many months experience on L.C.C. cars before their own were delivered, Croydon avoided most of the teething troubles with their new cars.

With the change of livery, there was a renumbering of the Croydon fleet. The remaining four wheelers took the numbers 1-20, the old bogie cars became 21-30 and the new cars were delivered bearing the numbers 31-55.

Widening of Croydon High Street continued and the cost of doubling the tram track was estimated at £8,000. In February 1928, the Ministry of Transport sanctioned the borrowing of £39,765 repayable in 20 years, toward the cost of the fifteen new cars. This enabled the Corporation to reach a new agreement with the L.C.C., which was to remain in force until 30 September 1932. In 1928, Spurgeon's Bridge, which was a relic of Canal days, was rebuilt and widened, enabling the tramway department to lay a passing loop on the bridge.

In the meantime, although the new E/1 class cars were fully committed on week-days, one could usually be spared to work on the Thornton Heath route on Sundays, where it carried the route number stencil "2". It was soon found that its takings were higher than those of the open top bogie cars. Councillor Keys, now asked them to sanction the borrowing of £7,376 for the fitting of covered tops to the old bogie cars and to complete the track doubling in the High Street.

Work was already proceeding with the fitting of air brakes and two and one cushioned seats to the old bogie cars. Two of the four wheelers were also fitted with air brakes and they were kept as the emergency spares for the Thornton Heath route. In order to test out Councillor Keys' proposal, one of the bogie cars was fitted with a short-canopy top cover, cloth covered (not cushioned) two and two seats on the upper deck and two trolley poles, one for either direction of travel, as both terminals of the Thornton Heath route were in congested streets.

The trials were evidently successful and it was decided to fit the remainder of the class with similar top covers. The very exposed platforms and double flight staircases were retained and it must be admitted the cars looked rather ungainly.

Tom Goodyer evidently now felt that his task had been achieved and he retired on 30 September 1928, aged 62. (See Appendix C for Biography). He was retained as a consultant for several years at a fee of £500 per annum. Gordon V. Stanley, the Engineer, was appointed Acting Manager at once and was confirmed as Tramways Manager in October at a salary of £600 per annum. G. D. Morgan, the Chief Clerk, became Assistant Manager as well.

The first bogie to be top covered, No. 30 (new numbering) reappeared in service on 13 December and identical top covers were fitted to the remaining nine bogie cars during 1929 and 1930. They were painted in the new red and grey livery. The provision of top covers for the old bogie cars cost £4,000 and this was approved in March 1929. It was not possible to fit top covers to the four-wheeled cars, because of the low railway bridges at Selhurst Station, Selby Road and Penge West Station. However, as at Addiscombe, covered top double deck buses could just get under them and very soon Tilling introduced their version of the ST type bus, with covered top but open staircase on routes 12A and 75, both of which competed with the Penge trams.

In 1932, Coulsdon & Purley U.D.C. tried to persuade Croydon Corporation to move the Purley tram terminus from its position on the congested Brighton Road at the Fountain, to the small strip of land with shrubs, between Brighton Road and the High Street, where they ran parallel.

In 1932, the Southern Railway, who had been electrifying their lines in the Croydon area, decided to rebuild West Croydon Station. Until then there had been two separate station buildings, that for London bound traffic stood back in a forecourt from London Road, while the building for down traffic was at the far end of Station Road on the left and at the outer end of the platforms. West Croydon Bridge was rebuilt and widened with a new station building on a rafted site, with some shops on the east side of the bridge. There were also rafted shops on the west side adjoining Tamworth Road. Both old buildings were put to other uses, that in Station Road became a bus waiting room.

In the meantime, moves had been going on behind the scenes and in Parliament to unify the control of public transport in the London area (to be described in detail in another chapter). As a preliminary move, the East Surrey Traction Co. was reconstituted on 28 January 1932 as the London General Country Services Ltd. The L.G.C.S. took over the old station building as a waiting room. Several years later, the goods yard became a timber yard and the station building then became an associated wood shop, which it still is.

Thus, at last Croydon Corporation Tramways had been put in a sound position and takings were improving. The final improvements came in April 1933, when the rest of the track in South End was doubled at a cost of £45,545 and nine sets of second-hand 35 h.p. motors were obtained for £340 per car set, a bargain price as they had only been in use for seven years. They were fitted to the Penge cars as they came in for overhaul. A left-hand crossover was purchased from Hadfields and installed just past the Davis Theatre (a large cinema) for the use of the Thornton Heath cars, now that the single track on which they had terminated, had been doubled. A crossover costing £225 was installed by the Clock Tower at the beginning of Thornton Heath High Street in 1932, so that short working cars could reverse there and various odd sections of track were relaid in the early part of 1933.

Unfortunately, Croydon Corporation Tramways were taken over to the new London Passenger Transport Board on 1 July 1933.

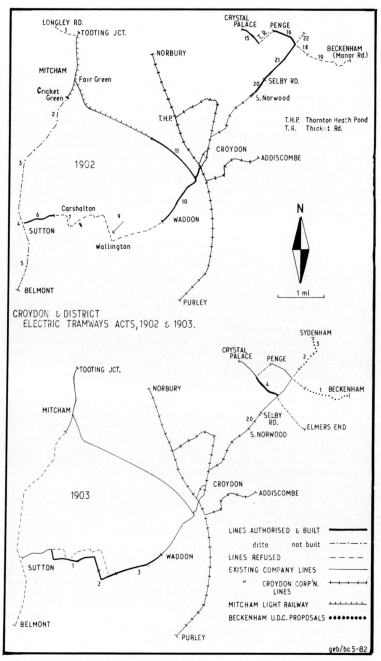

CROYDON & DISTRICT
ELECTRIC TRAMWAYS ACTS, 1902 & 1903.

T.H.P. Thornton Heath Pond
T.R. Thicket Rd.

1902

N

1 ml

1903

LINES AUTHORISED & BUILT
ditto   not built
LINES REFUSED
EXISTING COMPANY LINES
"   CROYDON CORP'N.
     LINES
MITCHAM LIGHT RAILWAY
BECKENHAM U.D.C. PROPOSALS

geb/bc 5-82

(Maps). The tramways permitted by the Croydon & District Tramways Acts of 1902 and 1903.
(Drawn by B. Connelly

CHAPTER FOUR

THE SOUTH METROPOLITAN ELECTRIC TRAMWAYS & LIGHTING COMPANY, LIMITED

The Areas Served

It is usual to begin an account of this nature, with a brief description of the area served by the undertaking concerned. In the case of the South Metropolitan Company, this does present a certain difficulty, since it served not one, but three distinct areas, each with its own particular character. From its terminus in Tamworth Road, West Croydon, the company had a route running to Mitcham and Tooting, while another ran to Wallington, Carshalton and Sutton. Separated from these by three miles of Croydon Corporation track, were two more routes in the Urban District of Penge, and these were, in fact, the first part of the company's system to be opened to traffic.

Penge, which includes the area known as Anerley, was the smallest Urban District in the Greater London area, it was, until 1855, a detached part of Battersea. It then became a part of Lewisham, but obtained a separate entity as an Urban District on the 15 May 1900. A large part of its small area is taken up by the grounds of the Crystal Palace and by a residential school. For its size, Penge has quite an imposing Town Hall, erected in Anerley Road, between the station and the aforementioned school, in 1879. Although mentioned by Conan Doyle as a quiet village to which one of Sherlock Holmes' clients retired, and the birthplace of Mrs. Beeton, of cookery fame, Penge owes its development mainly to the re-erection of the Crystal Palace at the top of Anerley Hill, in 1854, when it was removed from the Great Exhibition of 1851 in Hyde Park.

The three main streets of Penge, Croydon Road, Anerley Road and the High Street are of ample width, and while the two former are lined with Victorian houses, many of which are now, sadly in want of repair, Beckenham Road and the High Street form a compact but well appointed shopping centre, with street markets held in the adjoining Maple Road, and until the war Penge Empire Theatre. There is also a shopping centre in Upper Norwood, which although partly in Croydon and partly in Lambeth, adjoined the Crystal Palace terminus of the trams. Historians say that Anerley Station was named after a villa owned by a Scots merchant and meaning "Lonely" and the area is said to have been developed between 1853 and 1858. Thornsett Road, near the Selby Road boundary, where the present writer was born, was developed entirely by Thomas Crapper, inventor of the lavatory cistern.

To return to the lines on the other side of Croydon, the Tooting line, on leaving Tamworth Road terminus ran through the older part of the town in very narrow streets, until it passed the barracks in Mitcham Road. After this, that thoroughfare became wide and straight and was not built-up until the 1920's apart from the provision of a cemetery near the borough boundary. On leaving Croydon, the road pursued a straight course over the wide expanse of open scrubland known as Mitcham Common. After about a mile, a humped-backed bridge crossed the L.B.S.C. Railway and the road entered the old township of Mitcham, then still part of the Croydon Rural District, which was not disbanded until 1914. Mitcham which contains a number of interesting Georgian houses, is now a separate borough* and is well known for its historic cricket green and its lavender factory. After passing the Fair Green with its small clock tower, the tramway negotiated a rather narrow section of street, with shops, before crossing Figges Marsh, an open space of lesser proportions than Mitcham Common. Although the company's cars proudly carried the destination "Tooting", they in fact only reached the fringe of the area of that name. Tooting itself lies within the Metropolitan Borough of Wandsworth, in the County of London. The boundary at the point in question was on the North side of the humped-back bridge at Tooting Junction Station.

The tramway to Wallington, Carshalton and Sutton left the Mitcham line at Elis David Place at the western end of Tamworth Road, West Croydon, and after negotiating two rather sharp corners in Church Street and passing Croydon Parish Church, ran along Epsom Road, flanked on one side by the railway as far as Waddon Station. From this point onwards, the tramway did not follow the existing road to Carshalton, which was in places very narrow and winding. Instead it kept to the south thereof serving roads whose development was contemporary with the construction of the tramway. In later years, Croydon by-pass was crossed and the ugly black corrugated iron north wall of the aerodrome followed soon after passing Waddon station. From here on, until the old road was rejoined at the "Windsor Castle", Carshalton, the area served was entirely good-class residential housing, much of which was not built until after the 1914-18 war. Park Lane, Carshalton, was still open country in 1917. The line terminated at the "Grapes" public house in Benhill Street, Sutton, at right angles to the High Street and some little distance from the town centre.

The reader will recall that the British Electric Traction Co. Ltd., a powerful group controlling many tramway systems throughout the country, were thwarted by an injunction from obtaining control of the Croydon Tramway Co. at the turn of the century when electrification was first proposed. However, the B.E.T. did succeed in persuading Croydon Corporation to let them work their tramways on a lease and shortly afterwards, they had the opportunity to take over two new tramway schemes, outside but adjoining Croydon boundaries.

In 1901, soon after the B.E.T. had commenced working the Croydon Corporation system, the Croydon Rural District Council (a separate authority controlling areas surrounding the Borough), submitted the Mitcham Light Railway Order to Parliament for approval. This comprised three street tramway lines based on Mitcham, one of which was extended to the Croydon Borough boundary. Fortunately, this scheme was approved in its entirety on 6 November and the three lines were:—

Railway No. 1—1 mile exactly, double line.

> Commencing in London Road, Mitcham, at its boundary with Tooting Graveney (Tooting Junction Station), across Figges Marsh to London Road, Mitcham, at Upper Green (now known as "Fair Green").

* This relates to before the formation of the Greater London Council in 1964, since when both Penge and Beckenham have been absorbed into the London Borough of Bromley, and Mitcham into the London Borough of Merton.

Railway No. 2—3 furlongs 3.78 chains, double line.
>Commencing at the terminus of Railway No. 1 at Upper Green and continuing along London Road, Mitcham, to a point 5.6 chains south of the junction with the Causeway (Cricket Green).

Railway No. 3—1 mile 6 furlongs 3.0 chains double line.
>Also commencing at the terminus of Railway No. 1 at Upper Green and continuing along Upper Green, Commonside West, Blue House* Bridge and Croydon Road, Mitcham Common to the Croydon Borough boundary.

As approved, these lines would be isolated from any other tramways, but it was hoped that at some future date, the L.C.C. would build a line to connect with the Tooting Junction terminus and Croydon Corporation would consent to Railway No.3 being extended to the centre of Croydon. No. 2 was a short branch to Mitcham Vestry Hall and the Cricket Green. It was intended to be the first part of a lengthy tramway to Sutton and beyond. Railway No. 3 was to run for over a mile across the open space known as Mitcham Common and was intended as a link between Mitcham and Croydon, with little expectation of intermediate traffic.

Having obtained legal powers to build itself a tramway system, Croydon Rural District Council then discovered that legislation at that time made no provision for a Rural District Council to own, operate, or perhaps more important, to raise the necessary finance to construct a tramway system. Therefore, after due consideration, the Council sold their powers in the Mitcham Light Railways to the British Electric Traction Co. for £1,000 on 15 January 1902.

The B.E.T. saw the Mitcham Light Railway as one step in the large tramway system they intended to build around Croydon and followed this acquisition by presenting a Bill to Parliament, containing their own proposals for the area. It was entitled the Croydon & District Electric Tramways Bill 1902. If accepted, this would enable them to construct a continuation of Light Railway No. 3 from the Croydon Boundary to the centre of Croydon. It was to be linked to a line from Croydon to Wallington, Carshalton and Sutton. There would also be a lengthy continuation of Light Railway No. 2 from Mitcham to Sutton and Belmont, making a large triangular system to the west of Croydon. There was also to be a small separate system in the Urban District of Penge, connecting the Croydon boundary at Selby Road with Beckenham and Lewisham. There were hopes that the London County Council would extend their lines in Lewisham to link up and Beckenham Urban District Council was currently formulating plans for a tramway system. One of the Penge termini was to be at the top of Anerley Hill, by the Crystal Palace, then in use as a large exhibition centre, which it was hoped would attract much traffic to the trams.

Since Croydon Corporation's tramway system was leased to the B.E.T., the fact that the Penge services and the Mitcham/Sutton services would be separated by about two miles of Corporation owned track was thought to be of little consequence and it was intended to work the whole system as one with lengthy through services, under the "Croydon & District Tramways" fleet name.

Unlike the Mitcham Order, the 1902 Bill did not pass through Parliament unscathed and when it became effective as an Act, on 31 July 1902, many sections had been deleted, largely because of the very narrow roads named in Carshalton. The narrowest, Pound Street, passed between a lake and an overhanging church wall (both features still exist in 1982—the roads to have been served were largely those served currently by London Country buses). There was also a low railway bridge in Wallington and some very narrow streets and awkward corners in the old part of Croydon, where the Sutton and Mitcham routes were to meet.

* Public houses at opposite ends of Mitcham Common were then known as "Blue House" and "Red House", now "Ravensbury Arms" and "Jolly Gardeners".

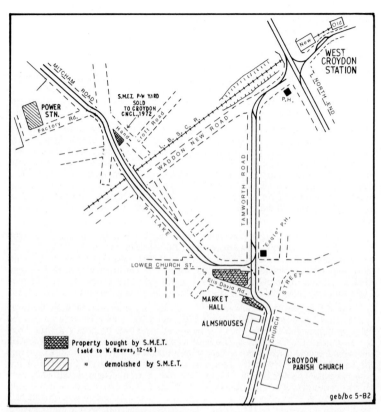

The S.M.E.T. track layout in the Pitlake area, West Croydon showing buildings to be demolished and those actually taken down. (Drawn by B. Connelly)

Although the sections through Carshalton were thrown out, strangely enough, the equally difficult sections in Croydon were accepted, provided that certain demolitions were carried out.

In the case of Penge, apart from one low and narrow railway bridge, there was no difficulty with narrow roads, since Penge had been developed much later than Croydon and its main roads were of ample width. There were some steep gradients, particularly Anerley Hill, leading up the Crystal Palace. The Act provided for a route commencing at the top of Anerley Hill, descending past Crystal Palace (Low Level) Station to Thicket Road, a turning on the left, which led through to the top end of Beckenham Road, Penge. The route was to proceed along Thicket Road and Beckenham Road as far as the Penge/Beckenham boundary. Another route was to start at Selby Road, the Croydon boundary and proceed along Croydon Road and Green Lane, Penge where it met a small enclave of Beckenham before the Lewisham Boundary. The two routes would cross at right-angles at Penge Police Station at the junction of Beckenham Road, Croydon Road and Green Lane. There were railway bridges close to the Beckenham boundaries, that at Beckenham itself being too low for double deck cars.

There was subsequent correspondence with the Board of Trade, enquiring whether Parliamentary Powers and an inspection would be necessary for those lines which led to depôts and on which a public service would never be provided. The Board's reply said in effect, they do not require authority, but we would like to know about them. It was intended to construct a depôt in Aurelia Road, West Croydon, not far short of the Mitcham boundary and one in Torr Road, Penge, by the railway bridge, before the Lewisham boundary. That for the Sutton route would be entered directly from the running track.

There was a good deal of discussion in December 1902, as to who was responsible for the cost of road widening, the B.E.T. or Croydon Rural District Council. Mr. Sidney Morse, the B.E.T's solicitor, reminded the Council that the company had paid £1,000 for the Mitcham Light Railway Powers and that in his view, that specifically exempted them from the provisions of the road widening clauses contained in the Bill.

Croydon Corporation were entitled to object to Tramways Nos. 10, 11 and 20, which lay within the Borough and were granted protective clauses. That relating to No. 20 in South Norwood was described in the Corporation Chapter. The Company were permitted to construct Tramways Nos. 10 and 11, but under Section 43 of the Act, they retained the right of compulsory purchase at a later date. If this right was exercised, then the Corporation must lease the lines back to the Company and grant them full through running rights. They must also reimburse the company for any widening and road improvement carried out. Owing to the large amount of work demanded, this would be quite a considerable sum. The Corporation demanded to see and approve all drawings. They also said "The position, design and colour of all posts, standards, brackets and attachments and the positions of all feeder cables constructed by the company, within Croydon, shall be subject to the reasonable approval of the Corporation".

With so many sections refused in the Act and the various restrictions imposed by the local authorities, the B.E.T. and their Parliamentary advisors took a long hard look at the powers which they held and decided that the 1902 Act as it stood, could not make a viable tramway system, even when grafted onto the existing Corporation system. There were also some doubts about the link up with other tramways in Beckenham and Lewisham. In the circumstances, another Bill was presented to Parliament, entitled The Croydon & District Electric Tramways (Extensions) Bill 1903, offering alternative routings to those thrown out in the 1902 Act. (The separate "Tramways" enumerated in the 1902 and 1903 Acts are set out in Appendix B).

Between Sutton and Wallington, the route now proposed was to avoid the centre of Carshalton, by following new roads to the south, some of which were not yet constructed; although this routing was opposed by some frontagers in Sutton, the company was assured the co-operation of the Carshalton Park Estate Company, who were developing the area at the time. Although there had been correspondence with the Beddington and Wallington Council about the low bridge in Manor Road, Wallington, the new routing avoided that too. In Penge, the routing via Thicket Road was convenient for a direct service from the Crystal Palace to Beckenham, but if that did not materialize, Thicket Road was too roundabout for a direct route from the Crystal Palace to Croydon. Therefore, the new Bill contained provision for a continuation of the line down Anerley Hill and Anerley Road to meet the Croydon Road line at the "Robin Hood". However, the line would cross Croydon Road and continue down Elmers End Road to the Beckenham boundary, but there would be connecting curves at the Robin Hood.

There was provision for any line constructed under both the 1902 and 1903 Acts, shown as single track on the Deposited Plans, to be laid as double track, provided that certain necessary road widenings were carried out. A very wise provision, under which practically the whole South Metropolitan system was laid with double track. Agreements were reached between the Company and Penge Urban District Council concerning the construction of tramways in Penge, on 29 September 1902 and 21 August 1903. Like Croydon, Penge U.D.C. had the right to purchase its tramways in each seventh year on granting six months' notice, but if it did, it had to lease them back to the Company. The whole of the 1903 Act was passed.

In the meantime, Beckenham U.D.C. did apply for powers to construct a tramway system. It asked for powers to use animal or electric traction and trams or motor buses. If electric, the tramway was to be worked by overhead wire or slot conduit systems. The Council wished to borrow £55,000 to pay for their construction, and the tramways were to be leased to the B.E.T. for 28 years, under the terms of an Agreement dated 21 October 1902, which also mentioned the use of buses.

The three Tramways described in the Bill were:—

Tramway No. 1—1 mile 75 chains, commencing at the Penge boundary in Beckenham Road and continuing to a point in Beckenham High Street at the west end of Manor Road.

Tramway No. 2—53.9 chains, a continuation of the B.E.T. line in Green Lane, Penge, along Thesiger Road and Kent House Road to the Lewisham boundary at Sydenham.

Tramway No. 3—13 chains entirely within the Borough of Lewisham, to continue along Kent House Road to its junction with Sydenham High Street.

The London County Council opposed Tramway No. 3, but agreed to permit through running if they constructed such a tramway themselves. The Act of Parliament permitting the construction of Tramways Nos. 1 and 2 received Royal Assent on 11 August 1903.

Thus, under the umbrella title "Croydon & District Tramways" the B.E.T. was now in a position to build up a large network of tramways centred on Croydon, which it was hoped would attract passengers and business from a wide area to Croydon. Unfortunately, as already described, Croydon Corporation saw things rather differently and thought they would stand to lose financially. Their objection came to a head on two points in particular. Tramway No. 20 of the 1902 Act, entirely within the Borough, they insisted on building and owning themselves. On 15 June 1905, they refused the B.E.T. permission to enlarge Thornton Heath depôt to accommodate the additional cars which would be necessary to work the enlarged system and to provide an entrance in Whitehall Road.

Although Tramways Nos. 2, 3, 4 and 5 of the 1902 Act, the Mitcham—Sutton line, were accepted, there was much objection from frontagers, particularly at the Sutton end and it appeared that single track would be necessary at Rose Hill, where the road was in a cutting. In the end, Sutton Council withdrew their support and no work ever started on the Mitcham—Sutton—Belmont route, except for the short stub, Mitcham Light Railway No. 2. The Company had to pay Croydon Corporation £1,000 towards the rebuilding of Pitlake Bridge in the old part of Croydon. It has recently been discovered that the Company purchased a small plot of land on the north-east side of the bridge for use as a permanent way yard. It was not track connected. (Details only came to light in 1972, when London Transport received a compulsory purchase order, in connection with a further rebuilding of the bridge.) The Company had to contribute £3,000 (and no more) towards the cost of rebuilding and widening Goat House Bridge in South Norwood and the bridge over the road near Selby Road; although both were on Tramway No. 20, within the Borough of Croydon and claimed by the Corporation. Penge U.D.C. asked the Company to pay about £250 for widening the bridge at Anerley Station but it eventually cost £1,750. The Company had to pay £4,600 toward road widening in Penge and Anerley.

As the intentions of the British Electric Traction Company became clearly known, relations between them and Croydon Corporation became strained. It was thought that the existing arrangement by which the B.E.T. retained direct control of the "Croydon & District Tramways" might not work well if the new lines had to be separated administratively from the Corporation system, so they decided to set up a subsidiary company as they had done in other areas. The County of Surrey Electrical Power Distribution Co. Ltd. was registered on 19 April 1899; it had very widespread objectives, but was not yet operative. The B.E.T. obtained control and by a special resolution on 3 August 1904, the name of the Company was changed to the "South Metropolitan Electric Tramways and Lighting Company Limited", the longest name of any tramway undertaking in the London area. (The title "South Metropolitan Tramways Co. Ltd." had already been registered as a subsidiary of the London Tramways Co. in 1879, but came to nothing.) The Company already had powers to provide electric lighting throughout the Sutton and Cheam districts and to it were made available the powers conferred by the Mitcham Light Railway Order and the Croydon & District Tramways Acts of 1902 and 1903. The B.E.T. appointed C. G. Tegetmeier as Chairman and James Devonshire, Emil Garcke and George Offor as Directors. Mr. G. Ratcliffe Hulme* was appointed Manager in April 1905. The original Capital was £50,000 in £10 shares. This was increased to £200,000 on 29 March 1905 and increased again to £400,000 in May 1906.

The Company had a generating station built in Wellesley Road, Sutton, some distance from the proposed tramways. This was to supply the lighting network and part of the tramways. Although Beckenham U.D.C. had powers to construct a tramway system, which they might have leased to the B.E.T., and had built a power station in Churchfields Road, they now had second thoughts about tramways and were thinking in terms of permitting the B.E.T. to run buses in their area. (Beckenham appears to have been the only municipal authority in the London area to have held motor-bus powers.) Nevertheless, they did conclude an Agreement on 15 June 1905 to supply electric current to the Company's Penge tramways at 2 pence per unit from Churchfields Road Power Station. Current within Croydon was to be supplied from the Corporation's own power station in Factory Lane off Mitcham Road.

During 1905, there was a constant flow of correspondence between the B.E.T., the Board of Trade and the various Local Authorities concerned, about the widening of roads. Croydon Corporation were reluctant to permit double track in Stafford Road by Waddon Station and in Tamworth Road. To the latter, the company replied that as Tamworth Road was to be used by both the Mitcham and Sutton routes, single track there would slow up the whole service. The Board of Trade were of the opinion that the Corporation's permission to lay double track was not necessary. The Rural District Council wanted "single pole" construction. The B.E.T. replied, "We cannot agree to single pole construction, from which we presume you mean bracket arm construction, in place of span wires." The B.E.T. hinted that the Council were too late to object, as span wires had already been approved by the Board of Trade, who objected to bracket arms over 16 feet in length, which might be necessary if the roads were widened.

Plans were put on view at the Parish Office, Vestry Hall, Mitcham on 13 May 1905. There were very strong objections from one landowner and frontager and much pressure was brought to bear on him by both the company and the Rural District Council, who announced on 9 September that he had accepted their conditions. The road across Mitcham Common was to be widened on the north side only. Like the horse tramways, the company had lengthy arguments with the local authorities as to where the road surface should be paved with stone setts and where wood blocks. Croydon Corporation were insisting on specially dressed stone setts.

In June and October 1905, there were proposals in other quarters to build tramways from the Crystal Palace to Thornton Heath and from the Crystal Palace along Crystal Palace Parade. No more was heard of these schemes, but on 9 August Croydon Corporation served notice on the B.E.T. that it intended to terminate the Lease of its tramways and henceforth work them itself. The leasing arrangement was to end on 1 June 1906.

* Gilbert Ratcliffe Hulme was also a Director of the "Northmet" Power Co. and had been District Superintendent N.E. Lancashire for the B.E.T.

With regard to the contretemps over the connecting link between South Norwood and the Penge lines at Selby Road (Tramway No. 20), the Croydon Corporation Road Surveyor announced on 9 November, that he had now started work on this line by direct labour. Thus encouraged, the B.E.T. set about a campaign to try and persuade the Croydon voters to get the termination of the lease reversed. They offered to increase the rental paid to £4,000 per annum, lobbied householders and produced a coloured map of the intended complete tramway system, all of which was of no avail. A site in Aurelia Road, near West Croydon Cemetery, was sold to the Company by West Croydon Estate Co. for a depôt on 14 December.

During 1905, work was commenced on the various lines which were to form the South Metropolitan system, starting first on the Selby Road—"Robin Hood"—Penge High Street section, then the Mitcham Light Railways. Penge U.D.C. were quite happy with the proposed double track throughout, as they thought it would help if there was ever a prospect of through running with the London County Council. They demanded bracket construction for the overhead wires, but this was turned down for the same reasons as those in Mitcham. An Agreement for wood block paving was reached with Penge U.D.C. in 1905.

Although the Board of Trade had been notified that the company proposed to construct a depôt in Torr Road, Penge, this site turned out to be on a section of route which it was no longer intended to construct, so another site had to be found. The company entered into negotiations for the purchase of a site in Raleigh Road, Penge. Access would have been through Southey Street, a narrow alleyway leading off the High Street close to the "Crooked Billet". (Part of Beckenham Road had now become High Street, Penge.)

In June 1905 an order was placed with the Brush Electrical Engineering Company (which was associated with the B.E.T.), for thirty two cars on long wheelbase radial trucks. They were thought to be suitable for working on any part of the system. One pole at the Crystal Palace was in Lambeth.

The only important road works that had to be carried out on the Penge lines comprised widening and strengthening the bridge over the railway at Anerley Station, cutting back the forecourts of Penge Police Station and property adjoining Penge Station (L.B.S.C. Railway). Here the main London Bridge—Brighton railway crossed over the road on a very low four track bridge, under which the roadway had to be considerably lowered, but the pavements were not lowered and were protected by railings. It was impracticable to widen the road here and interlaced track had to be laid. This started at the centre line of Crampton Road and although most of the interlaced track was in Tramway No. 15, the first few yards were in Tramway 16. Where the track became double again, there was another bridge carrying the Crystal Palace—Sydenham branch line over the road. This bridge was a high brick arch viaduct, well clear of the tramway. A few yards beyond this, the tramway turned left to terminate a few yards into Thicket Road, by the Penge entrance of the Crystal Palace grounds. Apart from this short terminal stub of single track and the interlaced track, the whole of the Penge system was laid with double track. No track was ever laid along the rest of Thicket Road, thus dividing Tramway No. 15 into two separate parts.

Unfortunately, the negotiations for a depôt site in Raleigh Road fell through and at the last minute, the company had to seek another site. One was found in Oak Grove Road, near the "Robin Hood", where some new development was in progress. This site was acquired on lease from a Mrs. J. Clarkson on 8 February 1906. Dick, Kerr Ltd. were asked to build a depôt on the site with all possible speed. Oak Grove Road slopes down sharply from Croydon Road and houses had already been built nearly half way down. A gateway and single storey office block were built adjoining the road and the depôt itself stood well back parallel to the road. Later, more houses were built obscuring the building from the street and the position of the office block prevented passers-by from seeing inside. As it was on such a steep gradient, a large basement was built under the rear end to give a level floor for the tracks. The freeholder demanded a clause in the lease precluding unnecessary noise, to which the company replied that there should be no noise, as the depot was to be used only for the storage of tramcars. In fact, maintenance was carried out there and in later years the basement was used as a rifle range for the staff and brass bands used to rehearse there for competitions at the Crystal Palace.

The agreements with Penge Council required the company to contribute £6,100 towards the reinstatement of pavements and any road widening necessary and to pave the whole width of the road with wood blocks in front of all places of worship. The Council agreed that the company should not be held to the requirement to construct the line from the "Robin Hood" down Elmers End Road to the Beckenham boundary, unless Beckenham U.D.C. constructed a continuation to Elmers End Station.

In the meantime, Tramway No. 20 was opened by Croydon Corporation on 14 December 1905 and was worked as a short extension of the South Norwood line. The contract for the construction of the lines on the Penge side of the boundary was awarded to W. Griffiths & Co. Ltd., and the laying of underground conduits and cables for the power supply to British Insulated and Helsby Cables Ltd., but in an agreement dated 25 September, it was arranged that the B.E.T. would supply the manhole covers. The work was supervised by the Company's Engineer (Charles Wright Durnford).

The rails and overhead wires were joined at Selby Road, but there was a marked contrast between the surroundings; from the Goat House Bridge to Selby Road, there was single track with one passing loop in a narrow road between three storey terraced houses and a few converted to shops, between the over-bridge and the boundary. The road widened suddenly at Selby Road and from there up the hill to the "Robin Hood" and to Penge Police Station, there was double track, between fairly large mansions with front gardens. Holy Trinity Church stood on the corner diagonally opposite the "Robin Hood". Span wire construction of the overhead suspension was used throughout (except in Oak Grove leading down to the depôt).

The section of tramway from Selby Road to the "Pawleyne Arms" just before Penge Police Station was ready for inspection on 7 February 1906 (Tramway No. 21) and Penge U.D.C. was the only local authority involved. It was inspected by Lieut. Col. P. G. von Donop on 10 February. Afterwards, he expressed surprise that the Post Office had not been invited to send a representative. When advised, they did insist on guard wires at several points. The Colonel pronounced the route fit for public service on 13 February. The Company had been under an obligation to complete the line by 15 August 1905, but obtained an extension of time when it was discovered that the power supply from Beckenham would not be ready until 1 April 1906. Evidently the section breaker at Selby Road, to separate the two undertakings, must have been temporarily bridged and current drawn from Croydon since the line opened without ceremony immediately following receipt of the certificate. As the lease still had a few months to run, this section was worked as a further extension of the South Norwood line, using Croydon Corporation Milnes four wheelers.

In the meantime, in order to prepare to work the system themselves, the Corporation wished to be rid of the fifteen cars that were the property of the B.E.T., and asked them to remove them forthwith. The Corporation had ordered fifteen new cars to replace them and to make space in the depôts, took the B.E.T. cars one at a time on horse drawn flat trucks, along Canterbury Road and Mitcham Road to dump them on the site in Aurelia Road, which the company had purchased for a depôt. As many as possible were covered by tarpaulins. To everybody's embarrassment, the first eight new cars which the Company had ordered, were then delivered to Thornton Heath Depôt. They were long wheelbase four wheeled cars in a dark green and ivory livery. As none of the Company's depôts was yet ready, they pleaded that they had nowhere to put them and after discussion, the Corporation agreed to let them remain at Thornton Heath until their own new cars arrived, provided that they were permitted to use them in service on their main

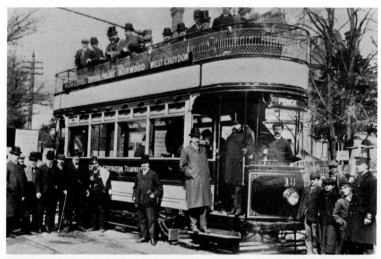

S.M.E.T. No. 13, on the terminal stub in Thicket Road, Penge with Col. von Donop on the platform. Note "Croydon Corporation Tramways" on board fixed to waist panel.

(Courtesy Penge Public Library

line, to compensate for the mileage worked by Corporation cars in Penge. The waist panels of the eight South Metropolitan cars were covered by chocolate coloured boards, which were lettered "Croydon Corporation Tramways", concealing the B.E.T. magnet and wheel device. The Company's own lettering had not yet been applied to the rocker panels. By the time the Corporation's new cars were ready for delivery, Penge depôt in Oak Grove Road was sufficiently advanced for the cars to be stored there, together with the remaining eight of the first batch.

The difficulty over these cars had arisen because the Brush Co. had demanded an appropriate charge if they were expected to store them at their works in Loughborough. In the correspondence arising therefrom, it was agreed that the next sixteen cars which the South Metropolitan Co. would require should be of a smaller type, making a saving of £58 per car. This was agreed in February 1906 and at the same time the order for a further 14 cars of the smaller type, to work the Sutton route, was cancelled when it was realized that the fifteen "Croydon & District" cars dumped on the site of Mitcham Road Depôt (Aurelia Road) would have to be taken into the South Metropolitan fleet. One of a batch of large bogie cars, delivered to Gravesend where they were found to be too large, also found its way onto the Aurelia Road site, to be tried out when the line opened. It did prove suitable for the Mitcham route and in due course three more were acquired.

On 7 April 1906 it was announced that current could now be obtained from the Beckenham Power Station and that guard wires as required by the Post Office had now been fixed near Penge entrance to the Crystal Palace. There was disagreement with the Corporation as to whether the track in Tamworth Road, Croydon, common to the Mitcham and Sutton routes, should be connected with the Corporation rails on West Croydon Bridge. The Corporation protested to the Board of Trade, who replied on 27 April, "Although we disagree with your views, we will not press for a junction with Station Road. To avoid being unfair or unjustified, we will instruct the company to terminate Tramway No. 10 a few yards short of the junction." (In fact about one yard!).

Col. von Donop visited the area again on 10 April, to inspect the rest of the Penge system. In his report delivered the next day, he observed that the road surface was not yet completed and that only drivers with at least six years' service could be employed on Anerley Hill. Cars 11 and 13 were used for the inspection which included braking tests on Anerley Hill. Both these cars were fitted with Spencer track brakes, which could be wound down onto the rails when descending the hill. It is not certain whether all cars of this batch (Nos. 1-16) were delivered with track brakes, but most probably were. The inspection commenced at the Penge entrance to the Crystal Palace grounds, where the Colonel was welcomed by Mr. P. W. Greetham, Chairman of Penge U.D.C.

The lines were opened for service the next day, 12 April, from the "Pawleyne Arms", along Penge High Street to the Thicket Road terminus and from the "Robin Hood" to Low Level Station. The steep section on Anerley Hill could not be opened until the company had persuaded sufficient drivers with at least six years' service to transfer from other undertakings. This was achieved and the line up the hill opened on 28 May 1906.

A Mr. Tremlett transferred from the police and was appointed Inspector covering the Penge area lines, a task which he performed efficiently throughout the life of the trams.

While the Penge lines were being completed and opened, work was already in hand on the Mitcham route. The line commenced on the Mitcham side of the London/Mitcham boundary, immediately beyond the hump-backed bridge on which Tooting Junction station was located. The Tooting shopping centre was over half a mile away and was the terminus of the first L.C.C. tram route to be electrified in 1903. The depôt in Aurelia Road, West Croydon, always referred to by the Company as "Mitcham Road Depôt" was built round the cars dumped on the site, by W. Taylor & Co. It was to hold 26 cars. The construction of both the Tooting Junction and Sutton lines was undertaken by the Brush Electrical Engineering Co.

In the meantime, as predicted, Croydon Corporation terminated the lease and from 1 June, the service provided by their cars was cut back to Selby Road, on the South Norwood route. Using their radial trucked cars (1-16) the Company then provided services Crystal Palace—Robin Hood—Selby Road and Crystal Palace—Robin Hood—Penge. The triangular double track junction at the "Robin Hood" made this possible. There were close links between the Brush Electrical Engineering Co. Ltd. and the B.E.T. Group. J. S. Raworth, who was a director of both, invented a system of regenerative control, by which a car descending a steep hill, could use its motors as brakes and generate current which passed back into the overhead wires to be used by other cars ascending. It necessitated cars used on the route to be fitted with special controllers and other electrical equipment. One of the radial trucked cars was appropriately fitted out and performed trials on Anerley Hill on 25 June, in front of an invited audience of senior representatives of the tramways industry. It was stated that the car on a 9 ft. 6 in. truck was carrying 58 passengers and weighed 12½ tons loaded. It was fitted with two 40 horse power motors. It was also stated that in future, the Penge routes would be operated by sixteen cars, eight with regenerative equipment and eight without, but all would have track brakes as required by the Board of Trade for Anerley Hill. Regular regenerative working would have to await the fitting of more cars.

The ex-Croydon & District cars reposing at Mitcham Road depôt were renumbered and the B.E.T. badge replaced the Croydon Coat of Arms, but they were not repainted and remained in the chocolate and ivory livery. The ten small Milnes four wheelers became Nos. 17-26 and the bogie cars, both ex-Croydon & District and ex-Gravesend were numbered indiscriminately between 27 and 35. The smaller Bush four-wheelers on order were to be 36-51. The Company's accounts state that Nos. 36-43 were to be delivered with track brakes but without regenerative equipment and cost £617 10s. each. (In fact they were delivered in September or October without track brakes and received them later.) Nos. 44-51 were to have regenerative equipment and track brakes and cost £707 each. Regular regenerative operation on Anerley Hill must have awaited the delivery of these cars, probably in December 1906. The water car transferred at the same time was not numbered.

Work continued on the construction of the Mitcham route and the Company notified the Board of Trade that Mitcham Light Railways and part of Tramway No. 11 was ready for inspection on 11 May. It was inspected by Lt. Col. von Donop on 18 May, from Tooting Junction to Mitcham and Canterbury Road, Croydon. He also inspected the Cricket Green branch in Mitcham. He commented on the fact that a representative of Croydon Corporation was not present, although part of the line was in the Borough. He did not permit the line to open until several telegraph posts which had been left standing in the roadway when the road was widened, were removed. The company reported on 30 May that this had been done.

However, the Colonel had not waited for this confirmation in writing and issued his certificate on 24 May, so the line opened on 26 May without ceremony, the company taking their pick of the 19 cars stored in Mitcham Road depôt. The remainder of Tramway No. 11 was inspected on 7 July and the Colonel asked about the gradients on the approaches to Pitlake Bridge. After consultation, the representatives of the Company told him that the gradients were 1 in 18.9. On the Croydon side of this bridge, at the foot of the approach, there was single track in the very narrow Lower Church Street. For the time being, this single track was to be used as a terminus for the service. A representative of the Corporation was present on this occasion and objected strongly, saying that cars waiting in this narrow street would cause obstruction. The company explained that this was necessary until the line was further extended into Tamworth Road. Cars had to use the single line to cross over from one track to the other when reversing. To this, the Inspecting Officer concurred, provided that not more than one car ever stood in Lower Church Street. This was accepted and the line opened to passenger traffic on 14 July. This temporary terminal arrangement was in use for about three months. Some demolition of property and setting back of frontages was completed, but by no means as much as provided for in the Act. An old Market Hall remained, with small minaret-like towers at each end and the adjoining small house was made into the Company's office. (114 Lower Church Street). The remaining demolition was carried out in 1978! The Market Hall was demolished at that time, exposing the flank wall of No. 114, on which was sign-written the times of cars to Mitcham and Sutton.

The track in Tamworth Road, to be shared with the Sutton route, was completed and inspected on 9 October, enabling cars from Tooting & Mitcham to reach their ultimate terminus opposite West Croydon Station. The Company were not permitted to construct Tramway No. 10A, the connecting curve with the Corporation's main line, nor a line crossing North End to join the Norwood service in Station Road. The connecting curve from Lower Church Street continued as single track to join the down track from Croydon in Tamworth Road and there was a crossover for up cars to rejoin their correct track. This very awkward junction was signalled with three lamps in a small wooden box on the first traction post in Tamworth Road and another in Lower Church Street. As originally laid there was also a single line curve from Lower Church Street towards Sutton, but it was rarely used and removed after a few years. In accordance with the Protective Clause in the Act the traction posts within Croydon had bases, scroll work and finials like those used by the Corporation, with the coat of arms on the former and were mainly of bracket construction. Those used on the remainder of the system were of a rather heavier design.

In the meantime, work was proceeding on the Croydon—Sutton line and the time limit specified in the Act was due to run out by the end of the year. As already indicated, the Brush Electrical Engineering Co. was the contractor for the construction of this line and with regard to the haste with which it had to be built, *Brush Budget,* their house magazine, had the following to say, "For legal reasons it became necessary to build the line very quickly and the Brush Company laid ten miles of track in six weeks. The first rails were rolled on 20 June, the first car ran on test on 8 August, followed by the Board of Trade Inspection on 10 August. Since the tracks were not completed into Croydon, a

S.M.E.T. No. 23 arrives at Tooting Junction Station.   (Courtesy "Len's of Sutton"

S.M.E.T. No. 31 and L.C.C. 371 face each other at Tooting Junction. This photo is taken at the same point as the photo above, but looking the other way.   (Courtesy J. B. Gent

No. 38 off the Crystal Palace route, at the "Windsor Castle", Carshalton. Note wall of convent school which had to be set back. (Photo F. Merton Atkins (Courtesy E. R. Oakley

car had to be taken by lorry to Wallington and off-loaded onto the track there". Presumably "10 miles" refers to single track, as the whole route was not ten miles long. The car was No. 25, one of the small Milnes cars and in those days a "Lorry" was a flat truck drawn by horses.

A site for a depôt was leased from A. Ross on 23 July 1906 and work was put in hand at once by Dick, Kerr Ltd., to erect a building capable of holding 60 cars. As Mitcham Road and Penge depôts were each built for 25 cars, the South Metropolitan company spaciously provided accommodation for double the number of cars its fleet ever reached, presumably with other extensions still in mind. The depôt was located on the north side of Westmead Road, just short of the Carshalton/Sutton boundary, but always known as Sutton depôt. It was entered through an arched gateway, with single track curves in both directions directly from the running track onto the depôt fan.

The section completed for the Inspection on 10 August ran from Croydon/ Wallington boundary to Ruskin Road. There was some difficulty over widening in Stafford Road, which was already partly built up with houses and shops where it passed through Wallington. Beyond, the line turned right into Boundary Road, crossed over the railway on the Wallington/Carshalton boundary, where the bridge had to be widened. Beyond the bridge, the road descended as Park Lane on a steady gradient. There was a sharp left turn at the bottom into Ruskin Road. At the time, neither Ruskin Road nor the following Beynon Road had been made up or developed and for some time, the trams ran on what in effect was reserved track. At the far end of Beynon Road, opposite the "Windsor Castle" public house, the high wall of a convent school had to be set back. At the top of the next gradient, the line crossed over the railway by some timbered cottages and then turned right again and descended Ringstead Road which was narrow and on a steep gradient. It was laid entirely with interlaced track. As the maximum gradient was 1 in 12, the Inspecting Officer said he was entitled to insist on the use of cars with track brakes, but as the road flattened out before the bottom, he would not insist on this occasion. Two bogie cars were not allowed to pass each other on the curve at the top of Ringstead Road. They were not normally used on the Sutton route, but had to use the depôt for overhaul facilities.

The next section from the Croydon boundary through Waddon and the working class district around Croydon Parish Church to join the Mitcham route in Tamworth Road, together with the section from Ruskin Road to the depôt in Westmead Road, were inspected on 10 November. Once again a representative of the Post Office demanded guard wires and in subsequent correspondence, the Board of Trade enquired which was Elis David Road and which was Lower Church Street, as they were too small to show clearly on the map. On receipt of the Colonel's verbal assurance, the Company was able to provide a service the next day, from West Croydon terminus to Sutton depôt and it was hoped to complete the final section to the "Grapes" in Benhill Street, just off Sutton High Street by Christmas.

In the meantime, the first eight of the smaller Brush single truck cars had been delivered to Sutton depôt (without track brakes). They were numbered 36-43. Work continued apace and Colonel von Donop appeared again on 21 December to inspect the final section, which he did in car No. 36. He assured the Manager that all was well and that his certificate would be posted without delay, so the public service commenced later the same day, thus the whole South Metropolitan system was opened in 1906, making 13.36 route miles.

Before the year was out, small Brush cars Nos. 44-51 were delivered to Penge Depôt. They were identical to 36-43 except that they were fitted with track brakes and regenerative equipment, for regular use on Anerley Hill. The Raworth regenerative system could only be properly tested if the whole service was worked by regenerative cars and this was now possible. The service from the Crystal Palace alternately to Penge or to Selby Road had not proved suitable to public requirements, so from early 1907, services were provided, Selby Road— Crystal Palace with cars 44-51 and from Selby Road to Penge using some of Nos. 1-16. The rest were moved to Sutton depôt to work on the West Croydon— Sutton service. As the tracks were not connected at West Croydon, such transfers proved rather difficult and cars had to be moved at night, using temporary rails to bridge the gap at the top of Tamworth Road.

Agreements were reached with Croydon Rural District Council on 26 November and Penge U.D.C. on 13 September 1906 for rails and drain boxes to be cleaned out regularly for £45 and £15 per annum respectively. On 9 April 1907, Mr. Durnford, the Engineer, reported on the working of the Penge system. He said the radial trucked cars were causing excessive wear on the junction and curves at the "Robin Hood". The regenerative cars had not shown the expected economies and indeed they were responsible for excessive current consumption. Consequently, Nos. 1-16 were removed one at a time to Sutton depôt, where the track brake gear was removed and fitted to 36-43, which took their place at Penge depôt. Regenerative working ceased and the equipment was gradually removed from Nos. 44-51 and they were provided with ordinary equipment. The regenerative equipment was all removed by 1909 after which Nos. 36-51 were identical. From then on, Nos. 1-16 always worked on the Sutton route, where Nos. 36 and 51 were retained for short workings sometimes assisted by one of the Milnes cars.

Unfortunately, one of these Milnes cars working on the Sutton route, was the victim of the South Metropolitan's only really serious accident. On Easter Monday, 1 April 1907, No. 19 was running as an extra car to Sutton with a full holiday load of passengers, when it got out of control on Wallington Railway Bridge and ran away down the gradient in Park Lane. It overturned on attempting to take the sharp corner into Ruskin Road and fell on its side in front of a doctor's house. Two people were killed and thirty injured. The accident occurred at about 3.30 p.m.*

Naturally, the Board of Trade held a searching inquiry and issued a report on 4 July. Major J. W. Pringle reported that he had examined the car and found that the body had separated from the truck and there were a number of deep

* One of those killed was Mrs. Wilhelmina Suhr for which Croydon Corporation mistakenly apologised!

chips on the outside edges of the tyres of the wheels. He estimated that the car must have been doing at least 18 miles per hour on the curve where it overturned. The conductor stated that there were 22 passengers inside the car and 33 outside, plus an unknown number of children. The driver, who was normally employed as a fitter, but had some driving experience with the Corporation, was acting as a relief driver and was found to be principally to blame for the accident, because of his lack of experience, which resulted in his letting the car take the curve at too great a speed and the conductor for applying the hand brake at his end so as to lock the wheels; he had received no instruction on the proper procedure.

It became evident to both the Corporation and the Company, that the Selby Road frontier was of little use as a terminus for either. Relations between the two having improved in the meantime, an agreement for through running was reached on 14 April 1907. From 24 June, a service was provided with Corporation cars running from West Croydon to Penge terminus and a service from West Croydon to the Crystal Palace, using only South Metropolitan cars, which had the track brakes demanded for Anerley Hill.

From then on, South Metropolitan cars only ran to Penge on odd occasions, usually as football extras on Saturday afternoons, or for track maintenance. The Company produced a new rule book, instructing crews that when working over the section from Selby Road to West Croydon, they must avoid altercations with Corporation staff at all costs and behave as though they were employees of the Corporation themselves. A multi-coloured array of through tickets was devised (see Chapter on Fares and Charges). Unlike joint services in many other places, the crews seem to have got on well together. Eight cars were provided by each undertaking and gave a five-minute service from West Croydon as far as the "Robin Hood". Later a crossover was installed in Anerley Road and extra cars ran in peak hours from the "Robin Hood" to the Crystal Palace, from 1912.

Turner's Automatic Points were installed at the Robin Hood junction, and cars coasted to take the corner for Anerley, but continued under power for the straight road to Penge. There was a cabinet on the pavement beside the traction pole, in front of Holy Trinity Church, with a cable emerging from a hole in the top, which passed over a pulley near the top of the post and worked the overhead point, in conjunction with the rail point. There was a skate on the overhead wire where the driver had to cut out to turn and another one round the corner to reset the points for the straight road. Because of the slight gradient, these points often gave trouble, when drivers misjudged when to cut out and sometimes ran back. The conductor would then leap down and tug at the wire on top of the cabinet. When the apparatus functioned properly, it did so with a loud clonk that the writer could hear from his home near Selby Road. A Turner's Controller was also installed at Pitlake junction at the bottom of Tamworth Road and was interlocked with the signal lights on traction posts in Tamworth Road and Lower Church Street.

As the depôt was near the "Robin Hood", in the mornings, one would often see drivers' small children waiting with a blue enamelled jug of steaming tea and sandwiches in a red handkerchief, for their father's breakfast. The stop sign at Low Level Station was inscribed "Last Stop before the Crystal Palace" and on passing here, the driver would set his controls to climb the hill and sit on the stairs to consume his repast.

It was fortunate that the longer wheelbase cars had been removed to work on the Sutton route as they were longer and of larger capacity than the Corporation cars and would certainly have given trouble on the section between Selby Road and West Croydon, which was all single track with short passing loops. Owing to the difficulties of transfer, full maintenance facilities were installed in Penge depôt, as well as Sutton.

On 13 October 1907, the London County Council opened a branch line from their Streatham—Tooting line to Tooting Junction. Their tracks met those of the company end on but were not connected. In any case the L.C.C. used the slot conduit system and the Company used overhead wires.

In March 1908 a crossover was laid near the top of Tamworth Road, so that a second car could reverse when one was standing on the terminal stub. On 4 June the Company introduced a parcels carrying service, using the front platforms of Mitcham & Sutton cars. *Light Railway & Tramway Journal* says the following: "The S.M.E.T. made a new departure on Tuesday by inaugurating a Tramway Parcels Express, in connection with the service of cars between Tooting and Penge, Croydon and Wallington, Carshalton, Sutton and Mitcham. Conductors receive packages at any of the recognized stopping places, or they may be left with certain agents and they are dealt with by special messengers in uniform. The rate for collection and delivery within half a mile of any part of the lines vary between 7 lb. for 3d. and 56 lb. for 7d."

The Manager, Mr. Ratcliffe Hulme, resigned and was replaced in July, by A. V. Mason from Devonport, who became Manager and Engineer of the S.M.E.T. C. W. Durnford, the S.M.E.T. Engineer then became Manager at Devonport.

So far, the British Electric Traction Co. had held all the capital and completely controlled the expenditure and policy of the South Metropolitan undertaking, just as it had when it worked the Corporation system. However, from 1 November 1908, the B.E.T. legally assigned the rights in the Mitcham Light Railways and the Croydon & District Tramways Acts of 1902 and 1903 (excluding the benefits of Tramway No. 20 of the former) at a book value of £43,500 to the South Metropolitan Electric Tramways & Lighting Co. Ltd. The company was then permitted to act as an autonomous subsidiary of the B.E.T., like the many other systems which they controlled throughout the country and abroad. All management decisions were then left to Mr. Mason, at 114 Lower Church Street, Croydon.

On 21 September 1909 an agreement was reached with Penge U.D.C. for the carriage of parcels in their area, in exchange for permitting the Council to fit gas lighting attachments to the traction posts. (The drawing attached to this document, showed a traction post quite unlike those used by the South Metropolitan! It did resemble those used on certain other B.E.T. subsidiaries.)

On 26 September 1910, Penge U.D.C. granted the Company a Temporary Building Licence for a passenger shelter at the top of Anerley Hill. It was a small timber building against the back edge of the pavement on land belonging to the Crystal Palace authorities and was set level with the scissors crossover, now installed at the terminus. There were two doors in the front with a window between them. Inside there was a cabinet against the window with a clock facing outwards so that it was visible from the cars and a telephone in direct communication with the depôt. The seats arranged round the three sides of the interior, were slatted benches like those on the cars and above them were picture frames carrying the Company's advertisements and notices. Above the doorways there was an enamelled iron plate on a board, proclaiming "S.M.E.T. TRAM SHELTER". An agreement was signed with Penge U.D.C. on 14 November, for cleaning out the shelter for £1 per annum. This shelter was in use throughout the life of the trams and trolleybuses and was subsequently used as an office by the author of the "Fares & Tickets" chapter of this book. In 1965 it was condemned as unsafe and locked up. It was destroyed by vandals in August 1980. An open fronted shelter was also erected in 1910, on Mitcham Common opposite the "Blue House" (now "Ravensbury Arms"). There is still a shelter on the site.

In July 1911, the All Red Railway was opened in the Crystal Palace grounds. (See Appendix B for details). The parcels carrying service proved unsatisfactory and was given up on 31 December 1911.

In January 1912, A. V. Mason was promoted to General Manager and Engineer, and A. E. Wray became Assistant Manager. Following complaints from the Local Authority, repairs had to be carried out on the paving between the rails on the Tooting line, early in 1912.

In April 1912, the possibility was considered of running trolleybuses between the "Angel" Benhilton and the "California Arms", Belmont, part of the route originally proposed and vetoed by Sutton Council. However, Sutton Council objected again. Nevertheless, as the law then stood, their consent was not necessary for motor buses. It was proposed that seven B.A.T. buses be ordered to work a route Mitcham—Sutton—Belmont, covering the whole of the discarded tram route. A site was sought for a garage, but before the matter could be taken further, there came news of a possible change in control of the company and things were left in abeyance for the time being.

S.M.E.T. No. 24 at Fair Green, Mitcham in late 1920s. Note staff uniforms.
(Photo Dr. H. A. Whitcombe, courtesy Science Museum

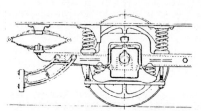 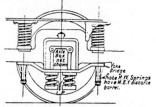

(*Left*) The Lycett & Conaty radial gear, with which S.M.E.T. Nos. 1-16 were originally fitted and (*right*) the Warner gear which replaced it in the 1920s. ("Tramway & Railway World"

CHAPTER FIVE
THE LONDON & SUBURBAN TRACTION CO. LTD.

In 1912, as well as controlling the South Metropolitan Electric Tramways and Lighting Co. Ltd., the British Electric Traction Co. also controlled the Metropolitan Electric Tramways Co. Ltd., with its subsidiary bus undertaking.* It operated a large tramway system in North-West London, with over three hundred cars. Although the B.E.T. had a controlling interest in many important tramway systems throughout the country, their only other interest in the London area was a small motor-bus company using the fleet name "British".

Apart from the London County Council and the various municipal tramway systems, the all powerful organization in the London area, was the UndergrounD Group (Underground Electric Railways Co. of London Ltd.), who as well as controlling all the underground railways except the Metropolitan and Waterloo & City lines, controlled the London United Electric Tramways Co. in South West London and from January 1912, controlled the huge London General Omnibus Co. Ltd. which even then operated several thousand buses all over the London area. This group had few interests outside London.

The B.E.T. at first tried to compete by introducing its own motor bus services, but then managed to conclude a non-competing agreement with the UndergrounD Group, so a new tramway holding company was set up, in which both would hold shares. This was the "London & Suburban Traction Company Ltd." registered on 20 November 1912. The B.E.T's holdings in the Metropolitan Tramways and the UndergrounD Group's holdings in the London United Tramways were transferred to it forthwith. The South Metropolitan Company's turn came later and it was transferred with effect from 14 June 1913. Mr. Mason remained in management at 114 Lower Church Street, Croydon, with A. E. Wray as Superintendent.

It was not long before the South Metropolitan Company's omnibus proposals came up again and ten Daimler double deck buses were ordered in 1913, but Daimler were unable to complete them on time and ten L.G.O.C's "B" type chassis with Brush bodies were substituted in July. They were painted dark blue, with the fleet name "SoutherN". One advantage to the S.M.E.T. of becoming a member of the UndergrounD Group, was that their tram routes were protected from competition from the "GeneraL" buses of the L.G.O.C. (Thomas Tilling had a working agreement with the GeneraL). The same applied to the country services operated by "East Surrey", who had a service from Croydon, passing through Carshalton and Sutton, but followed different roads to the trams (largely those rejected by the 1902 Act). This was important, as by this time good class housing was developing in Wallington and Carshalton.

* The Tramways (M.E.T.) Omnibus Co. Ltd.

When delivered ready to start running on 1 August 1913, the ten "SoutherN" buses were integrated with the L.G.O.C. fleet and allocated to Streatham Garage, from which they normally worked on route 59, (Oxford Circus and South Croydon) which competed directly with Croydon Corporation trams, emphasising Croydon's weakness in not having through running powers to work to London. After a letter of protest from the Corporation, the buses were transferred to Twickenham Garage to work on routes which did not come anywhere near Croydon. In due course GeneraL buses worked between Mitcham, Sutton and Belmont. (The road from Sutton to Belmont is still a tree lined avenue not completely built up, in 1982.) No change was made to the livery of the cars at this time.

On 6 May 1914, a Tilling bus collided with a Carter Paterson's lorry in front of the Crooked Billet, Penge and overturned. It held up tram traffic for several hours, while the police investigated the cause.

Directorship of the three London Tramway companies was shared among the existing directors of the B.E.T. and of the UndergrounD Group. A. L. Barber of the B.E.T. became Secretary of the London & Suburban Traction Co. In April 1914, Mr. Wray left the S.M.E.T. to become Manager of the Gravesend & Northfleet Tramways. He was not replaced immediately. In June, the L.C.C. became interested in a proposal to ask the Company for through running facilities for their cars to Mitcham, but because of the outbreak of war soon afterwards, it did not reach the stage of a definite request to the Company.

In March 1915 at a discussion between London Tramways Managers, Mr. Mason said he did not think women were suitable to conduct large open top cars, but in the New Year, the Company had to employ them, as so many men were being called up in the forces. For the use of women staff, wooden stools were provided on the platforms and canvas screens fixed against the stairs to keep out draughts. In December, the fitting of side lamps on all vehicles, including trams, became compulsory and the Company's cars were modified similarly to those of the Corporation. Head lamps were obscured and a simplified livery adopted. (Still green and ivory).

An event of greater importance occurred in December 1915, when an aerodrome was opened at Waddon alongside Stafford Road, just beyond the Croydon/Wallington boundary on the Sutton route. It was on the site of two farms and became the London Area Headquarters of the Royal Flying Corps. From then on, Stafford Road was flanked by a long black corrugated iron fence. Subsquently, a munitions factory was erected on the Croydon side of the aerodrome, with both railway and tramway sidings leading into its yard. The railway crossing was protected by imposing level crossing gates where it crossed the tram line. When the factory came into use, a special tram service was provided, using the bogie cars which displayed the destination "Waddon Workman". (National Aircraft Factory opened May 1918.)

In March 1916, it was announced that the S.M.E.T. had contracted with the County of London Electricity Supply Co. for bulk supply of current, both for lighting and for that part of the tramways which they supplied. Henceforth, part of Sutton Power Station became a substation and the rest was leased away. The Crystal Palace and its grounds became a Training Centre for the Royal Navy. The service on the Penge route was curtailed at the "Pawleyne Arms" and the Cricket Green service at Mitcham was given up. From 7 April 1916, South Metropolitan staff came out on strike against the employment of women drivers. It spread to the Corporation staff but was over by 20 May.

Starting on 10 August, Beckenham had a bus service, Route 109 (now 227) from the "Crooked Billet", Penge to Beckenham, Bromley and beyond. It was worked by petrol-electric single deck buses, which because of varying agreements, appeared at different periods either lettered "GeneraL" or "Thomas Tilling".

The Market Hall at Pitlake, Croydon, still not demolished, was leased to two gentlemen with foreign names as a cinema, the "Electric Theatre". The Head Office of the London & Suburban Traction Co. was established at

Electric Railway House (now 55 Broadway, Westminster) in 1916 and W. M. Wright became Secretary of the S.M.E.T. As a wartime measure, it was suggested to Croydon Corporation, that local routes in the area should be given service numbers and evidently they were offered the numbers 1-3 for their local routes. The services in which the Company were interested were numbered thus:—

Route 4—West Croydon—South Norwood—Penge (Corporation Cars).

,, 5—West Croydon—South Norwood—Crystal Palace (S.M.E.T. Cars).

,, 6—West Croydon—Mitcham—Tooting Junction (S.M.E.T. Cars).

,, 7—West Croydon—Wallington—Sutton (S.M.E.T. Cars).

The Corporation ignored this scheme and the company did not display the numbers on the cars, but they were shown on the folder maps issued by the three companies from 1916. The Metropolitan Electric Tramways already allocated class letters to their cars (always referred to as "Type" letters); the other two companies were brought into line as follows:—

Type J—Nos.	1-16	Brush radial truck cars.
,, K— ,,	17-26	Milnes single truck cars.
,, L— ,,	27-29) 31 & 35)	Brush bogie cars.
,, M— ,,	36-51	Small Brush single truck cars.
,, O— ,,	30 & 32-34	ex-Gravesend Bogie cars.

The letter P was used later and these Type letters were painted on the solebars on one side of the car only. Time schedule running letters were introduced and displayed as red letters on white enamelled iron plates on the rearmost window pillar of the cars.

Because of the difficulty in placing a trolley wheel on the wire during the blackout and the risk of knocking passengers' hats off or worse, when pulling the pole down, or the risk of a broken spring inside the trolley mast, one of the J Type cars was fitted with metal hoops over the ends of the upper deck in August 1916. In due course they were fitted to all the rest of the fleet and gave quite a distinctive appearance to South Metropolitan cars. In 1917, bogie car No. 31 derailed in Tamworth Road and ran into the front of a house.

A case was heard in Croydon Magistrates' Court on 6 December 1917, described in the press as "Boy's dangerous prank". Some boys had been jumping on the backs of trams, when the conductor's attention was distracted, giving the emergency bell signal, stealing cash boxes and jumping off. Mr. Mason was called to give evidence.

In the autumn of 1918, following the resignation of Mr. A. H. Pott, the Manager and Engineer of the Metropolitan Electric Tramways and the London United Tramways, C. J. Spencer, the Bradford Manager, currently absent on war service with the Admiralty, was invited to take over the management of the three London tramway companies. From 1 November, he was appointed Manager of the Metropolitan and London United undertakings. He could not take over the South Metropolitan until a suitable post had been found for Mr. Mason. This came about on 18 December, when Mr. Mason accepted the post of Assistant Manager and Engineer to the three companies. No doubt Mr. Spencer was pleased to note that S.M.E.T. Nos. 36-51 were equipped with track brakes which he had invented many years ago at Bradford. On 28 January 1919, Mr. Spencer was promoted to General Manager, Tramways. Soon afterwards, J. B. Mackinnon was appointed Traffic Superintendent and E. Boys, Secretary of all three Companies. Penge Urban District Council asked for the electrification of all suburban railways.

A regulator's box was erected on the corner of Croydon Road and Elmers End Road opposite the Robin Hood, in the front garden of No. 103 Croydon Road in accordance with an Agreement reached with Mr. S. G. Gee, the owner of the property, on 16 May 1918, for £5 per annum. It was like a sentry box, with half doors, so that a regulator could stand inside with the top half open and note the passing of the trams. It was surmounted by a small clock and like the shelter at the Crystal Palace, was in direct telephone communication.

Diminished revenue was reported on the trams, but increasing profits on the lighting side. There was also a report that Metropolitan Vickers had a large financial interest in the Company. (Most companies in the UndergrounD Group were heavily mortgaged.) On 12 December, the Company obtained freehold ownership of the site of Penge depôt from W. Clarkson for £960.

The MetropolitaN tramways in North London had evidently over-estimated the number of single deck cars required to serve Alexandra Palace and offered two on loan to the South Metropolitan Co. in 1920. On 1 August Nos. 145 and 150 were transferred and pushed across the gap in the rails at Norbury, whence they were able to travel under their own power to Penge depôt. They arrived, painted in a red and white livery, bearing the coat of arms of Middlesex and the legend "County Council of Middlesex", as part of a fleet which the M.E.T. worked on behalf of that County. When the news got back to them, on 27 September, the County Council were extremely annoyed that two of "their cars" should be loaned outside the County and demanded their immediate return. This was not done, but the arms and title were obliterated before they went into service. Early in 1921, No. 150 was used on the Robin Hood—Crystal Palace short workings and 145 was transferred to Sutton depôt for short workings from there. For reasons explained in the rolling stock chapter, they were not entirely satisfactory and were returned at the end of 1923.

In 1920, Croydon Aerodrome became a civilian airport, operated by Imperial Airways (the local Council thought it should be called Wallington Airport). From 1920 onwards, the B.E.T. began to relinquish its holdings in London and Suburban Traction Co. which eventually became an entirely UndergrounD Group subsidiary, in 1928. (The B.E.T. itself became a subsidiary of Government Stock and Other Securities Investment Co. Ltd., in 1920.)

On 10 November 1921, a new agreement was drawn up between the Company and Croydon Corporation for maintenance of track within the Borough and to permit the construction of a curve at the top of Tamworth Road, only to be used for the transfer of cars. This replaced an agreement of 15 May 1907.

(a) For the first year the Company will pay the Corporation £2,532 14s. 10½d. and sums calculated by the Borough Surveyor in subsequent years (with certain safeguards). For this the Corporation would maintain the whole of the surface of those roads in the borough served by the Company's cars.

(b) The Corporation would construct a single track connecting curve between their own tracks on West Croydon Bridge and the Company's tracks in Tamworth Road. It would then be regarded as the property of the Company who were then permitted to run cars over it, only between the hours of 9.00 p.m. and 9.00 a.m. They must not carry passengers or goods except the Company's own stores.

(c) South Metropolitan cars must not remain unnecessarily on Corporation tracks.

(d) Twenty-four hours' notice must be given to the Corporation of any proposed movement of cars across the West Croydon Junction.

The Company had hoped to be allowed to run cars across in service, but this would have necessitated Parliamentary Powers, which were not needed if a line was never to be used for passenger carrying. A curve branched off the terminal stub, less than a car's length from the end of the track and joined the Corporation's main line on West Croydon Bridge. The connecting curve was laid in and usable by September 1922, making it possible to maintain the whole South Metropolitan fleet at Sutton depôt, so the equipment in Penge depôt was dismantled. Nos. 36 and 51, retained at Sutton for short workings, were transferred to Penge, as any car from that batch could be sent to Sutton at short notice when required. A start was now made in painting the company's trams and buses in the UndergrounD Group's red and white livery.

In December 1921, the L.C.C. proposed to extend their route from West Norwood to the Crystal Palace, but this was strenuously opposed by Lambeth

Council and came to nothing. The Company was always alive to the traffic potential of sporting and other events, not only at the Crystal Palace and as well as running extra cars on Saturday afternoons between the "Pawleyne Arms" Penge and Selhurst for football traffic, all spare cars available from both depôts were pressed into service between West Croydon and "Cold Blows", Mitcham Common, when Mitcham Fair took place each year. In July 1922, the Company enquired whether either of the other two companies had any covered top cars to spare, which they could borrow, to see if their own cars could be fitted with top covers. Unfortunately, they had none to spare.

While at Bradford in 1911, Mr. Spencer had been a pioneer with trolleybus development and with his permission, the Associated Equipment Company (another UndergrounD Group subsidiary), demonstrated a single deck trolleybus of quite modern appearance for the time, somewhere on the South Metropolitan system during 1922, presumably with one trolley on the wire and towing a ball and chain. A. C. Ingram became Assistant Secretary to the three tramway companies in 1922.

There was an accident on 16 March 1923, when a steam traction engine pulling a very large boiler on a flat truck, collided with and overturned a tram in the narrow part of London Road, Mitcham. There were no serious injuries, but other traffic was very much delayed.

Also in March, the L.C.C. wrote to the Company, proposing through running between their two systems, but the Company was not interested. However, on 2 June, the Town Clerk of Mitcham (which was now a separate borough) wrote to the Company complaining that although Tooting Broadway was the nearest large shopping centre to Mitcham, there was no direct tram service to it. Shoppers were forced to go to Croydon, which was much further, in fact over two miles away. He asked if, in the circumstances, the South Metropolitan service could be extended to Tooting Broadway, only half a mile beyond the Tooting Junction terminus. On 8 June the Company sent a copy of this letter to Mr. Bruce, of the L.C.C., asking for his observations.

No agreement was reached between the two parties on this occasion, but discussions continued throughout 1924 and into 1925.

In August 1923, the "Southern" bus fleet was augmented by the transfer of three K type open top buses and one S type from the L.G.O.C. and several of the B type were withdrawn.

At midnight on the first Saturday in August, Inspector Charles Binfield, who was in charge of the paying-in office at Mitcham Road depôt, was attacked by two men and knocked unconscious. They stole £97 12s. 5d.

An agreement was reached on 5 January 1925 between Croydon Corporation, Beddington & Wallington Urban District Council and the South Metropolitan Company for the reconstruction and widening of Stafford Road, Waddon. The two authorities each promised to reimburse the tram company for the realignment of the rails in its own area.

In June 1925, the Ministry of Transport (which had replaced the Transport Department of the Board of Trade in 1919) took note of the poor condition of the track and road surface on the Cricket Green spur at Mitcham, which had not been used since the war. The Company's management evidently came to the conclusion that the only effective way to avoid the expense of lifting the rails, was to come to a speedy agreement with the L.C.C. for through running and persuade them to use the spur as a terminal stub.

The question of through running with the L.C.C. was a matter which exercised the other two companies, particularly the Metropolitan, who had quite a number of through services to various L.C.C. terminals in North London, mainly over conduit equipped track. Terms and policy were discussed at regular meetings between the UndergrounD Group and the L.C.C. The matter of through running to Mitcham was raised at a meeting on 8 June, attended by Messrs.

No. 23 at Fair Green, Mitcham. Note Clock Tower and track to right, leading to the Cricket Green, just beyond the block of shops.   (Commercial postcard, Courtesy "Len's of Sutton"

Spencer and Mason, for the Companies and Messrs. Bruce, Croom-Johnson and F. Scothorne for the L.C.C. It would be necessary to bring the tracks of both authorities into line and join them at Tooting Junction, but there remained the hiatus over the different methods of current collection and the L.C.C. thought the South Metropolitan Company should bear the whole cost of £1,650 for installing a changeover point. (See Croydon Corporation, Chapter 3, for details of change-over procedure.) It was eventually agreed that each would pay half this cost and as the junction between the two systems was on a rather narrow section of road at the foot of a hump-backed railway bridge, the boundary was not a suitable place for a change point. Consequently the change point was to be constructed several hundred yards back on L.C.C. track at a widening of the road, where a new police station was under construction. This did present a problem, as of the three services which the L.C.C. had terminating at Tooting Junction, only one was to be extended through to Mitcham and it would not be practicable for the cars on the other two to change over to trolley operation for such a short distance. Therefore, a special change point had to be designed, incorporating a point blade in the conduit, which by the operation of a lever, could either deflect a plough onto the change point or permit it to pass unhindered to the old terminus. The overhead wires were extended from the South Metropolitan side to just beyond the change point, making a section of dual equipped road, on which through cars would use the overhead wires and cars terminating would remain on the conduit.

It was agreed that as the company had no cars suitable for running on conduit track, a service to the Cricket Green was to be provided only using L.C.C. cars.

The Company was, therefore, to curtail its service from Croydon to Mitcham Fair Green and the L.C.C. would virtually take over completely, the section Cricket Green—Fair Green—Tooting Junction, providing the cars and crews that worked over it as part of a through service from a central London terminus. The Company was to provide power and maintain the track. Each Authority was to fix the fares in its own area and receipts taken on the section concerned were to be divided equally between the L.C.C. and the Company. The Agreement was for five years and matters of detail were to be settled between the respective managers.

While these negotiations were going on, the General Strike occurred in June 1926. The Trade Unions did not have quite the grip on the economy that they have today and its effects were not absolute. The South Metropolitan tramways were not brought completely to a standstill and Sutton depôt kept cars on the road.

The track to Mitcham Cricket Green was refurbished and the traction poles painted silver, while span wire replaced bracket suspension, in readiness for the L.C.C. to take over. It appears that the L.C.C. made some trial runs to Mitcham on 1 September.

Victor Matterface, the Brakes Inspector of the Metropolitan tramways, who later became a well-known Tramway Engineer elsewhere, describes how he was called on to visit South Metropolitan depôts as well as in the 1920's. He was told about Sutton and Penge depôts which he visited and found well run, particularly Penge for fear of losing face with the Corporation, who maintained high standards. Quite by chance he heard that they had another depôt off Mitcham Road, West Croydon and on visiting that found quite a different state of affairs. Conditions were quite chaotic and standards of maintenance were poor. Moreover, he noticed an electric lighting cable passing over the wall to an adjoining house, which he found was occupied by a senior official. Mr. Matterface made a report to Head Office and the official was dismissed.

With the curtailment of the service provided by the Company, at Mitcham, there would be the opportunity to make a number of economies. The original Milnes four wheeled cars were now getting very decrepit and it was found that the nine bogie cars would be quite sufficient to provide the normal service between West Croydon and Mitcham, so a number of Milnes cars were stored away in the back parts of the other two depôts. It will be recalled that Sutton depôt was built to house 60 cars, but up to now had rarely held more than 20, so even with the overhaul facilities, there was plenty of space to spare. Therefore, the nine bogie cars and a few four wheelers were transferred to Sutton and worked the Mitcham line from there. Mitcham Road depôt closed on 5 October 1926. It was offered for sale and although the Corporation, who were always short of depôt space, were approached, they rented it as a mortuary.

At the same time, most of the office work was concentrated by the Group at Electric Railway House (now 55 Broadway). The Company's office at 114 Lower Church Street was closed and leased away to Reeves the furnisher, together with the adjoining Market Hall, which the Company was supposed to have demolished for road widening in 1906! Two bays in Sutton depôt were screened off and such office work as still had to be done locally was done there.

From 22 September 1926, all cars on the Penge route ran right through to Thicket Road.

Through running by L.C.C. cars to Mitcham commenced on 4 November 1926. Their service 8 was extended, becoming Victoria—Tooting—Mitcham (Cricket Green). The extension was one mile long and required five extra cars. It was worked by "standard" E/1 Class cars, like those used on the service to Croydon and Purley and sometimes by the slightly older but almost identical E Class, using 15 cars per hour in each direction. The Company then provided a service from West Croydon to Mitcham (Fair Green), with a car every nine minutes and a twenty minute journey time, normally using the bogie cars.

At the same meeting as the through service was decided upon, the possibility of through running over each other's tracks for access to overhaul works was also discussed and mutually beneficial arrangements worked out. As the Kingsway Subway had not yet been deepened, except for single deck cars, the L.C.C. system was effectively divided into two parts, North and South of the Thames. Their main overhaul works was at Charlton in South-east London and North London cars had to be maintained separately. The UndergrounD Group also wished to centralize overhaul facilities. The Metropolitan Tramways had a well-equipped works at Hendon and there was a connection at Acton with the London UniteD tramways who had a slightly less well-equipped works at Fulwell. The South

London United 278 on loan, crosses Mitcham Common. (Photo G. Bendall

Metropolitan undertook such maintenance as they could in Sutton depôt. It was agreed that North London L.C.C. cars be permitted to make the lengthy journey out to Finchley and back down the other road to Cricklewood and Willesden, where they met other L.C.C. tracks at Scrubs Lane, which connected with South London and so to Charlton Works. Likewise, South Metropolitan cars were permitted to make the journey to Hendon Works over L.C.C. tracks. Of course, it was necessary for S.M.E.T. cars to be towed over L.C.C. conduit tracks and conversely, some L.C.C. cars did not have overhead gear. Advance notice of car movements had to be given, but no charge was made by either party and at last S.M.E.T. cars could be thoroughly overhauled at Hendon.

On 18 June 1927, there was a collision between two cars (presumably L.C.C. cars) in London Road, Mitcham, when they met on temporary track where relaying was in progress. There were no serious injuries, but one passenger was cut by flying glass and traffic was held up for over an hour.

One month later, the Company was able to purchase twelve cars from Croydon Corporation, with spare parts at the bargain price of £700 for the lot. The original intention was that they should replace the Mïlnes cars which were worn out. However, with the S.M.E.T. service cut back to Mitcham, it was found that only four would be required, so the best four were sent to Hendon to be slightly modified to resemble other S.M.E.T. cars. Soon the remaining six B-Class buses were withdrawn from the SoutherN fleet and were replaced by more ex-L.G.O.C. K Class buses.

During 1927 and 1928, most of the South Metropolitan track was relaid and as far as possible wood-block surfaces were replaced by tar-bound macadam. A small steam roller with a vertical boiler between twin rollers was used in Penge and Anerley. Other equipment was loaned by the L.U.T.

When the cars were sent to Hendon for overhaul, most lost their enamelled iron advertisements and received short term paper displays instead. (See Appendix A.) Several received other minor improvements, such as cushioned seats, but Nos. 17, 21 and 47 were condemned as unfit for further service. The first two ex-Corporation cars to be put into service were numbered 52 and 53 at first, but with the withdrawal of the three cars mentioned above, three ex-Corporation cars appeared numbered 17, 21 and 47. It is believed that 53 was renumbered 17 and 52 remained as an addition to the fleet. (See Rolling

Stock section.) Although they resembled the M Type they were usually found on the short workings on the Sutton and Mitcham routes. They were designated "Type P''. (They lacked track brakes.)

The Company's "SoutherN'' fleet of open top K type buses was now outdated and in urgent need of replacement and at a Board Meeting of the UndergrounD Group, it was decided that SoutherN fleet should be liquidated and in their place, ten more buses of a modern type be added to the bus subsidiary of the Metropolitan Electric Tramways. The ten K type buses were taken off the road one by one from 1 January 1928.

Early in 1928, the short workings from the Robin Hood to the Crystal Palace, were extended back to Selby Road in peak hours. These had always done quite well as buses were not then allowed on Anerley Hill. Both the Corporation and the Company had always turned trolleys with a hooked bamboo pole. One was kept at each terminus and at the Robin Hood, hung from a large hook near the top of a traction post. Like the city gentleman's umbrella, trolley ropes were kept neatly furled round the trolley pole, only to be undone in cases of dire emergency. Apparently the Company did not possess an additional bamboo pole for Selby Road, and the one from the Robin Hood had to be carried there resting on the backs of the seats of the upper deck of a car when required. Later, these short workings were numbered 5A. (When on his way to school, the writer was once asked to change seats!)

On 19 July, the L.C.C. withdrew service 8 from Mitcham and diverted their service 6 there in its place. It connected Mitcham with the City, instead of Victoria. Thus, the Company's service 6 and L.C.C. service 6 met at Mitcham Fair Green and the passenger was encouraged to think that one was merely an extension of the other. The combined maps issued by the three tramway companies used a symbol to indicate through services, under the description "Services are operated'', and the intending passenger might have been forgiven for expecting to see Company's cars working on them. The service from Mitcham to London was shown with this symbol, but so was a service from Tooting Junction to Willesden, over which the Company's cars had to run "dead'' to reach Hendon Works, but could not have run in service.

Really serious attention now had to be given to the reconstruction or replacement of the Company's rolling stock and although the ex-Croydon cars were in better condition than their own, it was decided to rebuild the J type cars on the Sutton route and not to commission any more ex-Croydon cars for service. No. 16, which because of the poor condition of its body, had already been re-pillared with five windows, was sent to Hendon in August or September 1928, stripped right down and rebuilt with flush sides, two and one reversible cushioned seats inside and a number of other improvements. On the return of No. 16 to Sutton, the remainder of the J type were sent to Hendon one at a time and similarly rebuilt, except that they retained four windows. Some other cars in the fleet were then less extensively refurbished, with long cushioned seats.

A model of a proposed new type of car was submitted to Lord Ashfield, but it was not approved. The railway line between the Crystal Palace (Low Level) and Beckenham, which had been closed during the 1914-18 war, was electrified and reopened in 1929. This was the railway which crossed over the Corporation tramway just short of the Selby Road boundary. A new station called Birkbeck, was built where it crossed Elmers End Road, but was not sufficiently near the tram route to affect their traffic. Just beyond the station, Elmers End bus garage was built and opened, also in 1929.

As overhauled cars returned from Hendon, route boards were fitted just below the saloon windows, where they were more accessible than in the old position on the upper deck. The new boards showed about five points with a route number in small figures at each end (the only place where route numbers were ever shown on South Metropolitan cars). Since the UndergrounD Group took over, the Company's cars had carried the statutory lettering at the bottom

S.M.E.T. No. 16 returns to Sutton Depôt after rebuilding.　　　　(S.M.E.T. Official photo

of the rocker panel, but had displayed no badge or fleet name. Late in 1929, the fleet name "SouthmeT" began to appear in gold letters on the waist panel. Crew's duties were signified by running numbers instead of letters and the livery was slightly simplified.

In January 1930, the L.C.C. entered into discussion with the Company about a huge housing estate and a very large hospital, which they were then building "out of County" at St. Helier between Mitcham and Sutton. The L.C.C. wished to persuade the Company to build the Mitcham—Sutton line included in their original powers and then permit them to run over it as far as St. Helier, as an extension of their Mitcham service. The Company was not really interested and explained that their powers had long since lapsed and costly new Parliamentary Powers would be needed. They were only prepared to consider the proposal if a bridge in the outskirts of Mitcham and some road widening were included in the scheme.

On 1 July 1930 the Agreement with Croydon Corporation for the supply of electricity in their area was renewed.

At a Board Meeting of the S.M.E.T. on 5 February 1931, it was proposed to increase the capital of the Company from £500,000 to £600,000 by the creation of 100,000 new ordinary £1 shares. This was carried. A Bill before Parliament to unify public transport in London, received its second reading on 23 March, amid great opposition from the independent bus operators and the trade unions.

On 27 August, the air liner *Normandie* of Imperial Airways, overshot the runway at Croydon Aerodrome and crashed through the fence onto Stafford Road, narrowly missing SouthmeT tramcar No. 15.

Also on 7 August 1930, a firm was given the contract to repave the roadway between the rails, between Fair Green and Cricket Green at Mitcham. Unfortunately, the firm went bankrupt before the work was completed and another firm had to be called in to finish it, (Carpave Ltd. 1 June 1933). Twenty five signs inscribed "To the Trams" and bearing an arrow pointing in the appropriate direction, were fixed to lamp standards in streets adjoining those served by the trams. (One such sign was observed by the writer in the forecourt of Penge East Station in 1944, ten years after trams had ceased to serve Penge!)

The question of borrowing covered top cars came up again in the autumn of 1931. Neither the Sutton or Mitcham route was crossed by any overbridge and it was stated that covered top cars would be a boon when crossing Mitcham Common in winter. This time the S.M.E.T. was more lucky, as the London United tramways had some in store. They had recently converted their Kingston area routes to trolleybus operation and had obtained some of the new Feltham type cars for their Uxbridge route. Ten of the London United "U" type covered top bogie cars were transferred to Sutton Depot to work the West Croydon—Mitcham route. They were ungainly vehicles with double-flight stairs and short canopies, but they had top covers and Brill 22E bogies, which were more reliable than the Brush bogies under their own cars. Being only on loan, they retained the L.U.T. livery and fleet numbers.

They normally worked on the Mitcham route, but had to run over most of the Sutton route to reach the depôt. When they were installed to start working on 24 October 1931, the Company's nine bogie cars and one or two Milnes four wheelers were then taken into store at the L.U.T's Fulwell Depôt, never to turn a wheel in service again.

The Company suffered from the industrial depression of 1931 and at a meeting of the directors in May, the following proposals were considered:—

1. To abandon the Penge section, which suffered heavily from bus competition. (Bus routes 12 and 75.)

2. To lease the remainder of the Tooting route, i.e. Mitcham—West Croydon, to the London County Council, to be worked as part of a through route.

3. To convert the Sutton route to trolleybus operation and to make an agreement with Croydon Corporation for the working of the Crystal Palace route.

However, as it now seemed certain that the Company would be taken over by the new authority that was to unify public transport in London, before very long, these projects were left in abeyance. Nevertheless, Mr. Pybus, the Minister of Transport, announced in February 1932, that the London Transport Bill was dead and he had no intention of forcing it on an unwilling House of Commons. However, another slightly amended Bill was soon prepared.

On 1 July 1932, the electricity undertaking of the South Metropolitan company was handed over to the London & Home Counties Joint Electricity Authority, who already supplied the current in bulk. Mr. Mason, who was Chief Engineer to both the electricity and tramway departments, claimed and received heavy compensation for severance. Mr. Mason remained with the Tramway companies, but the three electric-lighting offices and show rooms were handed over to the new authority. They were at:—52 High Street, Sutton; 47 Woodcote Road, Wallington; The Square, Carshalton.

The Wallington Office had a direction sign, like an UndergrounD Group stop sign pointing to it.

Flushed with the success of his trolleybus venture in the Kingston area of the London United Tramways, Mr. Spencer obtained permission in July 1932 to apply for powers to run trolleybuses on the Sutton route of the South Metropolitan company, so that he could implement the third item of the proposals put forward in 1931.

However, the days of the South Metropolitan Electric Tramways and Lighting Co. Ltd., were now numbered. It had already been stripped of the lighting side of its business, the more profitable side, and now the tramway undertaking was to be absorbed into the unified transport system, of which so much had been heard.

Ex-Croydon Corporation No. 346 at the Crystal Palace. Note passenger shelter and hooked bamboo pole on traction post. 21 August 1935. (Photo O. J. Morris

L.C.C. No. 1 near Purley on the famous journey from Waltham Cross, with Mr. J. W. Fowler standing in front of car. (Courtesy J. H. Meredith. Photo O. J. Morris

CHAPTER SIX

THE LONDON PASSENGER TRANSPORT BOARD

As early as 1929, Herbert Morrison of the London County Council was pressing for the L.C.C. to take over all public transport in the London area and placed a Bill before Parliament early in April, to enable this to happen. Later he moved over and took his seat in Parliament, where he was able to exploit even grander notions, that public transport be nationalized and another Bill was placed before Parliament, with this in mind, at least in so far as London was concerned. The uncertainty caused by this atmosphere put a damper on further developments of public transport in London, as those desiring to make improvements felt that the fruits of their endeavours would pass to others.

A Bill of Parliament received its second reading on 23 March 1930, but by February 1932, there had been a change in the government and Mr. Pybus, the new Minister of Transport, decided to drop the Bill. However, by then things had gone so far, outside Parliament, that some change was necessary. A new Bill was presented, on similar lines, but instead of handing everything over to the L.C.C. or the State, everything was in effect handed over to the UndergrounD Group, under a new name.

Lord Ashfield remained Chairman and Frank Pick, who had become Managing Director of the Group in March 1928, became Deputy Chairman. John Cliff, a former Trade Union leader, was to be the member nominated by the L.C.C. These and others were named as Members of the new London Passenger Transport Board in May 1933, but moves had been taking place behind the scenes from the beginning of the year. Each tramway undertaking in the London area was sent a questionnaire, asking for details of operating methods, rolling stock, fares and tickets, and other assets such as depôts and any other properties. These questionnaires were much resented and the L.C.C. refused to complete theirs. Tramways belonged to eleven local authorities and three companies, but not all the local authorities operated their tramways themselves.

The "appointed day" when all tramways had to be handed over to the Board, was 1 July 1933. The major bus undertakings and the UndergrounD railways (including the Metropolitan) were also taken over on that day, and the minor bus operators were drawn in one at a time later, but the main line railway companies (including their suburban services) were excluded. There was some sort of pooling arrangement with them.

We are only interested in the tramways operated by the London County Council, Croydon Corporation and the South Metropolitan Company. In the case of Croydon Corporation, on the night of 30 June, a fresh coat of grey paint was applied covering the gold title "Croydon Corporation Tramways" and a small red label inscribed "London Passenger Transport Board, 55 Broadway, Westminster S.W.1." covered the name of the Manager. The municipal coat of arms and fleet numbers remained for the time being. The South Metropolitan cars carried similar labels, but black on white. Otherwise, as the Company was already part of the group, it was not thought necessary to signify the change of ownership, in any other way.

The Board assumed legal ownership of all rolling stock, track, depôts and other assets on 1 July. Operating staff were transferred automatically. Administrative staff were to be offered equivalent posts to those they now held, but Corporation staff did have the opportunity of transferring to other departments of the Municipality. Miss Doris Allcorn, the Manager's Secretary, elected to do this. Other people at the Town Hall only spent part of their time working for the Tramways Department.

Croydon Corporation handed over to London Transport 55 tramcars, 1 welding car, 1 tower wagon, 2.24 miles of single track and 7.04 of double. The staff handed over comprised 11 administrative staff, 2 cash receivers, 1 depôt inspector, 6 inspectors, 4 regulators, 41 motormen, 32 conductors, 1 composite (could drive or conduct) and 20 workshop staff. The above were all covered by the Corporation Superannuation Scheme, but there are believed to have been more motormen and conductors who had not been long enough with the Corporation to qualify. (New uniforms ordered in January 1933 for 19 inspectors and regulators and for 201 motormen and conductors.)

The Administrative staff were:—

G. V. Stanley	—Tramways Manager.	F. S. Harding	—Secretary.
G. D. Morgan	—Assistant Manager and Chief Clerk.	A. E. Hunt	—Traffic Clerk.
		G. B. Tiller	—Ticket Ordering.
W. H. Troake	—Stores Superintendent.	T. E. Winscombe	—Statistician.
L. Marriott	—Draughtsman.	W. E. Miller	—Comptometer Operator.
F. Stapley	—Insurance Clerk.		
B. L. Constable	—Wages Clerk.		

Mr. Stanley was moved to an Engineering appointment at Chiswick Works. Mr. Morgan was given an administrative post in the Traffic Development Office (see Appendix C for biographies). Mr. Troake was moved to the stores at Charlton Works and Mr. Tiller went to the Fares and Charges Office at 55 Broadway. From subsequent events, it would appear that Mr. Marriott was given an appointment in electrical engineering. Very little information is available concerning the movement of ex-Company staff, who probably numbered fewer than those of the Corporation, but it is known that S. H. Weatherhead, the clerk at Sutton depôt, subsequently received an administrative appointment in Operating (Central Buses) at 55 Broadway. (All the above named were also named in a staff list of 1922.)

Croydon Corporation celebrated the parting with its tramway responsibilities by calling a meeting of the staff, at which the Mayor stated that their interests would be protected. Exactly what powers he had in that direction was not clear, but the Board did promise that no former member of the staff of an undertaking taken over would suffer any reduction of salary or conditions of service. However prospects of promotion were reduced. It was said that the ex-L.C.C. Tramways and Metropolitan Railway staff had the best conditions of all. Later ex-Croydon staff found to their cost that if they accepted promotion, they then came under London Transport conditions, which followed closely UndergrounD Group practices.

After a few weeks, a small letter E was applied after the fleet numbers on the dashes of ex-Croydon Corporation cars. Soon afterwards, the letter S was applied similarly to ex-South Metropolitan cars.

The new Board was known to hold strong views about the replacement of tram services, particularly those where there was single track in narrow streets or worked by outdated rolling stock. They were much impressed by Mr. Spencer's success with trolleybuses in the Kingston area of the ex-London United Tramways. Plans were prepared for trolleybus conversion on a large scale.

In order to find suitable positions for two very experienced and well respected tramways managers, the tram (and trolleybus) system was divided into two areas, with a General Manager over each. C. J. Spencer took charge of "North and West" and T. E. Thomas, General Manager of the L.C.C. Tramways since 1930, took "South and East". Geography was somewhat manipulated as Mr. Spencer's empire included the Metropolitan Electric Tramways, the London United Tramways, the South Metropolitan and Croydon Corporation Tramways, while Mr. Thomas had the L.C.C. Tramways and the other municipalities. Although this arrangement was short-lived, it did prolong the separate and different practices of the L.C.C. and the UndergrounD Group, as North and West cars continued to be overhauled at Hendon and South and East cars at Charlton, for some long time afterwards.

In October 1933, Mr. Spencer resigned and was appointed Resident Director to the North Metropolitan Electric Power Supply Co. Ltd., formerly part of the UndergrounD Group, but which London Transport could not take over. Before taking up those duties, he made a prolonged visit to South Africa to advise transport undertakings in Johannesburg, Bloemfontein and other places.

J. C. Mitchell, Secretary to the Board, was appointed liquidator of the UndergrounD Group and there were early reports of ex-Croydon and Walthamstow tramcars to be seen in a red livery similar to that of the L.C.C. (Croydon 34E and 55E then due for a repaint). Following Mr. Spencer's resignation, T. E. Thomas became General Manager (Trams and Trolleybuses) covering the whole system. Frank Pick was a very large man, well over six feet tall and broad shouldered. He only liked large men around him and must have looked askance at small Welshmen like T. E. Thomas and G. D. Morgan.

A map issued in November 1933, showed the trolleybus routes that the Board was to include in a Bill to be put before Parliament. These covered most of the "North & West" area, including Sutton—Croydon—Crystal Palace of the former SouthmeT. They also included Bexley—Erith—Dartford.

One of the first major changes to tram services, was to affect the Croydon area. Notices were posted on the sides of the cars, stating that the following changes would take place on the night of 6 December:—

(a) Route 4 — West Croydon—Penge was to be abandoned and competing bus services 12 and 75 were to be strengthened.

(b) Route 5 — West Croydon—Crystal Palace to be strengthened to a five-minute service by extending the former Robin Hood and Selby Road short workings through to Croydon.

(c) Route 6 — West Croydon—Mitcham to be replaced by an extension of ex-L.C.C. route 30, now to run Willesden—Tooting—Mitcham—West Croydon.

(d) Former L.C.C. route 6 to be cut back to Tooting Junction and the Mitcham Fair Green—Cricket Green section to be given up.

This made route 30, now over 14 miles in length, the longest tram route in London. About 40 cars were required, most of which were E Class cars from Hammersmith depôt at the other end of the route. However, Thornton Heath depôt had to supply seven cars and for this purpose cars of the 552-601 batch of E/1s took the place of the Penge open toppers there. These were in fact the old single deck Subway cars rebodied. As route 30 was regarded as an outer belt route with no severe gradients, both batches were "slow motored" cars. This was the only period when the connecting curve at the top of Tamworth Road was in regular use. The far destination at College Park, was shown on the blinds of the cars as "near Willesden Junction", but was in fact some distance short of that important railway station.

In order that the Crystal Palace service could be strengthened, to the 15 cars available (36-51s, less 47s) were added three ex-Croydon Corporation cars, Nos. 1E, 2E and 3E, which because of the reversal of numbers of the single

Ex-Croydon Corporation No. 370 in Brigstock Road.   (Photo by E. G. P. Masterman

truck cars at the 1927 renumbering, they were the newest. They were quickly fitted with track brakes and put back into service on the Crystal Palace route still in Croydon Corporation livery, in which they ran for several weeks, before being sent to Hendon in turn for repainting and renumbering.

The use of small suffix letters after the fleet numbers of the cars from municipal fleets, was only regarded as a temporary measure and it was decided to renumber them, either in gaps in the L.C.C. fleet numbers or above the highest L.C.C. number. Most of the ex-municipal cars were accommodated in the former part, but Walthamstow and the three companies were given numbers in the 2000s above the highest L.C.C. car. Croydon cars were allocated the numbers 345-399. Nos. 2 and 3 were sent for repainting first and they carried the numbers 346 and 347 in small plain gold figures. No. 1 was sent away a little later. It was renumbered 345. No. 5 was evidently repainted at Charlton, fitted with magnetic track brakes, numbered 349 and transferred to Erith. No. 19 was retained at Thornton Heath and fitted with fixed snow brooms. Although later painted red, it was not renumbered and remained 19E. Nos. 4, 6-18 and 20 were taken to Brixton Hill depôt for scrapping without being renumbered, but the trucks under some of them reappeared later under other cars (see Chapter 7). Because of their unusual livery and high standard of maintenance, they stood out proudly among the motley collection of cars, mainly ex-Bexley and Erith, awaiting the hammer at Brixton Hill depôt.

Before long, the old Croydon bogie cars on the Greyhound—Thornton Heath route were painted London Transport red and cream and renumbered 365-374. At the same time they were given standard L.C.C. combined tail lamp and route number stencil carriers, fixed under the landings of their double-flight staircases. For the time being these carried the route number 2. When the turn of the modern bogie cars came to be repainted, they took the numbers 375-399 and retained their colourful enamelled iron advertisements. No ex-South Metropolitan car was ever renumbered, although a number were repainted in the official London Transport livery. The ex-London United cars which had been working on the Croydon—Mitcham route were now transferred to the Sutton route, to work alongside the J type cars (1s-16s), four of which were withdrawn and sent to Brixton Hill. In due course, several of the ex-L.U.T. cars were renumbered in the 2000s, as though still working as part of that fleet.

92

Route 16/18, Embankment—Croydon—Purley was not affected by any of the changes going on. In December 1933, London Transport came to an agreement with the various local authorities for the lifting of rails on sections of tramway abandoned.

In February 1934, George F. Sinclair, ex-L.C.C., was appointed Rolling Stock Engineer (Trams and Trolleybuses). He had designed L.C.C. car No. 1, the modern car, which was to have been the forerunner of a new fleet.

In May it was announced that the fleet name "London TransporT" would be used and it began to appear on the waist panels of cars as repainted. The livery for trams was to be red and cream similar to the L.C.C. style.

One of the matters brought to light by the plans to operate trolleybuses, was the need to rationalize electric current supply and with that in mind a new agreement was drawn up with Croydon Corporation. The main points of this agreement reached on 17 January 1934, were:—

(1) The sub-station at Thornton Heath depôt to be given up.
(2) Drovers Road sub-station, South Croydon, to be retained.
(3) Croydon Corporation to build a new sub-station in Tennison Road, Norwood, and lease part of it to London Transport at a peppercorn rent.
(4) Croydon Corporation to contribute £4,500 towards new high tension cables to Mitcham and Sutton.

The new sub-station at Tennison Road would be suitable for the trolleybuses when they materialized. It was built without delay, a short distance into Tennison Road, alongside a small market garden. The Bill authorizing the conversion of a number of tram routes to trolleybus operation received Royal Assent on 31 July. This included Sutton—Croydon—Crystal Palace.

Although bus route numbers had been regulated by the police for a number of years, there were still several separate numbering systems among the tramway undertakings taken over. The L.C.C's system predominated, using odd numbers north of the Thames and even numbers to the south, with pairs of even numbers for routes making the loop round the Embankment. In theory, local routes in the Croydon area were numbered 1 to 7. As already noted, until about twelve months earlier, there had been two routes numbered 6 meeting at Mitcham. Thus a scheme was worked out by which any route which duplicated a number in the L.C.C. series would be renumbered, into what was then a gap in the L.C.C. series on 3 October 1934. The only change affecting the Croydon area was the Greyhound—Thornton Heath route, which had lately carried the number 2. It became 42. At the same time it was decided that single deck bus services would be numbered in the 200s (Route 109 at Penge became 227) and trolleybus routes would be numbered in the 600s. (Later some numbers in the 500s were used as well.)

Croydon Corporation was not satisfied with the compensation which it received for the loss of its tramways and went to arbitration. This was decided on 29 October, by Joshua Scholefield, K.C. Land adjoining Purley depôt, which had been acquired for an extension which did not materialize, was to be excluded from their considerations. The Corporation was awarded £7,674, of which £5,000 had already been paid. There were outstanding loans of £198,599 3s. 2d. on the assets of the transferred undertaking, which had to be paid by London Transport.

In March 1935, it was announced that the Sutton—Croydon—Crystal Palace route was to open in October. London Transport decided to standardize on a 70 seater six-wheeler, but the first batches for the Croydon area and Bexley area, were to be slightly smaller and 60 seaters. They too were six-wheelers. Those for the Croydon area route were ordered from Leyland, with Birmingham Railway Carriage & Wagon Co. bodies.

In June, one of the few remaining sections of single line on the main road in Croydon was doubled, that between Aberdeen Road and Parker Road, South

End. This still left the more notorious section of single track at Crown Hill, between North End and High Street.

The Crystal Palace tram terminus was on a gradient and it was ruled that if the crew wanted to take their break there, in the busmen's canteen round the corner on the Parade, they must go one at a time and not leave the car unattended. However, a car was left on 25 October 1935 and began to run away down Anerley Hill. It was stopped by a passenger, Mr. Leonard Tofield, of Elmers End Road, who strained his wrist applying the hand brake. Another passenger jumped off and was slightly injured. This event was in contrast to the exemplary record of the South Metropolitan Company, who never had an accident on Anerley Hill, despite the steep gradient.

The contract for erecting the trolleybus wires between Sutton and the Crystal Palace was awarded to Messrs. Clough, Smith & Co., who claimed that it would be necessary to renew 80% of the traction poles.

In spite of the trolleybus programme, it was announced in August that 250 trams of the E/1 Class were to be modernized, i.e. fitted with windscreens, flush-panelled sides and inset route and destination boxes. There were to be no mechanical or electrical improvements. They have often been referred to as "Rehabilitiated" cars or "Ashfield rebuilds", but neither term appears to have been recognized officially. In fact, only 154 cars were treated thus, but these did include four ex-Croydon cars.

Trolleybus replaced the trams on the West Croydon—Sutton route on 8 December 1935. The rest of the J type cars joined the four which had already been withdrawn, at Brixton Hill depôt, where they were scrapped, but the lower saloon seats retained for further use. Six of the London United cars were moved to North-West London. Although it had been intended to convert right through in one operation, the Crystal Palace section was not ready. In order to find suitable locations for turning loops, the route was extended slightly at both ends. In Sutton, the wires came out into the High Street and ran a short distance to the right to run round a small green at Bushey Road. At West Croydon, the wires crossed over the main road into Station Road and terminated in a loop at a triangular widening at the entry to St. Michael's Road, opposite the old station building. (At the time there was a church on the corner, now there is a Bus Station.) This extension, overlapped the Crystal Palace tram route by a few yards.

The new 60 seater trolleybuses were numbered 64-93 and although full-fronted, the driver sat in a half-cab inside, with a single passenger seat over the wheel-arch alongside him. This arrangement was soon found to be unpopular with the staff, as a passenger sat there could distract the driver. (At their first overhaul, this batch were given full internal bulkheads and an extra seat was squeezed in on the top deck.)

There were insufficient vehicles in the first delivery to work the whole service between Sutton and Croydon and several of the earlier 1-60 batch ex-L.U.T. trolleybuses, known as "Diddlers" because of the clicking noise their contactors made, had to be used during the first few weeks.

Sutton depôt was completely rebuilt to hold 40 trolleybuses, with a combined traverser and turntable. The arched gateway disappeared and an office block was erected alongside the entrance. When the opening of the Sutton—Croydon section was announced, it was stated that the route would be extended to the Crystal Palace, "when certain works were completed". In fact, there was still quite a lot to do on that side of Croydon. There was some pretty rough weather during December 1935 and the writer recalls seeing ex-Croydon Corporation No. 19E sweeping snow at Selhurst Station, while work was still going on erecting the double overhead wires.

One effect of wiring for trolleybuses was that the two pairs of wires were accommodated in troughing under the bridges at Selhurst and Selby Road. They were located above the centre of the road instead of being drawn out to one side, as they had been for the trams. The high destination boxes of the three ex-

Corporation cars just cleared the troughing under these two bridges, but the hoops of the ex-SouthmeT cars did not and had to be sawn off and the upper deck lamps were wired onto the handrails. The following instruction was issued to the staff:—

> "Drivers must stop their cars immediately before passing under railway bridges at Selhurst Station and Selby Road and conductors must mount the stairs and ascertain that all passengers are seated and warned of the danger."

Several trial runs were carried out on Anerley Hill, to test the special anti-run-back brakes, with which they were fitted, using trolleybus No. 65, which was purposely dewired several times on the hill to make sure that the brake really worked and for the benefit of the press. A roundabout was built at the top of Anerley Hill to provide a run-round loop and was said to be located partly in five different boroughs. (Lambeth, Croydon, Penge, Beckenham and Lewisham.)

Although span wire overhead construction was used for most of the route, bracket suspension, using peculiar curved bracket arms, was used in Northcote Road and on the approaches to Goat House Bridge. At last the trolleybuses commenced running through to the Crystal Palace on 9 February 1936. The whole service was provided from Sutton depôt and the trams were broken up where they stood in Penge depôt. The agreement for their sale to Cohens was dated 12 October 1935, and must have been signed while it was still hoped that the line would open right through from Sutton to the Crystal Palace in one operation. When their last remains had been cleared away, the depôt was leased to a potted meat manufacturer on 29 September 1936. (Sold to him 4 January 1946.)

The new trolleybus service was numbered 654 and for the first time there was a through service crossing the main road at West Croydon. Route 30 continued to serve West Croydon with trams and Tamworth Road now had both trams and trolleybuses, the trams using the trolleybus positive wires.

The conversion of tram routes to trolleybus operation continued in North and West London and London Transport set up its own team of experts to undertake the overhead wiring work, instead of letting it out to contract. This team was largely drawn from the former municipal tramways and included G. V. Stanley and L. Marriott from Croydon Corporation. Unfortunately, while working at Southall in 1936, both were knocked down by a private car and seriously injured. (See Biography of G. V. Stanley.)

Mitcham Road depôt in Aurelia Road, West Croydon, remained closed and empty, the connecting curve, which joined the main road towards Mitcham had been taken out on 8 December 1935. It was now decided to use this depôt for breaking up some of the cars displaced by the trolleybus conversions and the connection was reinstated on 2 June 1936, but this time facing towards Croydon. A number of London United cars were broken up including at least one still in blue livery. There were also some L.C.C. E Class cars from North London. In October, they were joined by the ex-Croydon old bogie cars Nos. 365-374. They were replaced on route 42 by ex-L.C.C. cars. (See Rolling Stock Chapter 7 for details.)

In September 1936, London Transport purchased five more B/1 type 60 seater trolleybuses. Several of them were used to supplement 64-93 on the Sutton—Crystal Palace service. They were numbered 489-493 and could be distinguished from the earlier batch by their black rubber rear wings.

In spite of being wholeheartedly committed to trolleybus conversion, there were still some minor improvements to the tram facilities. The terminus at Thornton Heath was at the busy junction where the High Street met Grange Road and Whitehorse Lane. A few yards of the old Whitehorse Road line were brought back into use and a crossover installed at Talbot Road, so that cars could stand clear of the busy road junction, as from 17 November.

A major disaster occurred in the next month, when the Crystal Palace was burned to the ground on the night of 5 December, when over 500 firemen were

Ex-S.M.E.T. No. 40s at Selhurst Station, with hoops removed from top deck during last month in service. The wall in photo on page 28 is now covered by advertisements.

(Photo E. G. P. Masterman

Ex-L.C.C. E/1 Class car on route 30 on temporary track on Blue House Bridge, Mitcham.

(Photo O. J. Morris

required. The trolleybuses were unable to get up the hill for much of the next day. There was no intermediate turning loop, so a reversing triangle was later installed into the mouth of Versailles Road, the turning opposite Thicket Road. In fact, the gradient favoured a trolleybus reversing and they could be seen performing the exercise without putting their poles up on the wires. It had been intended to provide turning facilities at the Robin Hood, but no suitable place could be found. Nevertheless, short workings to Versailles Road showed "Anerley— Robin Hood" on the destination blinds. When the writer protested, this was altered to "Anerley via Robin Hood". The loop at West Croydon was retained for short workings and one was installed round a small traffic island at Boundary Road Corner, Wallington, also at Waddon Station.

One other event in the summer of 1936, which temporarily affected the tram service on route 30 was the rebuilding of Blue House Bridge, Mitcham. One carriageway and parapet was built first alongside the old bridge and a single tram track laid on it, reached by temporary crossovers and single track on the grass verge of the bridge approaches. The "half-bridge" was available to trams and pedestrians only. Cycles had to be pushed. Other traffic was diverted. The old bridge was then demolished and the other new half erected in its place, with a second tram track. It is said that as route 30 was high on the list for trolleybus conversion, the rails on the new bridge were laid in shallow troughs, from which they could easily be removed, when the tram route was abandoned.

Now that trolleybuses were established on the Crystal Palace route, the regulator's sentry box at the Robin Hood was no longer required and the lease of the site was terminated on 24 May 1937. The houses on the corner of Elmers End Road were pulled down and a large block of flats erected on the site. Soon afterwards, it was announced that although no more trams were to be "rehabilitated", the light timber framed windscreens, devised for these cars, would be fitted to other cars as overhauled. In due course they were fitted to all the ex-Croydon E/1 type cars, which by this time were the only ex-Croydon cars still in service.

With the spread of trolleybus conversions across West and North London all the older ex-L.C.C. and ex-Metropolitan types of car were scrapped and everything from the London UniteD Tramways was scrapped except the Feltham type modern cars. These had originally been delivered in two batches, 46 to the London UniteD and 54 to the MetropolitaN tramways. They were externally identical, but had different electrical equipments, the only obvious difference was that the MetropolitaN cars were equipped with conduit plough carriers and the London UniteD cars were not. These latter worked on route 7 to Uxbridge and a few weeks before that route was to be converted to trolleybus operation, they were each fitted out with plough carriers and the necessary switch gear for conduit operation, so that they could make their own way under power to whichever depôt they were sent. All ex-L.C.C. depôts had traversers instead of track fans (except Brixton Hill). The only depôt which had sufficient clearance without obstructions either side of its traverser to accommodate the Felthams which were longer than any other London cars, was Streatham (Telford Avenue) and it was here that they came. They were able to work on all the routes allocated to that depôt, including 16/18. So, they were to be seen regularly in Croydon from then on. They were capable of a good turn of speed on the straight stretch between South Croydon and Purley. They had front exits and were of slightly lower seating capacity than the E/1s. They had spacious vestibules at both ends to give a large standing capacity, which regulations never permitted to be used to the full. The Uxbridge route was converted on 15 November.

Ex-L.C.C. tram route 6, which had been cut back to Tooting Broadway on 6 December 1933, was re-extended to Mitcham on 30 May 1937, but as the Cricket Green branch had already been lifted, it terminated at the Fair Green. However, this was to be short lived as on 12 September, there was another trolleybus conversion, which involved route 30. It was replaced by trolleybus route 630, which ran from the existing loop at West Croydon to College Park, Harlesden, still described as "Near Willesden Junction". Part of tram route 12 was also converted and extended, running as 612 from the "Prince's Head" Battersea to Mitcham, Fair Green, largely over the same roads as 630. 612 made a loop round the Fair Green as a terminal. Route 630 was operated by 32 of London Transport's standard 70 seat trolleybuses, all based on Hammersmith depôt. Now that Aurelia Road depôt was cut off from live tram track, it was cleared of the cars being scrapped there and closed on 22 November. It was subsequently sold to Croydon Corporation and used by their Refuse Department. As Thornton Heath depôt no longer had to supply cars for the Mitcham Road, it could take all the cars necessary for routes 16/18 and 42 and Purley depôt was closed.

The 70 seater trolleybuses experienced no less difficulty in negotiating Pitlake Corner into Lower Church St. than the bogie trams had done and the signal lights were retained until replaced by ordinary traffic lights. The conversion of route 30 saw the end of the SouthmeT tramway system.

In March 1938, the former L.C.C's blue painted car No. 1, was transferred from Holloway to Telford Avenue depôt and painted red. Henceforth it was to be seen from time to time on route 16/18. The Light Railway Transport League made history on Sunday 15 May, when No. 1 was hired and made the return trip from Waltham Cross to Purley, with a tea break at Purley. At the time this was the longest journey which could be made by tram in London and owing to rapid trolleybus conversions, the last occasion on which it was possible.

In June 1939, Mr. Sinclair was appointed Chief Engineer (Trams & Trolley-buses) on the retirement of Mr. Mason and J. H. Parker became Chief Electrical Engineer; he had been with Croydon Corporation in 1915. During 1939, following the trolleybus conversions in North London, a number of rolling stock changes were made. The ex-Croydon Corporation E/1s continued to provide the Thornton Heath complement on route 16/18, but ex-L.C.C. E/3 all-metal cars began to appear on the Thornton Heath route 42. The ex-MetropolitaN Feltham cars followed their ex-L.U.T. brethren to Telford Avenue and some were allocated to Brixton Hill depôt which was now regarded as an annexe to Telford Avenue and had no traverser. These cars already had conduit gear and did not need modification. Telford Avenue was now practically cleared of ex-L.C.C. cars and the few remaining spaces there were filled by ex-Walthamstow cars, contemporary with the ex-Croydon E/1s and closely similar to them. (See Chapter 7).

War broke out on 3 September 1939 and had a very speedy and profound effect on London's tramways. It overshadowed two other events; A. L. Barber, former Secretary of the London & Suburban Traction Co., retired and J. B. Mackinnon, the Schedules Superintendent, died suddenly on 13 September.

Blackout precautions were introduced almost immediately and on the trams, side lamps were rendered ineffective and the headlamps masked. These masks only allowed a small amount of light to escape through a central slot, which could be covered by a red slide to convert it to a tail lamp. Interior lights were hooded. Later the collision fenders were painted white to be seen in the blackout and sticky netting fixed to the window glass to prevent splintering; there was a small diamond shaped hole in the centre, through which passengers were expected to discover where they were. The London Passenger Transport Board was put under the direct control of the Government through the Railway Executive Committee. There were no immediate changes to the tram services, but they gradually assumed greater importance as fuels for other forms of transport became more scarce. Just as in the 1914 war, the first effect to be felt was that of large numbers of operating and engineering staff joining the forces and London Transport had its own Territorial Unit who went to camp in August 1939 and were sent straight overseas without returning to work. The remaining operating staff had to work long hours preparing and implementing an evacuation programme

* At first leased to the Corporation and sold to them on 29 April 1946. Cohen's men had complained that the roof was unsafe.

for school children, an exercise in which the trams played their part in getting them to the main line railway stations on the first part of their journey away from London.

In spite of the war, trolleybus conversions continued for the time being in other parts of London, but did not affect the Croydon area directly. Some men conductors were trained as drivers and women conductors were first recruited in October 1940. Frank Pick retired in May.

Purley depôt was put into use as a store for war damaged cars, plus a few cars in running order, which had not yet received windscreens to the driver's platforms. Also to be seen there in 1940, were Works Cars 014 and 015, together with Snow Brooms 031, 032 and 034, these latter still in the old L.C.C. dark lake and cream livery. Ex West Ham No. 328 was there too.

Being in a direct line between the coast and London, Croydon and Penge were early among the places to suffer from heavy bomb damage. The through service to London was interrupted on 10 and 11 September 1940, by bomb damage outside Croydon, and a shuttle service was provided by Thornton Heath depôt running as far as Norbury Station. The service was interrupted again on 17 September. On Thursday 3 October, a bomb caused a large crater in London Road, Thornton Heath, between Dunheved Road North and Dunheved Road South, cutting the depôt off from the rest of the Croydon system. Cars from London terminated at Thornton Heath Pond and all other traffic was diverted. A shuttle service was provided after two days, just south of the crater, to Purley, using four of the unvestibuled cars stored in Purley depôt; they were Nos. 1484, 1741, 1765 and 1776, all standard ex-L.C.C. E/1 type cars. One track was relaid across the gap by 15 October. The overhead wires at Warwick Road, in the same area, were damaged on 18 October. Both tracks at Dunheved Road were restored by 20 October.

A high explosive bomb fell in Thornton Heath High Street near the Clock Tower, damaging the eastbound track on the night of 5 November and the service was curtailed at the Clock Tower, for several days, with one car providing a shuttle service in the High Street. There were several other incidents in Streatham and Brixton which interrupted the through service to Croydon and Purley and occasionally cars had to be lent to other depôts. It is said that two Feltham type cars, cut off from Telford Avenue depôt, had to spend a night in Thornton Heath depôt.

Another bomb fell in front of the bus garage at South Croydon on 10 May 1941. Ex-Croydon Corporation car No. 396 was destroyed and the conductor killed. On more than one occasion, Telford Avenue depôt was cut off.

There were few air raids in 1942 and 1943 and a more or less normal tram service could be maintained in Croydon. Their contracts evidently having run out, the distinctive enamelled iron advertisements were removed from the ex-Croydon cars in 1942. Supplies of bright red paint ran out in 1943 and several cars appeared painted "indian red", this was a red oxide, that rather resembled the oxide used for trucks by many other undertakings. Croydon 391 is believed to have been one so treated. In December 1943, T. E. Thomas became General Manager (Operation), taking charge of the Central Bus as well as the Tram & Trolleybus Departments. Mr. W. H. Troake, former Stores Superintendent of Croydon Corporation Tramways, retired from Charlton Works in 1943.

Until removed to another site during the recent redevelopment in Croydon, the "Greyhound" public house stood on the east side of the High Street, not far from the Crown Hill intersection. Since the introduction of through working on the main line in 1926, cars on the Thornton Heath service had shown the destination "Greyhound" as their southern terminus, but had in fact reversed at the Davis Theatre (a large cinema) a little further down the High Street, near South End. Even this was in quite a congested area and from 25 October 1944, the cars carried on, out of service to the Coombe Road crossover and reversed there.

It was found that one additional car was required on route 42, to cover the slightly extended journey time. At the same time, three serviceable E/1 Class cars were allocated to Purley depôt, for use on route 16/18. The allocation of cars on 25 October 1944, was as follows:—

(Monday to Friday peak hours)

Route	Depôt	Cars required
16/18 Embankment—Croydon—Purley	Brixton Hill	15 Cars
,, ,, ,, ,,	Telford Avenue	16 ,,
,, ,, ,, ,,	Thornton Heath	18 ,,
,, ,, ,, ,,	Purley	3 ,,
16/18 ex Various short workings	Brixton Hill	29 ,,
,, ,, ,, ,, ,,	Telford Avenue	2 ,,
42 "Greyhound"—Thornton Heath	Thornton Heath	12 ,,

The short workings were mainly from the London end, hence their allocation to Brixton Hill. This arrangement lasted only until June 1945, when the three cars allocated to Purley were moved to Telford Avenue depôt. A few more war damaged cars and non-standard cars for which spare parts were not available were moved into Purley depôt. On 8 May, the war in Europe came to an end.

T. E. Thomas retired in October 1945 and the title General Manager (Operation) was allowed to lapse. Goathouse Bridge was widened in March 1946. Experiments were carried out at Pitlake junction with an electric induction frog setting device, from 18 January 1947.*

From 16 August 1946, the extension of route 42 to Coombe Road was officially recognized and passengers carried, but this again necessitated the use of one more car. In November 1946, the pre-war decision to get rid of the trams, was reaffirmed, but they were to be replaced by motor buses and not trolleybuses. However, the existing bus fleet was if anything even more worn out than the tram fleet and would have to be replaced before the tram conversion could commence. This might take 5 years.

On 26 December, 114 Lower Church Street and adjoining properties which had been leased to W. A. Reeves, the furnisher, since the offices were given up by the South Metropolitan Company, were sold to him.

In March 1947, T. W. Towers replaced T. J. Tilston as Operating Manager (Trams and Trolleybuses). Both were ex-L.C.C. men, but UndergrounD Group terminology continued to prevail. Around this time, as it was evident that the trams in London would have to be kept going for a few more years, visible external truss rods and other strengthening devices began to appear on many of the cars. A few, including ex-Croydon No. 391, received flush external panelling, without the other accoutrements of "Rehabilitated" cars. However, London Transport was unwilling to go to the expense of refitting proper external lighting and the headlamp masks were never removed, as they incorporated red slides for display at the rear end of the car and the combined side lamps-tail lamps and route numbers had been removed or rendered ineffective at the beginning of the war.

In 1947, Government was in the hands of the Labour Party and in August they brought in a Bill to nationalise all public transport, including the main line railways, the larger bus companies and London Transport.

The Act of Parliament received Royal Assent and from 1 January 1948, the London Passenger Transport Board became the London Transport Executive as one of the integral parts of the British Transport Commission. From then on all legal powers, etc., were held in the name of the Commission and not by the individual executives. (This led to some very difficult unscrambling more recently when the Commission was dissolved.) Lord Ashfield became a Member of the Commission and Lord Latham took his place as Chairman of the new

* Jackson Automatic Electric Controls Ltd. Trolleybuses 66, 88 and 90 had aerials.

L.T.E. Apart from the change in the official title in small letters on the sides of the vehicles, there were no noticeable or immediate changes. The fleet name "London Transport" was retained and preparations for the tramway replacement programme continued unabated behind the scenes. However, it gradually became apparent that from now on, London Transport was to be ruled by politicians, rather than by people who had any knowledge or experience of how to run a public transport undertaking.

In March 1948, Croydon Corporation had discussion with London Transport about plans for the widening of the main road at the corner of North End and Crown Hill, so that the tram track could be doubled at this last remaining section of single track on the main line. The "Crown" public house on the corner opposite the Alms Houses lost its licence and became an emporium for "Surplus Stores" on a short lease, so that it could be demolished without delay when the go-ahead was given. However, there were no further developments during the remaining life of the trams and the road was not widened until 1967.

The overhaul of trams to catch up on wartime neglect was taking longer than anticipated and it was decided that Purley depôt, still standing out of use, should be cleared of the war damaged cars collecting dust in its interior and be brought back into use as an annexe to Charlton Works where painting and certain other work could be undertaken. Doors were fitted and it came into use on 7 September.

A minor event during 1948, in connection with a series of experiments in overhead current collection, three cars were fitted with carbon skid trolley heads like trolleybuses. They were Nos. 378, 382 and 387, all three ex-Croydon Corporation cars. They remained on the cars for about a year, working regularly on route 16/18. At the end of the experiments, ordinary swivel trolley wheels were refitted.

During 1949 as the first stage of the tram scrapping programme was drawing near, V. J. Matterface, formerly of the Metropolitan Electric Tramways and now Tramways Engineer to Leeds City Transport, was able to persuade his new masters that the modern Feltham cars might be a good buy when London Transport had finished with them. No. 2099 was taken out of service and removed to Charlton Works for preparation for the journey and left for Leeds on approval on 20 September. That City's coat of arms was applied, but it retained its number and London Transport shade of red.

Late in 1949, it was decided that Thornton Heath depôt with its narrow entrance and awkward shape, would be quite unsuitable to convert as it stood to a bus garage. It was therefore to be demolished, together with the two adjoining houses, which Croydon Corporation had used as offices. A new bus garage would then be built on the cleared site and would have to be ready for use by the time the trams in Croydon were abandoned. Purley depôt was deemed to have completed its task as an annexe to Charlton Works by 29 November 1949 and was available to take the cars now housed at Thornton Heath. There was only one difficulty, apart from the various standard cars overhauled there and put back into service, there were seven Feltham type cars awaiting spare parts. They were Nos. 2067, 2091, 2130, 2163, 2165 and 2167. The last two were non-standard cars. There must evidently have been some panic to get the depôt clear in time to reopen for service cars. No other home could be found for these cars at short notice, so Cohen's men were called in with oxy-acetylene torches to break them up on the spot. The pieces were deposited in Purley Station goods yard. At least three of these cars would have been useful to Leeds, when the remainder were sold to them, if only as a source of spare parts.

A small canteen was installed in the rear part of the depôt, slightly reducing its capacity for tramcars and the building was ready for occupation by 1 January 1950. During the preceding night, the trams moved from Thornton Heath to Purley depôt, the move of stores and equipment being effected by three lorries and the tramcars themselves. In all, 35 tramcars, 100 crews and 50 mechanical staff were affected. Purley depôt was then called upon to provide on Monday-Fridays, 10 cars on the 16/18 through service, 6 cars on 16/18 short workings and 13 cars on route 42. Because of the now limited capacity of Purley depôt, West Norwood depôt was called on to provide two cars daily on the 16/18 short workings. These were invariably "rehabilitated" cars, with which that depôt was largely equipped. They came into service via Effra Road, Brixton. By this time, Telford Avenue and Brixton Hill were regarded as one depôt for administrative purposes, they were not very far apart and were no longer shown separately in car allocation lists.

The war memorial tablet on the wall of Brigstock Villa was removed to a place of safe keeping before tram operation from Thornton Heath ceased, but as soon as the depôt was cleared of cars, demolition contractors moved in. A newspaper reporter described the scene at Thornton Heath on 3 February. "A bulldozer, a mechanical shovel and a gang of highspeed demolition workers have turned Thornton Heath tram depôt in a matter of hours into something resembling a blitzed site. All that remained of Brigstock Villa, shortly after work started last week, was a pile of rubble".

There was no intention of converting Purley Depôt to a bus garage, as although of a more regular shape, its only entrance was on a busy part of the main Brighton Road and over the years there had been a number of near misses with other traffic, when trams were entering or leaving and the local press had conducted a campaign against its dangerous location. In the meantime, work was pressed forward as quickly as possible in providing a modern purpose-built bus garage on the site of Thornton Heath depôt and Brigstock Villa. When remarking that it was to have an entrance from Whitehall Road, we may recall the stenuous objections by the Corporation when the B.E.T. wanted to provide this facility for the trams.

In connection with the Festival of Britain Exhibition, that was to be held at South Bank in 1951, some major road works were carried out between West-minster Bridge and Waterloo Station, streets in that area being made "one way" at the same time. This did affect route 16/18. From 11 June 1950, the service was diverted (towards Croydon).

On 22 October, corresponding alterations were made for trams and other traffic proceeding towards the Embankment.

As a prologue to the final abandonment of trams in London, the separate operating departments of "Trams and Trolleybuses" and "Central Buses" were amalgamated under one Operating Manager, J. B. Burnell on 12 July 1950. From that date, certain tram and trolleybus depôts and bus garages were renamed, in cases where there had been one of each bearing the same name. In the area in which we are interested, there was a "Sutton Garage" and a "Sutton Depôt", the latter actually being located a few yards across the boundary into Carshalton. So from the above-named date, it became "Carshalton Depôt". Buses had always carried code letters alongside their running numbers, to indicate the garage to which they were allocated. For historical reasons, Sutton bus garage used the letters "A" and the use of these letters was now extended to trolleybuses, Carshalton depôt using "CN". It was not thought worthwhile extending the practice to trams, which continued to follow the L.C.C. practice of using a white number on a small blue plate hung on the first window pillar.

In the same month it was announced that the abandonment of the trams would take place over two years, in stages, by groups of routes working from West to East, so that Charlton Works and the nearby tram graveyard at Penhall Road could remain open until the last stage. It was originally stated that there would be eight stages. At each stage there was to be a reshuffle of cars in depôts, so that the worst cars in the fleet were scrapped first and the better cars from a depôt closing were moved to another one. This included bringing in ex-L.C.C. cars to replace the Felthams as they were moved to Leeds.

Although an accident caused one isolated abandonment before the scheduled date of commencement (damage to Battersea Bridge), the first official stage of abandonment occurred on the night of Saturday 30 September 1950 and affected the Wandsworth and Battersea areas. This did affect the Croydon area indirectly, by the withdrawal of tram route 12. This route which had formerly run from London Bridge to Tooting Junction, had been divided when route 30 was converted to trolleybuses and had become tram route 12 London Bridge—Battersea—Wandsworth and trolleybus route 612 Battersea—Wandsworth—Tooting—Mitcham. The replacing bus route 44 reinstated the through facility from London Bridge to Mitcham. At first this bus route ran a few yards further than the trolleybuses, which had run round the Fair Green, and terminated on a small patch of prepared ground alongside the pond at the beginning of Mitcham Common. 612 was the only trolleybus route to be abandoned with the trams and before 1959.

Leeds Corporation having agreed to purchase 92 Feltham type cars, they were taken out of service and moved to Charlton Works one at a time, so that conduit equipment could be removed and an articulated aircraft carrier lorry was specially adapted to carry each of them to Leeds. 2109 and 2113 had been war casualties and written off, five standard Felthams scrapped at Purley depôt as already described and in November 1950, while the move was in progress, Nos. 2144 and 2162 caught fire and were burned out. Their remains were dumped on the site at Penhall Road, near Charlton, which London Transport had leased as a graveyard for its tram fleet. It is believed that their bogies were sent to Leeds as "spare parts". To replace them, it was agreed that car No. 1 should go to Leeds, when the Croydon routes were abandoned. Work started on rebuilding Telford Avenue depôt late in 1950, but for the brief remaining period, the Felthams as they came out of service were replaced by E/1 and E/3 class cars displaced by other route abandonments. The Feltham cars were sold to Leeds at £720 each.

The second stage of the conversion scheme took place on the night of 6 January 1951 and involved routes serving Tooting and Wimbledon. This resulted in a reduction of trams on the London—Brighton road north of Streatham.

Croydon's turn came in the third stage on the night of Saturday 7 April 1951. This of course involved the trunk route 16/18, from the Embankment via Kennington, Brixton and Streatham to Croydon and Purley, which still carried very heavy traffic. Croydon was the last ex-municipal system to be abandoned in the London area apart from the L.C.C. and included the Thornton Heath branch, the last bastion of typical suburban routes with its sections of single and interlaced track and bracket overhead suspension, the clock tower and a typical suburban high street. However, on the last day, the Light Railway Transport League hired car No. 1 and 70 menbers made the journey from Highgate in North London, through the Kingsway subway, out onto the Embankment and via route 18 to Croydon and Purley. On the return journey, the Thornton Heath branch was covered and at Telford Avenue depôt, the party changed to another car and No. 1 had completed its last public journey in London, to be prepared for sale to Leeds. The tour continued on ex-Metropolitan Feltham No. 2079 to Southwark, Embankment and Victoria before returning to Telford Avenue depôt. Two days later 2079 left Charlton Works for Leeds. During the evening, the Streatham Chamber of Commerce hired car No. 947, ex-L.C.C. and Croydon Chamber of Commerce hired 839 for tours. This latter was actually the last car to leave Purley terminus, following the official last car. The proceeds were given to the Croydon branch of the Infantile Paralysis Fellowship, the fare being 5 shillings.

The official last car was E/3 Class, No. 1941, which left Purley terminus at 11.24 p.m. crowded to capacity and there were crowds all along the road. R. M. Harmer, author of the Corporation section of the first edition of this book, placed himself in such a position as to be issued the last ticket (for a 6 pence fare). Among the passengers was Mr. W. H. Troake, former Stores Superintendent of Croydon Corporation Tramways, who is said to have ridden on the first electric

Brigstock Villa and cramped entrance to Thornton Heath Depôt. Note map of "Shilling All-day Ticket" availability on roof, war memorial tablet and regulator in front of hut, working the point lever with one hand and a cord for the overhead point with the other!

(Photo London Transport

Ex-Croydon No. 375 (formerly 30) at Crown Hill. Note the "Crown" public house, now on a short lease, ready for demolition and road widening which did not take place until the trams had gone.

(Photo J. H. Meredith

car in Croydon. The driver was Mr. W. S. Stout, who had joined Croydon Corporation in 1909 and the conductor, A. G. T. Allen.

As mentioned, 1941 was closely followed by 839, decorated overall, with wreaths and bunting and carrying some civic dignitaries of Wandsworth. Older cars were used because of the fear of souvenir hunters and vandalism, which did in fact occur when the cars stopped outside Thornton Heath depôt. The ex-Croydon Corporation E/1s were still in sound condition and lived to see another day; they were transferred to New Cross depôt. Several of the Feltham type cars were in use to the end and were driven to the demolition site at Penhall Road, temporarily, while awaiting transport to Leeds.

The new bus garage at Thornton Heath was sufficiently advanced in construction for the bus service to start from there the next morning, using London Transport's then standard RT type buses. It had been intended to number the main service 109B and 109W, for Blackfriars and Westminster respectively, as had been done in the case of the Wimbledon services, but there was a change in heart at the last minute and the buses were delivered with blinds numbered 109 only. (The B.&W. disappeared from the Wimbledon buses soon afterwards.) The Thornton Heath service was numbered 190 and has undergone various extensions at the Croydon end in more recent years. Unfortunately, the 12.35 a.m. tram journey on route 16/18 was not replaced by a corresponding bus journey from Westminster to Purley.

Purley depôt stood empty until 23 November, when it was sold for £20,000, passing subsequently to Messrs. Schweppes Mineral Waters as a store. It has changed hands again recently and has received a new façade. The cast-iron gate posts with the coat of arms have disappeared, but the main structure of the two buildings remains.

The 23 remaining ex-Croydon cars were soon put into service on the various routes based on New Cross depôt, but 396 had been a war casualty and 376 damaged beyond repair in an accident just after the war. Nos. 384, 387 and 398 were taken out of service at the fifth stage of the conversion on 16 October 1951 and the rest survived until the sixth stage on 5 January 1952, when they were scrapped at Penhall Road.

The trolleybuses on routes 630 and 654 continued to operate without change, but in May 1952, the Electricity Board closed Beckenham Sub-Station. This was the former Churchfields Road Power Station which had continued to supply the Selby Road—Crystal Palace section. London Transport attempted to have its closure postponed and there was great consternation. Eventually they were able to obtain a small site in Bourdon Road, off Elmers End Road, not far from the old Oak Grove Road depôt and built a temporary sub-station using second-hand equipment.

The final abandonment of trams in London took place on 5 July 1952, with a closing ceremony at New Cross depôt by Lord Latham. W. R. Robertson, the Public Relations Officer, was in attendance, assisted by G. D. Morgan, ex-Croydon Corporation and the present writer.

Trolleybus routes 630 and 654 continued to operate unhindered and without modification until 1958, when it was announced that as many of the vehicles were now over 25 years old (including those on route 654), they needed replacement and what better than the "more flexible" motor bus. In fact, because of Police and Trade Union restrictions, a motor bus running in London is allowed very little more flexibility than a trolleybus. Work started late in 1958 on the removal of the traverser from Carshalton depôt and the installation of fuel tanks, but it was not found necessary to alter the construction or layout of the building again.

It was intended to use the new "RM" type buses to replace the trolleybuses as they were larger than their predecessors and almost comparable in capacity.

Although displaced by 70 seaters in the Bexley area, the 60 seaters were retained to the end in the Croydon area, Nos. 64-93 and latterly all of the 489-493 batch.

These were the only trolleybuses fitted with the special "run-back" brakes for Anerley Hill. A scotch was kept near the shelter at the top of Anerley Hill, and put under the front wheel when the crews took their break in the Crystal Palace canteen. The vehicles were definitely wearing out now, Nos. 64 and 72 had already been withdrawn in 1955, 490 was withdrawn in June 1957 and 71 in May 1958, followed by 489 in September 1958. This must have left Carshalton depôt with insufficient vehicles to cover emergencies and on 9 September, following damage by flooding, several of the remaining trolleybuses were put out of action. Therefore four 70 seaters, Nos. 1049, 1050, 1051 and one other were borrowed from another depôt. Croydon Airport closed in 1959.

Trolleybuses ceased to run on route 654 on the night of Tuesday 3 March 1959, when an official last run was made at the instigation of the Wallington and Carshalton Advertiser. No. 65 was used for this run; it was the one which had made the trials on Anerley Hill before public service commenced. This time it made the trip from West Croydon to Sutton and passengers included the Mayors of Sutton and Cheam and of Beddington and Wallington. The conductor was Mr. L. Lambert, who had started conducting with Croydon Corporation in 1919 and for many years had been their union representative. A tower wagon was waiting at the Lower Church Street corner to remove the junction in the overhead wires as soon as the last trolleybus had passed and replace it with plain wires leading only in the Mitcham direction. The trolleybuses were replaced by two motor bus routes, 154 and 157, which ran from the Crystal Palace beyond Sutton to Morden and 157 continued to Raynes Park. 154 followed the same routing as the trolleybuses, but 157 covered different roads between Wallington and Morden. In addition, for a short time bus route 64 was extended from West Croydon to the Robin Hood and to Elmers End Garage, but there proved not to be a demand for this service and it was soon cut back again. London Transport did not wait for the delivery of the RM class buses and used the existing RT type for several years. In April 1981, route 154 was diverted to a new estate on the site of Croydon Aerodrome and only 157 serves South Norwood and Anerley.

For the time being, route 630 continued to run between West Croydon and Harlesden, but its turn came on 20 July 1960, when it was replaced by bus route 220, with the same routing. This time RM type buses were used. With the same conversion, bus route 64 which had been running between West Croydon and Addington, was extended from Croydon to Tooting, supplementing route 220. At first it was worked by a mixture of RT and RM type buses. With a later reorganization of services, Carshalton Garage was closed on 28 January 1964 and its buses redistributed between Sutton and Merton garages. It was offered for sale at £13,500, but was eventually leased away as a small factory, which it remains*. More recently, bus route 220 has been cut back to Tooting, leaving 64 alone to serve Mitcham and Croydon. Hammersmith trolleybus depôt disappeared in a redevelopment programme of that area. No. 5 Bourdon Road was leased to Vickers from 18 March 1975 to 25 March 1977.

Thus ended an era of electric street transport in Croydon which had lasted sixty years. With its disappearance there have been many changes in the face of Croydon and changes are continuing. The first changes were brought about by war damage; for example, the "Gloster" public house was destroyed and was replaced by a new building bearing the name "Gloucester" in full. Once war damage had been repaired, the rebuilding programme gained momentum, largely when the Whitgift School moved away from behind North End and was replaced by a large shopping centre, backing onto Wellesley Road, which has been widened, with a fly-under where it crosses George Street. The "Greyhound" and other enterprises with well known names, such as "Turtle's", "Stockwell & Oxford", Wilson's Coffee House and others have moved to streets nearer the shopping centre. Very recently the Pitlake area has been redeveloped and a large housing estate built on part of the former Croydon Airport.

* It was sold 26 February 1981; remains in use as factory.

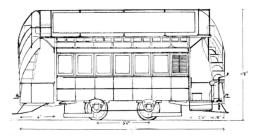

Stephenson horse car

Information about the horse cars is on page 26.

CHAPTER SEVEN
ROLLING STOCK LISTS

Croydon Corporation Tramways

Nos. 1-35   Built by G. F. MILNES & Co., at Hadley, Shropshire, in 1901.

Dimensions:—   Saloon 16 ft. long 6 ft. 2 in. wide over sills.
Overall length 28 ft. Height over trolley plank 9 ft. 11 in.
Seating 22 inside, 30 outside.
Half turn reversed staircases.
B.T-H. B.18 Controllers.
General Electric G.E.52 motors. 27 horse power.
Trucks—Sixteen cars on Peckham No. 9 cantilever trucks.
Nineteen cars on Brill 21E trucks.
(Both types 6 ft. wheelbase).
Braking—Hand and rheostatic only. Unladen weight 7½ tons.

These were the original fleet of cars delivered before the opening of the system. They cost £650 each and Nos. 1-5, 7, 9-11, 13-22 and 25-35 were delivered to Pitlake Generating Station (bodies only) in April 1901, while Nos. 6, 8, 12, 23 and 24 were delivered later directly to Thornton Heath depôt, where in due course all were fitted out and mounted on their trucks.

Sixteen were mounted on Peckham cantilever trucks and nineteen on Brill 21E trucks indiscriminately. The Peckham trucks are said to have given the better ride, but being built up from a number of separate parts, required more frequent maintenance than the Brill trucks, whose main component was a solid forging. When a report was made just after the 1914-18 war, Nos. 1-8, 11, 12, 15, 23-26 and 35 were mounted on Peckham trucks, while 9, 10, 13, 14, 16-22 and 27-34 were on Brill trucks.

The saloons with three side windows with opening lights above, were of conventional design for the period, with lincrusta flat ceilings and long bent plywood benches for eleven passengers each side. Small holes were drilled in the plywood making large circular patterns and there were panelled kicking boards under the seats. The side windows had curtains which could be drawn in sunny weather and above them the opening lights had radiused outer corners and yellow "Cathedral" glass (i.e. crinkled glass). The internal bulkheads were quite ornate, with a mirror in the top left-hand corner and a hole for a red "bull's-eye" lens to act as a tail lamp in the right-hand corner. The lintel board was in the form of a bevelled panel with a beaded edge. It was supported by elaborate capitals, running down the door sides. There was a single sliding door each end, with very rounded top corners and probably a Milnes maker's transfer on the panel immediately below the window. There were the usual bevelled panels on the lower part of the doors and bulkheads.

Lighting was provided by a main bulb in a brass-rimmed glass bowl in the centre of the ceiling, with other bulbs along the edge, one being placed conveniently near the bulkhead to illuminate the tail lamp bullseye. Electric signalling bells were fitted.

The upper deck was reached by wide sweep reversed stairs and there was two and two seating with single seats by the trolley mast. The seats against the stair well and at the end of the canopy were fixed, but the others were reversible. The trolley mast was of the Blackwell "Dublin" type with an exposed hinge and swivel at the top. At each end there was an "oyster" lamp on a stanchion to illuminate the upper deck. The platforms were reached by "Stanwood" fixed steps and were closed at the driver's end by "Bostwick" collapsible gates. As delivered, these cars were fitted with "Providence" spring steel lifeguards, which were very large and cumbersome. They had to be folded up at the rear end.

There was the usual headlamp in the centre of the dash.

Modifications

When the Inspecting Officer first visited Croydon's electric tramways, he was none too happy about the "Providence" lifeguards* and at the second inspection, they were condemned as unsuitable and they were replaced by Wilson & Bennett wire mesh gate and tray lifeguards. In later years, many of these were again replaced by Tidswell lifeguards, having a gate of two wooden slats.

The "Dublin" trolley masts which did not have caps over the swivelling tops, were found to let in water and the top parts were soon fitted with waterproof canvas socks. Loose canvas seat covers were also carried on the upper decks. The electric signalling bells did not give satisfaction and were gradually replaced by cord operated bells. The cords ran in brass eyelets above the saloon windows and on the batten separating the saloon windows and opening lights, there was painted an arrow and the inscription "When travelling in direction of arrow, pull cord this side to stop car". After the 1914-18 war, the Bostwick gates were replaced by leather covered chains, which hooked onto the saloon corner grab rail.

As delivered, these cars did not carry any destination equipment, but new cars delivered in 1906 and subsequently, had wooden destination boxes on tall stanchions above the ends of the upper deck. These cars were then similarly equipped. As these boxes had a small square opening at the back, glazed with opal glass, the Oyster lamps were removed.

It is said that Nos. 25 and 34 were taken out of service and loaned to the War Office for use as Searchlight cars. Subsequently they were canibalised to provide spare parts for other cars of the class. At the end of hostilities all cars of this class were in need of a major overhaul. In the case of Nos. 13, 25, 34 and 35, this amounted to a complete rebuild, including strengthened solebars. Nos. 25, 34 and 35 received normal half-turn stairs like the later cars, with revised seating on the upper deck. No. 35 was then mounted on a Brill 21E truck. No. 34 was repillared.

Disposal

All cars of this batch were withdrawn from service with the reorganization of services in the summer of 1927. They had to be disposed of quickly to make room in the depôts for the new cars on order to work on the main line. The four heavily rebuilt cars, 13, 25, 34 and 35 were included in a batch sold to the South Metropolitan Company.

In May 1927, 25 cars were sold to T. W. Ward & Co. for scrapping and are thought to have included most of those remaining from this batch. During the 1970s, the body of No. 8 was discovered, in use as a garden shed in Sutton. It was acquired by enthusiasts for preservation, but on examination by an expert, was found to be rotten beyond repair and scrapped.

(* Supplied by Dover Safety Car Fender Co.)

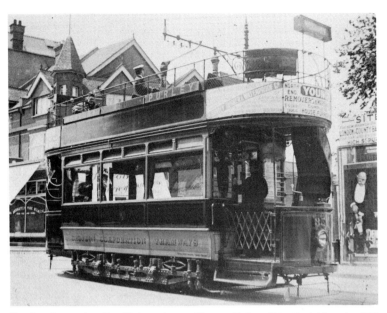

Croydon Corporation No. 35 in early condition at Purley. Note Bostwick gate, seat covers, sock over top of trolley mast and "Wilson & Bennett" wire lifeguard.

(Photo L. E. Brailsford

The fate of Croydon No. 34. Much rebuilt and with normal stairs, dumped with No. 35 and one other, probably 62 at Fulwell Depôt of the London United Tramways.

(Photo Dr. H. A. Whitcombe, courtesy Science Museum London. 5070

Nos. 36-45   Built by George F. Milnes & Co., at Hadley, in 1902.

Dimensions:—   Saloon 16 ft. 0 in. long, 6 ft. 1 in. wide over sills.
        Overall length 27 ft. 9 in. Height over trolley plank 9 ft. 9½ in.
        Seating 22 inside, 33 outside.
        Milnes "Exhibition" half turn staircases.
        B.T-H. B.18 controllers. G.E.52 motors.
        Truck—Milnes 6 ft. 0 in. girder type.
        Braking—Hand and rheostatic only.

Although numbered in the same series as the original cars, this batch in fact belonged to the B.E.T. and not to the Corporation.

The bodies were similar to Nos. 1-35, but contained a number of small improvements. Because the Metropolitan Police were objecting to reversed stairs which obstructed the driver's vision to the left, 36-45 had Milnes "Exhibition" staircases, which took a wide sweep in what is now known as the "Normal" direction, i.e. the bottom step just behind the controller and the top step close to and at rightangles to the bulkhead. The sweep was wider than that of most of their imitators. They had Tidswell lifeguards.

They carried the headlamp on the front of the canopy instead of on the dash and B.T-H. "B/2" trolley masts on which the pole could be turned through a full circle. Destination boxes were not fitted until just before their transfer elsewhere and there was a deck lamp on an upright stanchion near the stairheads.

With the break-up of the Corporation/B.E.T. Agreement in July 1906, this batch of ten cars was transferred to the new South Metropolitan Company, who over the years carried out a number of modifications on them. They are therefore described in detail in the section dealing with that company.

Nos. 46-55   Built by G. F. Milnes & Co., at Hadley, in 1902.   **Later Class B/2.**

Dimensions:—   Saloon 22 ft. 0 in. long, 6 ft. 0 in. over sills.
        Overall length 34 ft. 8 in. Height over trolley plank 9 ft. 9½ in.
        Seating 30 inside, 39 outside.
        "Robinson" double flight staircases.
        B.T-H. B.18 controllers. G.E.52 motors.
        Brill 22E maximum traction bogies.
        Braking—Hand and rheostatic only. Weight 9½ tons.

During 1902 it became evident that larger capacity cars would be needed for the main Norbury—Purley line and fifteen were ordered, ten to belong to the Corporation and five to the B.E.T. Those for the Corporation were ordered in February 1902 and delivered later in the year, costing £825 each.

They had long saloons with six side windows with two opening lights above each. Like Nos. 1-35, these lights had radiused outer corners. There were twin sliding doors in the end bulkheads, with a concealed chain over the top so that they opened and closed together. Seating in the saloon was again on perforated plywood benches. The double saloon doors had very rounded outer corners and were surmounted by large lintel boards with ventilation slits. There were mirrors on the upper panels of the bulkheads. The ceiling was of maple veneer, supported by ornamental brackets which carried lighting fitments as well as supporting grabrails with leather straps. On the outside of the bulkhead, under the half-canopy there was a glass bullseye lens with a red slide so that it could be used as a tail lamp. It was illuminated by a small bulb between the two thicknesses of the bulkhead. The body was supported on channel steel solebars. There were curtains in the windows.

As it had been suggested that these cars should resemble the London United bogie cars, they had short canopies and double flight stairs, changing direction at a small landing half way up. This arrangement necessitated long platforms. There was 2 & 2 seating on the upper deck, with a single seat at one side of the trolley mast. These cars had wooden roller blind destination boxes mounted on stanchions which curved outwards over the ends of the half canopies. As there were lights on the backs of these boxes, the cars did not have stairhead lamps. Like Nos. 36-45, they had B.T-H. "B/2" type trolley masts whose heads could be turned through a full circle.

These cars ran on Brill 22E bogies, a well tried design with the driving wheels nearest the ends of the car in the conventional manner. Axle-boxes were of the "Empire" roller bearing design with circular covers. There were fixed platform steps and Tidswell lifeguards with two slats to the gates. They had "Bostwick" platform gates as delivered.

The driver's platform beyond the stairs was completely open and unprotected and in all these were large ungainly looking cars, but typical of the turn of the century idea of what a high capacity bogie car should look like. Although insufficient to provide the full service, these bogie cars were worked hard on the main line and sometimes worked to Thornton Heath but never to Addiscombe or Penge, where they might have been too long for some of the passing loops on these lines.

Modifications

Being the main work-horses of the fleet and later being regarded, misguidedly, as suitable for through running to London, these cars underwent a number of modifications during their long lives. First of all, wire mesh gates were fitted between the bogies in 1903, no doubt on Police instructions. In later years these were replaced by wooden slatted gates. Then the "Empire" roller bearings evidently did not live up to expectations and were replaced by plain axle boxes. In 1910, the electric signal bells were giving trouble and were replaced by cord operated bells. With this arrangement, there was a push rod on the upper deck near the head of the stairs, which the conductor could use to operate the bell.

When in 1916, the Metropolitan Police insisted on all trams being fitted with side lamps, the remainder of the Croydon fleet had them fixed in small wooden boxes under the edge of the canopy. The bogie cars were unsuitable for this arrangement and the small boxes were hung from the top edge of the dash either side. The off-side one had a red bulb behind a white one, for use as a tail lamp. Around the same time, metal panelling was fitted round the stair landings. Later the bell push rod appears to have been replaced by a cord in a tube, with the top of the cord tied to the handrail.

In order, as they thought to render them suitable for through running to London, No. 55 was experimentally fitted with Westinghouse air brakes in August 1924. There were brake shoes acting both on the wheels and on the track. The equipment was removed at the conclusion of the experiments. In February 1926, following experiments with a four wheeled car, No. 48 appeared with 2 and 1 grey moquette cushioned seats in the saloon. There were transverse seats for two in each corner, reducing the seating by four. The moquette was of the same design as used by the UndergrounD Group (q.v.). In March new electrical equipment was ordered from B.T-H. for these cars and new trucks were considered, but turned down. As reconditioned they had new B.T-H. 509c motors and line switch attachments fitted to the controllers so that they could be used interlocked with air brakes. Air brakes were fitted to all ten cars in July 1927, this time acting on the wheels only. In that condition No. 47 was renumbered 22 and painted in the red and ivory livery and classified "B/1".

In 1928, following the success of the new L.C.C. type cars, it was decided to fit top covers to these cars. No. 55 was chosen for trials and a top cover only covering the saloon was fitted and had six windows each side to match the lower saloon. There was a small balcony at each stairhead, on which there was a small wheel and rod to open and close the upper saloon windows. The upper roof extended over the end balconies with deep valances which incorporated the destination boxes. The seating was reduced to 32 and the existing seats were cloth covered, but not padded! They were painted red and grey and renumbered 21-30. They were reclassified "B/2". All had 2 and 1 cushion seats inside.

Because both ends of the Thornton Heath route on which they now worked were in congested streets, two trolley poles were fitted, one for each direction of travel. No further alterations were made until after they passed to London Transport in 1933.

London Transport Days

They retained the Croydon classification "B/2" in white on the solebars. No. 21E (formerly 46) is recorded as being sent to Charlton Works for an annual overhaul in October 1933 and returned to Thornton Heath in "L.C.C. Standard Red" and the fleet number 365. At the same time a few modifications were made to bring these cars into line with standard practices, for example, the positions of the route board holders under the saloon windows were slightly altered to take L.C.C. type boards. The two side lamps on the dash were removed and replaced by a single side/tail lamp holder, with provision for a route number stencil, fixed to the underside of the stair landing. Before long the remainder of the class were overhauled, repainted and renumbered in the 365-374 series at Charlton. As "London Transport" fleet name transfers did not become available until May 1934, it is probable that they did not receive them until their next annual overhaul. They received hooks for L.C.C. type blue and white running number plates on the first window pillar behind the stairs.

During subsequent overhauls, Nos. 369 and 373 lost the rubbing strips between the waist and rocker panels and had them replaced by plain metal bands. 373 also had its solebars plated over.

In the meantime, trams in North London were being replaced by trolley-buses, making a large number of the earlier low powered ex-L.C.C. "E/1" Class cars available for disposal. London Transport held very strong views in favour of standardization, so when in 1936, the ex-Croydon cars were due for an annual overhaul and relicencing, they were withdrawn one at a time and replaced by E/1 Class cars between October 1936 and January 1937.

As they came out of service, they were driven to Mitcham Road depôt for Cohen's men to break them up as quickly as possible.

Croydon No. 55 at Purley. Note "Empire" Roller Bearings and wire "dog guard" between bogies.
(Photo L. E. Brailsford

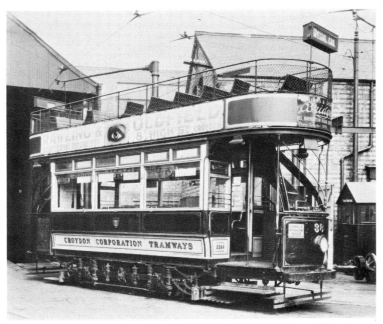

Croydon Corporation No. 38, after fitting with air brakes, two and one cushioned seats, channel steel underframes and "torpedo" side lamps, otherwise in original condition.
(Photo Walter Gratwicke

Nos. 56-60. Built by Brush Electrical Engineering Co. Ltd., in 1902.

Dimensions:— Saloon 22 ft. 0 in. long, 6 ft. 0 in. wide over sills.
Overall length 34 ft. 8 in. height over trolley plank 9 ft. 11 in.
Seating 30 inside, 39 outside.
Robinson double flight staircases.
B.T-H. "B.18" controllers. G.E.C. "52" motors.
Trucks—Brush "B" type bogies of 4 ft. 2 in. wheelbase.
Braking—Hand and rheostatic only.

Nos. 56-60 were the B.E.T. complement of bogie cars in the Croydon fleet and had bodies almost identical to the Corporation cars 46-55. However, there were a number of minor differences. The proportions of the decency panelling over the short half-canopies were different giving them a squarer appearance. There were no looped grabrail on the corner of the dash and there were typical Brush corner brackets supporting the landing half way up the stairs. They appear to have had metal destination boxes at first, soon replaced by wooden ones like 46-55. Trolley masts were of the B.1 type. These cars had Wilson & Bennett wire mesh lifeguards.

The greatest difference between these cars and 46-55 lay in the trucks. The former had conventional Brill 22E bogies with the driving wheels towards the ends of the car. Nos. 56-60 had Brush's own design of bogies, their "B" type, with the driving wheels towards the centre of the car. These proved less satisfactory than the Brill bogies.

While in use on the Croydon system, these cars normally worked on the Thornton Heath—Purley service and like 46-55 were probably too large for the Penge or Addiscombe services. However, in July 1906, together with Nos.

113

36-45, they were removed from service in Croydon, taken and dumped on the site in Aurelia Road, off Mitcham Road. In due course they were put into service on the South Metropolitan system and their subsequent history is therefore described in greater detail in the section dealing with that undertaking.

Nos. 36-45	(Second Series). Built by Brush at Loughborough in 1906.
56-60	(Second Series). Built by Brush at Loughborough in 1906.
61-70.	Built by Brush at Loughborough in 1907.
71-75.	Built by Brush at Loughborough in 1911.

Later Class W/1.

Dimensions:— Saloon 16 ft. 0 in. long, 6 ft. 2 in. wide over sills.
Overall length 28 ft. 0 in. Height over trolley plank 9 ft. 11 in.
Seating 22 inside, 32 outside.
Half turn "Exhibition type" stairs.
Westinghouse 90 controllers.
Westinghouse 200 motors. 21 horsepower each.
Trucks—Brill 21E (61-70), Brush 21E (71-75),
Mountain & Gibson 21EM (Nos. 36-45 and 56-60),
7 ft. 6 in. wheelbase.
Braking—Hand and rheostatic only. (Peacock hand brakes).

Nos. 36-45 and 56-60 were the cars which replaced those taken away by the B.E.T. in 1906, while 61-70 and 71-75 were purchased as additions to the fleet as traffic grew. All were virtually identical, certainly in so far as bodywork was concerned. By that time, G. F. Milnes & Co. had gone out of business and they were all built by Brush. Although of very traditional design and similar in appearance to Nos. 1-35, they were of rather more robust construction.

They had three window bodies with two opening lights above each. The only feature of the original 36-45 which impressed the Corporation, was the "Exhibition" stairs with which they were equipped. Consequently, the Corporation instructed Brush to fit staircases to the new cars, as nearly as possible like the Milnes stairs. As they came rather close to the dash, they had extra stringers above the normal ones, to protect passengers mounting the stairs from passing traffic. They cost £521 10s. each.

The saloons had perforated plywood benches like the Milnes cars, maple veneer ceilings with lighting along the sides only. There was a single sliding door at each end of the saloon, with only slightly radiused corners. There were ornate lintel boards above the doors, with ventilation slits. On either side in the upper part of the bulkheads there were mirrors. Both half bulkheads had windows, with a hinged opening part in the bulkhead nearest the platform step, which was of the Brush folding type. The head lamps were in the conventional position on the dash and there was a mirror under the canopy edge so that the driver could view the interior of the car without turning round and another just above the stair opening in the canopy, by which he could view the upper deck. Signal bells were operated by cords just above the saloon windows.

There was two and two seating on the upper deck, except for two single seats by the trolley mast. All could be turned over except that by the stair opening and at the end of the canopy. They had three plank solid backs, but the seats were made of thin laths set on edge and not quite touching, so that rain water could pass between them. The trolley masts were of the Brecknell, Munro B/1 type, but a late version which could be turned through the full circle. Destination boxes were set on high stanchions above the ends of the upper deck and had glazed openings in the back, so no deck lights were required.

As delivered, Nos. 36-45 and 56-60 were mounted on Mountain & Gibson 7 ft. 6 in. 21EM trucks, which were intended to be a copy of the Brill 21E design in defiance of American patents. Nos. 61-70 had genuine Brill 21E trucks and 71-75 had a Brush version of the same type, all to the same wheelbase. The Mountain & Gibson trucks appear to have been slightly less satisfactory than the other two types. They had Griffin 31 inch chilled iron wheels.

These were sturdy little cars and although used mainly on the Norbury—Purley and Thornton Heath lines in the early days, they could and did work anywhere on the system.

Modifications

Five more Brill 21E trucks were purchased immediately after the 1914/18 war and fitted to Nos. 36-40 in place of the Mountain & Gibson trucks which were disposed of. On all of these cars the small wooden side lamp boxes were replaced soon after the war, by neat metal side lamps, pointed at the rear end like a torpedo. Those of Nos. 1-35 that were rebuilt also received this type of side lamp.

In 1914, No. 36 had the plywood benches replaced by cushions, still running the length of the car. In 1924, Nos. 37 and 38 had their Westinghouse 200 motors replaced by B.T-H. 200 and B.T-H. 509 types respectively. In 1926, Nos. 38 and 39 were fitted with 2 and 1 cushioned seats in the saloon, thereby reducing their capacity to 18. The ceilings, bulkheads and window frames were painted white with black lettering. The seats were upholstered in Johnston's grey moquette like the bogie cars. They and No. 58 were mounted on channel steel solebars. In April and June 1927, Nos. 36 and 38 were fitted with Westinghouse air brakes acting on the wheels and on the track so that they could be used on the Thornton Heath route and run in conjunction with the bogie cars that were being similarly equipped. Presumably cars from 36-40 were chosen for these experimental features as they were on the newest trucks.

In June 1927, together with the four rebuilt older cars, eight of these, Nos. 43, 44, 62, 63, 64, 66, 67 and 69 were sold to the South Metropolitan Company at £700 the lot with spare parts. (See S.M.E.T. section for further details). Nos. 41 and 57 which must have had some defects, were sold to T. W. Ward for scrapping at the same time.

From then on, as they were repainted in the new red livery, the remainder were renumbered 1-20, in the reverse order of their old numbers. Hence, 75, 74, 73, 72 and 71 became 1-5, 70 became 6, 68 became 7, 65 became 8, 60, 59, 58 and 56 became 9-13. Nos. 45 became 14, 42 and 40 became 15 and 16. 39 with 2 and 1 cushion seats became 17, 38 also with cushion seats and air brakes became 18. No. 37 with Westinghouse controllers replaced by B.T-H.

Croydon No. 5 (formerly 71) in red and ivory livery, passing the Constitutional Club, Croydon Road, Penge. Most of these cars received hardly any modifications but remained in good condition.
(Photo N. D. W. Elston

115

Ex-Croydon Corporation No. 40E, with London Transport stickers on the rocker panel.
(Photo M. J. O'Connor

200 type became 19 and Nos. 36 with air brakes and long cushion seats became No. 20. From then on, Nos. 1-17 normally worked on the Penge route, 18 and 20 were the Thornton Heath route spares and No. 19 a general spare. They were classified "W/1" and nine received second-hand ventilated motors in 1932. No. 19 received magnetic track brakes, in 1927.

Disposal

No. 1-20 passed into the hands of London Transport and for the next few months continued to work as before. The small suffix letter E was soon added to their fleet numbers. Just before the Penge route closed one car was taken away to Charlton works, overhauled and repainted in the L.C.C. style. It is believed to have been No. 11E, then renumbered 355, with the L.C.C. style figures with black shading. (According to L.T. overhaul and inspection lists.) At the same time, Nos. 1E, 2E and 3E, were taken out of service for a short time, to receive a small modification—they were fitted with spare sets of track brake equipment, so that they could subsequently work to the Crystal Palace. They were not immediately repainted or renumbered. No. 5E was also sent to Charlton, repainted in the L.C.C. style and renumbered 349. It was fitted with magnetic track brakes, so that it could be tried out at Erith, where the local cars were in poor condition. (There

116

are reports that in fact No. 17 was substituted for No. 5 and became 349, because it had cushion seats. London Transport records are conflicting on this point.)*

When the Penge route closed on 6 December 1933, Nos. 1E, 2E and 3E were transferred to Penge depôt and took their place on the Crystal Palace route augmented service. After a few weeks, they were sent away one at a time to Hendon Works for repainting and returned renumbered 345-347.

London Transport adhered very strictly to annual inspection of cars and overhaul as necessary, ready for relicensing as Metropolitan Stage Carriages. As there were cars to spare, if one was found with a defect, for which a replacement part might cost more than the cost of a licence, it was withdrawn, particularly if the route on which it worked was nearing its closure. Thus, Nos. 4E and 7E evidently failed their inspection and were delicensed on 11 August 1933. The others were delicensed on abandonment of the Penge route. 19E was delicensed on 17 February, but instead of being put into store like the others, it was painted plain red and fitted with primitive snow brooms, which were no more than boards with bristles attached, fitted in place of the lifeguard gates and it was used for sweeping snow in the Croydon area until 31 March 1937. Nos. 345, 346 and 347 (1E-3E) survived until the Crystal Palace route closed and were delicensed on 14 February 1936. 349 (5E or 17E ?) remained available for service at Erith and with that system's own cars was transferred to Abbey Wood depôt, where it was delicensed on 28 March 1935.

London Transport's records show Nos. 5E-16E and 18E, 20E as being sold to Cohen's for scrapping on 9 May 1934. Nos. 11E, 18E and 20E were available for Cohen's men to inspect first at Thornton Heath depôt and the others in store at Brixton Hill depôt where all were to be broken up. 4E followed on 2 October. For some reason 17E did not follow until 12 June 1935 and 19E presumably some time in 1937. The three cars on the Crystal Palace route were sold to Cohen's at Thornton Heath depôt on 12 October 1935 and were to be broken up at Hampstead depôt, but they had to be held back until Crystal Palace route closed belatedly on 8 February 1936, when presumably they were broken up in Penge depôt with the South Metropolitan Company.

Nos. 11E, 18E and 20E with four others were sold to Cohens without trucks which were then used to replace unsatisfactory trucks under the seven Erith covered top cars, which were to remain in service a little longer. In fact, these Croydon cars were broken up at Brixton Hill, standing on Erith trucks.

Nos. 31-55 (Third Series)   **Class E/1 1927-1928**
Built by Hurst, Nelson & Co. Ltd., at Motherwell, Scotland.

Dimensions:— Saloon 22 ft. 2 in. long, 6 ft. 4½ in. wide at sills.
Overall length 33 ft. 10 in. Height over trolley plank 16 ft. 1½ in.
Seating 27 inside, 42 upstairs.
Quarter turn direct stairs.
G.E.C. K.B.6 controllers.
G.E.C. W.T.32 Q, motors (two 65 h.p.)
Trucks—Hurst, Nelson No. 4 (maximum traction swing bolster).
Braking—Hand, magnetic (on track) and rheostatic.

By 1926, the London County Council were insisting that any new cars purchased by adjoining undertakings and intended for through running over their tracks, must conform very closely to their own standard design, namely their "E/1" Class. At the time, their latest cars were a large batch numbered in the 1700s and 1800s, some built by Hurst, Nelson and the rest by Brush, all delivered in 1922. The L.C.C. was quite ready and anxious to permit their drawings for these cars to be used, in order to ensure that the design would be at least up to their standard and no doubt both Hurst, Nelson and Brush held sets of copies of these drawings. Walthamstow Corporation ordered twelve

---

* Recent research shows that 349 had the body of No. 17 and truck of No. 5.

The Croydon works car, as rebuilt for track welding, seen in Thornton Heath Depôt yard.
(Courtesy Rev. P. W. Boulding. Photo J. F. Higham

The former Croydon works car as London Transport 056, in the scrap yard at Walthamstow
Depôt, on 12 December 1937.   (Photo D. W. K. Jones

such cars in August 1926, closely followed by Croydon Corporation for ten cars in January 1927, only differing in small details from the Walthamstow cars. Croydon ordered fifteen more identical cars in January 1928. They were numbered 31-40 and 41-55 respectively.

The car bodies had four side windows on each deck and the upper deck canopies were enclosed, but not the lower deck, in deference to police regulations enforced in the London area at that time. The body framework was made of teak with mahogany panelling and walnut interior panelling. The interior trim was in light coloured oak, giving a bright cheerful interior. There was seating for 27 passengers in the lower saloon, with seats for three in each corner and two and one turnover seats for the rest, upholstered in UndergrounD Group style grey moquette. There was similar seating for 42 on the upper deck, 2 and 2 seats with curved seats in the canopies, all upholstered in grey moquette like the lower saloon. There were the usual pairs of opening lights over each saloon window, all each side being opened or closed together by a small lever. The upper deck windows could also be opened and closed together, with a rack and pinion device. There were two flat "Venturi" ventilators on the car roof. Upholstery and furnishings were supplied by G. D. Peters & Co. The seating capacity was slightly less than on their L.C.C. counterparts (69 instead of 73) and consequently it was more comfortable. Ceilings were matchboarded light oak.

The lower saloon was closed by the usual single sliding door at each end. There was a perforated sliding ventilator above the window in the door. A partition and hinged door closed off the head of the stairs at each end. Lighting was by means of 38 lamps with "Silvalux" 40 watt bulbs. Air operated "Numa" signal bells were provided by the Equipment & Engineering Co. in the saloon and on the platforms. Each bell push was surrounded by a red enamelled iron ring. Destination equipment had to be interchangeable with L.C.C. equipment, particularly in regard to such matters as route board brackets and the destination boxes on the ends of the car were of the L.C.C. standard "two line" type. However, Croydon did introduce one or two improvements in advance of the L.C.C. There were large opal glass plates against the front upper deck windows to which route number stencils (larger than those used by the L.C.C. at the time) could be fixed to show service numbers 16 and 18, with later 2 for the Thornton Heath service. Provision was made for L.C.C. standard side boards to be carried below the windows of both saloons. There were also, L.C.C. type combined tail lamp and service number stencil carriers on the underside of the canopy against the head of the stairs, which were of the quarter turn direct type.

The bodies of these cars were carried on channel steel underframes and there were steel platform bearers. In conformity with later L.C.C. E/1 cars these Croydon cars had folding platform steps, on the backs of which were side lifeguards, which came into position when the steps were folded up. There were the usual Tidswell type three slat lifeguards and Philipson type guards on the offside. The bodies weighed eight tons.

Hurst, Nelson supplied Mountain & Gibson type Maximum Traction bogies as supplied to the L.C.C. as their "Type 4". They were of longer wheelbase than the older Croydon bogie cars (4 ft. 6 in.) with cast steel side plates and swing bolsters instead of bogie pins. Springing was provided only on the bolsters and above the axle boxes giving a comfortable ride but a tendency to roll. Each bogie had a set of magnetic track brakes and the conduit plough carrier was fixed to an extension of one of the bogies with sufficient clearance to take the L.C.C. later type plough with sliding contacts on top. A changeover switch for conduit/overhead was fixed under the stairs at each end of the car.

All electrical equipment was supplied by the General Electric Co. and included fog lamps suspended under the front edge of the canopy (prior to fog lamps being adopted by the L.C.C.) There were two trolley poles, one for each direction of travel.

These were robust powerful cars, well suited to the trunk route from Croydon to London, but as noted elsewhere, they sometimes ran to Thornton Heath at weekends. To emphasize the similarity with L.C.C. cars, they carried "Class E/1" in small white letters on the solebars.

Modifications

Very few modifications were carried out on these cars while in the ownership of Croydon Corporation. By 1930 the L.C.C. had found that plough carriers mounted on one of the bogies tended to throw the ploughs about, particularly if the pony wheels were worn or had flats. To cure this trouble, they began to fit the plough carrier on brackets from the underframe of the car with adjustable bolts to allow for wear of the wheels and keep the plough head at the desired height above the rail. Croydon followed suit and began fitting body mounted plough carriers to their cars. Those on the Croydon E/1s differed from the L.C.C. ones in having side plates with large oval holes in them, which gave quite a distinctive appearance. By the time London Transport took them over in 1933, all but two had been so modified. Nos. 44 and 48 passed to London Transport still with bogie mounted plough carriers.

When taken over by London Transport in July 1933, at first these cars became 31E-55E still in Croydon livery. Nos. 34E and 55E were due for their annual inspection, servicing and relicencing, which took place on 15 and 27 July respectively. While at Charlton Works, they were repainted in the L.C.C. style of red and cream with the fleet numbers 378 and 399 in large gold figures shaded black. Nos. 36E, 38E and 54E followed in September while the remainder of the class were inspected between November 1933 and June 1934.

The later ones received the new style small gold unshaded numbers and from May 1934, they received "London TransporT" gold transfers on the waist panels. As they so closely resembled the later ex-L.C.C. "E/1s", hardly any modifications were necessary. In the meantime, the L.C.C. had adopted fog lamps, fixed to the side of the destination box and in due course, these replaced the Croydon lamps under the canopy edge. When 44E and 48E were overhauled on 1 March 1934 and 12 April 1934 respectively, they received L.C.C. type underframe mounted plough carriers without the additional side plates with oval holes, so characteristic of the ex-Croydon cars. They became 388 and 392. London Transport was inconsistent in applying the class title "E/1" to these cars and in general did not apply class letters to cars acquired from the smaller undertakings. (Dates quoted in this paragraph refer to the official list of annual inspections.)

Four ex-Croydon cars were included in the London Transport "Rehabilitation" programme in 1936, when they received flush panelled sides to both decks, inset route and destination boxes, white painted hardboard ceilings and one or two other refinements. Croydon cars already had cushioned seats of the highest standard on both decks and chromium plated handrails, so that they required less modification than the ex-L.C.C. cars rebuilt at the same time. Nos. 376 (32E), 379(35E), 380(36E) and 398(54E) were rehabilitated in November/December 1936 and returned to Purley depot. When the remainder of the ex-Croydon E/1s were next overhauled, they received higher dashes and light timber framed vestibule windscreens like the rehabilitated cars, but were not otherwise altered. All ex-Croydon cars had windscreens by the outbreak of war.

Inspections and overhauls were carried out at less frequent intervals during the war, as and when possible. Car No. 396 was destroyed by a bomb outside Croydon bus garage on 10 May 1941 and its remains dumped in Purley depot, to be officially written off on 30 November 1945. No. 376 caught fire on the Embankment on April 1945 and was officially withdrawn also on 30 November, reducing the Croydon rehabilitated cars to three. Like the rest, the ex-Croydon cars took on the visible signs of war, headlamp masks, white collision fenders and protective netting on the windows. With the side lamps, the side route number stencils against the stairs were removed.

All London trams were in dire need of a major overhaul after the war and many of the ex-Croydon cars emerged from this with various strengthening devices, including external diagonal trusses on the saloon sides. No. 391 (47E) was inspected and overhauled on 13 January 1948 and reappeared with flush panelling on both decks, that on the lower deck leaving the steel solebars exposed. It retained its old destination boxes and other appointments. Nos. 378, 382 and 387 received carbon skid trolley heads in March 1948, which they retained for twelve months.

With the closure of tram routes in Croydon on 7 April 1951, the Croydon E/1s were transferred to New Cross depot, to work on routes in South East London and only the two war casualties 376 and 396 were missing. However 384, 387 and 397 failed their annual inspections on 12 October 1951 and on 9 January 1952, the remainder were withdrawn and moved to Penhall Road scrap yard to meet their fate.

The B.E.T. Works Car

Unnumbered Water Car built by Brush Electrical Engineering Co. Ltd., in 1902.

Dimensions:— Overall length
                Water tank capacity 2,000 gallons.
                Brush HD2 type controllers.
                Truck—Brush "A" type 5 ft. 6 in. wheelbase.
                Motors—Brush 1000A 25 horse power.
                Braking—Hand and rheostatic.

This was a standard street spraying car, supplied to many B.E.T. Group tramways in the early days to deal with the problem of the very dusty streets which were to be found in most towns then in summer. No doubt in winter it could be fitted with snow sweeping equipment.

It belonged to the B.E.T. and therefore its stay in Croydon was short. It was removed with the rest of their stock to the South Metropolitan system in the summer of 1906 and its stay there seems to have been no longer. No

Ex-Croydon No. 386 at Thornton Heath terminus, after the track had been slightly extended by London Transport. (Photo W. A. Camwell

S.M.E.T. No. 7 in original condition, except for hoops over ends of upper deck, in Ruskin Road, Carshalton before it was built up. Probably August 1917. (Photo O. J. Morris

S.M.E.T. No. 14 as rebuilt, at the former site of Waddon Station. Like West Croydon, this station building was relocated, in this case nearer Croydon By-Pass. (Photo N. D. W. Elston

photographs of this particular vehicle are known to exist. (See the South Metropolitan section for further details.)

The Croydon Corporation Works Car

Unnumbered Water Car built by United Electric Car Co. Ltd., at Preston in 1907.

Dimensions:— Overall length 22 ft. 0 in. 6 ft. 2 in. over sills.
Water Tank capacity 1500 gallons.
B.T-H. B.18 controllers.
Brill 21E truck 5 ft. 6 in. wheelbase.
Height 10 ft. 10 in. to trolleybase. Inside height 6 ft. 1 in.
Motors—General Electric GE54 motors.
Braking—Hand and rheostatic.

When the B.E.T. took the other car away, the Corporation ordered another in July 1906. It was delivered early in 1907 and cost £619 10s.

It comprised a platform raised on baulks above the truck on which was mounted a rectangular water tank. There were dashes without headlamps at each end with access by climbing irons each side. Just ahead of each tank, there was a wheel operated valve for releasing water. Collision fenders were bracketed a few inches below the ends of the baulks. A domed roof was supported on steel pillars above the tank, concealing a small gantry which supported a B/1 type trolley mast. There was a lamp in a small box under the edge of the roof at each end.

The truck was of the usual Brill 21E design with truss rods, but carried an additional pair of wheels under the motor springs at one end with rail brushes.

In 1914, this vehicle was covered with slogans and coloured lamps for use in a recruitment campaign (see Chapter 2) and toured the system. In 1916, it was rebuilt as a welding car to carry equipment for track welding at night. The water tank was removed and a matchboarded body built in its place, with a sliding door and two windows each side.

A fixed platform step was provided below the sliding door with a ladder alongside it on one side only, for access to the roof and trolley mast. A curious looking hand rail was fixed to the roof above the ladder. Tidswell lifeguards with three slat gates were fitted and the lamp was removed from the roof; it was replaced by small side lamps in boxes like those on the bogie cars, but lower down on the dash. The vehicle appears to have remained in this condition for the remainder of its ownership by Croydon Corporation, but was rarely seen in daylight.

When London Transport took over and 19E was transformed into a snow broom, the welding car was moved to West Ham depot to replace one of their two works cars. It remained painted grey and was numbered 056. It was given a small head lamp in place of the Croydon side lamps.

It was sold to Cohens with another works car on 9 June 1937 for £40 for the pair and removed to Walthamstow depot yard for breaking up. It was seen there and photographed still intact by D. W. K. Jones on 12 December 1937.

The Tower Wagon

Late in 1917, to replace a horse drawn vehicle, Croydon Corporation purchased a set of parts from which to construct a battery powered electric tower wagon, costing £921.

The mechanical and electrical parts were supplied by Edison Ltd., and the tower was supplied by Rawlinson & Son of Blackburn. The chassis and body were fabricated in the Corporation's works at Thornton Heath. It was mounted on four solid tyred wheels and is believed to have been painted dark blue. It had an Edison A6 battery.

It was in regular use until London Transport took over in 1933. There was also a horse drawn pole planting wagon and a Ford van.

SOUTH METROPOLITAN TRAMWAYS

Nos. 1-16   Built by United Electric Car Co. Ltd., at Preston, in 1906. (for Brush Electrical Engineering Co. Ltd., Loughborough).

Later Type J

Dimensions:— Saloon 19 ft. 9 in. long, 6 ft. 0 in. wide over sills.
Overall length 31 ft. 10 in.
Height over trolley plank 9 ft. 10 in.
Seating 28 inside, 30 outside (before rebuilding).
Normal half-turn staircases.
Brush "H" type controllers.
Brush motors 40 horse power.
Truck—Brush 9 ft. 6 in. with Lycett & Conaty radial axle boxes.
Braking—Hand, rheostatic and Spencer track brakes.

The Company's initial order was to Brush for 32 cars of this type, but was cut down to 16 large cars and 16 smaller cars before the order was completed. Owing to pressure of work, Brush evidently purchased sixteen body shells from U.E.C. for the larger cars, which they fitted out and trucked themselves at Loughborough. In appearance they resembled the larger cars supplied by Brush to a number of undertakings around that time, with all the usual distinctive Brush features, such as canopy corner brackets, looped stair hand rails, cup shaped air extractors in the cantrail, swan-neck stairhead lamps and destination boxes under the canopy edge. They also had Brush's own design of upper deck wire screens with the wires crossed top and bottom, but parallel between.

The late Walter Gratwicke remarked that although apparently standard Brush cars, their detailed dimensions differed from any others supplied by that firm. (John Price discovered their U.E.C. origin after his death.) He also noted that they had narrow bodies, as the B.E.T. preferred to play safe and order bodies which could be transferred to a narrow gauge system if the standard gauge system for which they were ordered proved a failure. Hence there was very little "tumble home" to the rocker panels.

The contract price quoted was £605 per car, but the South Metropolitan company's accounts show £551 18s. 0d. per car, paid to Brush during 1906 and £388 6s. 0d. paid to B.E.T. Car Services on account of Nos. 1-16.

They were mounted on long wheelbase trucks fitted with Lycett & Conaty radial gear in which the axles pivoted about the motors and there were no motor support springs, but there were very large protruding axle-boxes. The body was supported on three-quarter elliptical springs at the end. By later standards they were rather slow cars, but the trucks gave a smooth ride on straight track. As they were built for use on the Crystal Palace route, they were fitted with Spencer track brakes, with a single pair of hard oak shoes under the centre of each truck and a brass wheel concentric with the hand brake staff on the platforms. Nos. 11 and 13 were used for the inspection of the Crystal Palace route and these cars took over the working of the Penge route as soon as the Corporation cars were withdrawn in June 1906 and in the same month, one of them was fitted with Raworth regenerative equipment for a demonstration on Anerley Hill for tramway engineers.

Unfortunately, they were found to cause excessive wear on the sharp corner at the "Robin Hood" and confined to the Penge route, until Croydon Corporation took over its working again. Some of the smaller cars were delivered to work the Crystal Palace route as soon as possible. From then on, Nos. 1-16 were transferred to the Sutton route in 1907, and on which they were employed exclusively for the rest of their days. The track brakes were gradually removed, but No. 10 retained them until after 1917.

The interior decor of these cars conformed to the usual Brush standard with oak trim. There were full length slatted benches and maple veneer ceilings in four panels, each with an elaborate gold transfer pattern in the centre and in each corner. A large brass rimmed glass bowl in the very centre of the ceiling contained the main light bulb, with six other unshaded bulbs disposed along the edge of the ceiling. There were also brass brackets supporting wooden grab rails with leather straps and eyelets for the bell cords. The car's number in gold shaded black and a maker's transfer appeared in the left hand upper panel of the bulkhead balanced by a glass bullseye in the right hand one, over which a red slide could be moved to act as a tail lamp. The left hand bulkhead window was blanked off to take a faretable frame. (When fitted, these frames were somewhat narrower than the space provided.) There was a single sliding door at each end of the saloon.

These cars had folding platform steps and there was a small mirror on the back of the destination box so that the driver could observe the interior of the car without turning round.

Because the bodies were designed for a narrower gauge, two and one seating was provided on the upper deck of Nos. 1-16. The double seats were all along one side and the single seats along the other with the trolley plank forming the gangway. The seats were all reversible except those at the canopy ends, which were fixed; they had three plank solid backs to foil pickpockets. The Brecknell-Munro "B/1 trolley mast was slightly offset towards one side and one end, although identical in appearance to those on Corporation cars, these could only be turned to one side and small arrows had to be painted on the bulkheads (later inside the headlamp.)

Modifications

Apart from the removal of the track brakes, few modifications seem to have been made to any of these cars before the 1914-1918 war. Like the Corporation cars, several of these had the right hand side bulkhead window modified with a hinged opening light at the top. In August 1916, a car of this class was fitted with large hoops over the ends of the upper deck to protect passengers from being struck by the trolley pole when being turned in the blackout or from a broken spring. The stairwell lamps were transferred to the hoops and their stanchions removed. In due course, all South Metropolitan cars were fitted with these hoops, which gave them a distinctive appearance. Those on Nos. 1 and 6 had flatter tops than the others.

By the end of the war, the bodies of these cars were found to be very worn and loose. Angle irons were fitted in the top corners of the windows and diagonal truss rods in the bulkheads. Evidently No. 16 was in worse condition than the others and was repillared with five windows instead. It was reclassified "Type J/1" (reports that No. 11 was similarly treated appear to be unfounded). "Philipson" side lifeguards were fitted under the platforms.

The Lycett & Conaty radial gear had not proved satisfactory and it seems that "Warner" radial gear was obtained from M & G Truck & Engineering Co. to replace it by 1912, but was not fitted to the cars until 1922 or 1923. The large protruding axle boxes were replaced by very small ones each supported directly on two coil springs without pedestals. They were found to be more satisfactory. (The earliest photos of cars on "Warner" radial gear, are of Nos. 1, 11 and 15, taken in 1924.)

Rebuilding

By the late 1920s these cars were really in need of drastic rebuilding and from 1927, it was possible to send them away to Hendon for this to be done properly. No. 16 was sent there early in 1928 and was gone for some time. When it returned it was completely transformed in appearance. The separate waist and rocker panelling were replaced by plain panelling, all painted red. A deeper dash was fitted and the upper deck wire mesh screens replaced by metal sheeting from the cantrail to just below the top deck rail, above which the destination box was fitted. It had a plain glazed back to illuminate the upper deck at night and the lamps were removed from the hoops. Long narrow destination boards with route numbers in small figures at the ends, were slotted into brackets just below the saloon windows, replacing those on the upper deck screens. Later an information board of triangular section was fixed under the canopy, where the destination box had been and the mirror for viewing the interior of the car fixed on a bracket behind it.

Instead of lining, a metal band about one inch deep and painted black, extended right round the side and dash just below window level and another just above the solebar level. The statutory lettering and "Type J/2" were in white and at a later date the title "SouthmeT" was applied to the centre of the side panel. As dash mounted advertisements would have spoiled the general lines of the car, they were removed, but later replaced by an advertisement board against the staircase, just above the dash. The "airscoop" extractor ventilators were removed from the cantrails. No. 16 was remotored with DK.31H motors.

The interior of the car was also transformed. The long benches were replaced by two and one reversible cushioned seats, with longitudinal seats in the corners. They were upholstered in Johnston's grey moquette with a green and black mesh pattern, of which the UndergrounD Group must have purchased many miles in its time (also used at Bristol, Glasgow and no doubt many other places). As there was no longer room for the resistances under the seats, they were placed in metal cabinets under the stairs. The ceiling was painted white and the central lamp bowl replaced by a disc of plywood. More powerful bulbs were put in the other positions. In place of a separate bell cord for each direction, a single cord was run along the centre of the ceiling to a bell on each canopy. For the benefit of the conductor, a short length of cord was spliced on and hung down over each doorway.

Following the evident success of No. 16, 1-15 were sent away in turn to Hendon and similarly treated, except that they retained the four window arrangement and classification "Type J". They remained allocated to the Sutton route. They received B.T-H. "B/2" trolley masts with sloping caps which could be turned through the full circle. (No. 16 did later).

Disposal

When London Transport took over, they remained confined to the Sutton route. The ten London United cars on the Mitcham route were displaced by an extension of route 30 to West Croydon late in 1933 and being shedded at Sutton, they took over a number of workings on the Sutton route, but not all. No. 9 evidently failed its inspection in March 1935 and was withdrawn and stored. Nos. 10, 11, 12 and 15 were withdrawn in October and stored in Brixton Hill depôt.* When the Sutton route was replaced by trolleybuses, the remainder joined them at Brixton in December 1935, but the contract with Cohens for their scrapping had already been signed on 12 October. They were broken up on the spot and only the saloon seats retained for further use.

* No. 12 was stored in Penge depôt early in 1935.

Milnes, maker's transfer on doors of S.M.E.T. Nos. 17-26.

(Drawn by F. K. Pearson. Courtesy David & Charles

Nos. 17-26   Built by George F. Milnes & Co., at Hadley, in 1902. **Later Type K.**

Dimensions:—   Saloon 16′ 9″ long. 6′ 1″ wide over sills.
Overall length 27′ 9″. Height over trolley plank 9′ 1″.
Seating 22 inside, 33 outside.
Milnes "Exhibition" half-turn staircases.
B.T-H. "B.18" Controllers. GE.52 Motors 25 h.p.
Truck—Milnes 6′ 0″ girder type.
Braking—Hand and rheostatic only.

This batch of cars was transferred onto South Metropolitan tracks in 1906, from the "Croydon District Tramways" system, having run since 1902 as Croydon Corporation Nos. 36-45, although always the property of the B.E.T.

They were closely similar to cars supplied to Bath and the South Lancashire systems at around the same time, three windowed double deck cars with flat internal ceilings. They were marginally more modern than Croydon Corporation's Nos. 1-35, supplied earlier by Milnes. As the Milnes company had recently come under German ownership, this batch of cars, together with the similar Bath, South Lancs. and some other cars were mounted on rigid two axle trucks of German design, made at the parent factory at Bautzen in Germany. Their main distinguishing feature was the solid pressed steel side frame, with a flange round the edge. There were the usual semi-elliptical springs at the ends supporting the body.

The saloons had polished plywood benches and backs, with patterns perforated in small holes. Like Nos. 1-16, they had maple veneer ceilings with patterned corners and a large brass rimmed lighting bowl in the centre, together with six unshaded bulbs along the sides. The lintel board over the door was more elaborate than those of Nos. 1-16 and supported on ornate capitals. There were similar capitals on each window pillar. A mirror formed the left hand upper panel of the bulkhead and the right hand panel carried a power consumption meter and a bullseye to form the tail lamp.

Like Nos. 1-16, these cars carried a narrow fare table board in the left hand bulkhead window position and some cars had a hinged opening light in the top of the right hand bulkhead window. There were very rounded top corners to the single bulkhead sliding door, which carried the Milnes gold transfer just below the window.

The upper decks were wide with two and two seating, except for a single seat by the trolley which was slightly offset. The mast was of the newly designed B.T-H. "B.2" design with a sloping cap; its principal advantage was that it could be turned through the full circle without damaging the internal cable. The canopies were wide and rather flat ended, with the headlamp mounted in the centre thereof, instead of on the dash. A small lamp was mounted on an upright stanchion near the head of each staircase.

As the Metropolitan Police took exception to cars with reversed stairs, these had the new Milnes "Exhibition" staircases, which were almost half-turn in the normal spiral direction, but took a wide sweep and were almost as easy to climb as the reversed stairs. They were even an improvement on the normal spiral stairs supplied by other manufacturers, some of which made an uncomfortably tight spiral. The front of the canopy was supported by a stanchion, just to the left of the controller, with an enormous fancy bracket on top. The stair handrails extended to this stanchion, there was no upright rail at the corner of the dash, but the grab-rail at the centre of the platform step had an equally large fancy bracket on top. There was a fancy grille like a wrought iron gate at the rear end of the dash under the stairs. The platform steps were of the fixed type and roller blind destination boxes were mounted at each end above the upper deck rails. The screens were of ordinary wire mesh.

When the S.M.E.T. accounts were separated from the B.E.T. Group General account, the cost of these cars was put at £495 6s. 8d. each.

S.M.E.T. No. 20, after the headlamp had been moved to the dash at the top of Tamworth Road, waiting to pull into the terminus, 4 August 1924.　　　　　　　(Photo F. Merton Atkins

S.M.E.T. No. 21 as rebuilt at Hendon, with new platforms and canopies and direct ¼ turn stairs, but dumped in the yard of Penge Depôt.　　　　　　　(Photo Walter Gratwicke

After the Carshalton accident in 1907, the staff were evidently rather reluctant to use these cars on the Sutton route and they spent the rest of their working lives on the Croydon—Mitcham—Tooting section, which had no gradients.

Modifications

Within a few years of transfer to the South Metropolitan system, all these cars had the headlamps moved from the canopy front to the usual position on the dash, one reason being that it enabled them to carry advertisements in the same positions as the rest of the fleet. Just after the 1914-1918 war, hoops were fitted over the ends of the upper deck and at the same time, the destination boxes were placed under the canopy edge. On these cars it was not possible to remove the stanchion which had supported the stairhead lamp as it was integral with those carrying the deck screens. Nos. 19, 20, 23, 24 and 25 received flat topped hoops like Nos. 1 and 6.

These were the oldest and smallest cars in the South Metropolitan fleet, were rather slow and because the Milnes trucks could not be lengthened, they were very subject to tail-wagging. By the late 1920s when it became possible to send cars away to Hendon for a thorough overhaul, they were all in really tired condition. They were sent away in turn in 1927 and No. 17 was at once declared to be beyond economic repair. It was withdrawn from service and probably scrapped. The others were at least made to look presentable again. Several were rebuilt to various extents, where necessary receiving replacements from the large stock of spare parts for Metropolitan cars, held at Hendon Works. Nos. 19, 20, 24 received new dashes and apparently new brake gear, with longer handles to the hand-brake, which necessitated a dash corner hand rail cranked outwards to clear it. Other cars received straight hand rails and folding platform steps.

No. 22 received Brush staircases similar to the "Exhibition" type and evidently taken from one of the ex-Croydon cars, which became a Metropolitan Works Car. No. 21 was more seriously modifed, receiving complete new ends, including platform bearers, collision fenders, dashes, headlamps and complete canopies, all of the MetropolitaN company's standard design. Even the staircases were replaced by the direct quarter-turn pattern, necessitating a rearrangement of the upper deck seating and stair hand-rails. Although drastic, this rebuilding was not a success, as presumably the main body structure was weak and the car was soon dumped in the back of Penge depôt "out of service". One report says that No. 26 was even more thoroughly rebuilt and re-classified "Type K/2", (the writer has seen no photographic evidence, but confirmed in official list).

Before work had been completed on the whole batch, it became clear that it might be cheaper to obtain replacement cars if any could be procured second-hand at a reasonable price. That opportunity arose sooner than expected in the Autumn of 1927, when twelve cars were obtained in good condition from Croydon Corporation.

With the arrival of these new cars, Nos. 20, 24 and 25 were dumped at Fulwell depôt of the London United Tramways and the others in the back part of Penge depôt. The company's accounts state that Nos. 17 and 21 were to be broken up in 1927 and although No. 17 had disappeared without trace, Walter Gratwicke saw two cars numbered 21 side by side in Penge depôt in 1932! (i.e. Milnes Car No. 21 and the ex-Croydon car which replaced it).

Although not further modified, No. 19 was later used as a breakdown towing car at Sutton depôt, still in full livery, but delicensed, with most of the paper advertisements peeling off. None of the others appear to have turned a wheel again. No. 19 survived long enough to become 19s, of London Transport.

Nos. 18-26 passed into the hands of London Transport in 1933 and their records show that they were sold to Cohens for scrapping on 17 May 1934, Nos. 18, 21, 22, 23 and 26 in Penge depôt and 20, 24 and 25 at Fulwell, where No. 19 followed on 2 October. Cohen's men broke them up on the spot.

S.M.E.T. No. 29 at Mitcham Fair Green in the late 1920s. (Photo G. N. Southerden

Nos. 27-29, 31 and 35. Built by Brush Electrical Engineering Co. Ltd., in 1902.

Later Type L.

Dimensions:— Saloon 22' 0" long, 6' 0" wide over sills.
Overall length 34' 8". Height over trolley plank 9' 11".
Seating 30 inside, 39 outside.
Double flight staircases with landing.
B.T-H. "B.18" type Controllers. GE52 Motors 25 h.p.
Trucks—Brush "B" type bogies, 4' 2" wheelbase.
Braking—Hand and rheostatic.

Like Nos. 17-26, this batch of cars was transferred to South Metropolitan tracks in 1906, having been built for "Croydon District Tramways" in 1902, and run as Croydon Corporation Nos. 56-60. Valued at £623 6s. 8d. each.

Although built by Brush instead of Milnes, the bodies of these cars were almost identical to those of Corporation Nos. 46-55. There were minor differences in the arrangement of the hand-rails, they lacked the loop at the end of the dash top rail and there were typical Brush brackets supporting the stair landings. They had six windows each side and the interior arrangement was similar to their predecessors, with long perforated plywood benches, etc. Unlike all other cars in the South Metropolitan's own fleet, they had double-opening doors to the saloon, with a concealed chain over the top so that the two always opened and closed together. As these doors gave a wide opening, the flanking bulkhead windows were correspondingly narrow. (It may be for this reason that all South Met. cars had very narrow fare tables. For the sake of standardization the London Companies always worked to the lowest common denominator!)

Like most cars with double-flight stairs, these had very short half canopies, with wooden roller blind destination boxes, each mounted on three stanchions above the end hand rail. Presumably there was a glazed aperture in the back to illuminate the upper deck. Upper deck seating was arranged two and two, except that there was a single seat beside the trolley mast, which was of the Brecknell, Munro & Rogers "B1" type, and slightly offset towards one side. There was no stairhead lamp and the wire mesh screens were of the Brush standard design.

130

There were originally Wilson & Bennett wire mesh lifeguards under the platforms, but no guard between the bogies. These cars had channel steel sills to the underframes. The biggest difference from the corresponding Corporation cars lay in the bogies, which were of Brush's own design and were reversed with the driving wheels nearest the centre of the car. They were not entirely satisfactory and had a tendency to derail on the very sharp corner at Pitlake. This was thought to be due to the fact that the smaller wheels were leading, but the Metropolitan Electric tramways which had some similar cars on almost identical bogies, turned the bogies round on one of their cars (No. 25) and it made no appreciable difference. It was subsequently noticed that the corresponding Corporation cars and the ex-Gravesend cars which ran on Brill 22E bogies did not suffer from so many derailments, even though the bogies of the latter were reversed. A special feature of the 22E truck was the Weight Transfer Device, which consisted of a specially shaped rubbing plate attached to the body of the car above the centre spring post. The latter was depressed slightly due to the movement of the truck, when rounding a curve; this increased the load on the pony wheels by approximately 20%. The Brush trucks did not have this feature. (We are indebted to Walter Gratwicke for this explanation.)

Modifications

These five cars received the least modifictions of any of the South Metropolitan fleet and in fact it was many years before they were even repainted, running in deep chocolate and ivory, with only the fleet numbers and badges altered.

The wire mesh life guards were soon replaced by the Hudson & Bowring slatted type and slatted gates fitted between the bogies. Under the Defence regulations in 1916, sidelamps in little wooden boxes were fitted to the top of the dash, like their Corporation counterparts.

In the early 1920s, the destination boxes were lowered to a position at the top of the end deceny panels and hoops were fitted over the canopies; these were all of the flat topped type and carried a stairhead lamp.

When sent away to Hendon, a few more modifications were made. The dash-mounted sidelamps were replaced by London United type lamps extending on tenuous stalks from the half-canopy and the stair landing hand rails. Folding platform steps were fitted, Philipson side life-guards under the off side of the platforms and the "B.1" type trolley masts replaced by the B.T-H. "B.2" type. One small feature which must have worried the authorities at Hendon, was that there was no wire screen over the stairside end decency panel. Nos. 28 and 31 were fitted with MetropolitaN metal scrollwork and 35 with solid panels in this position.

Walter Gratwicke states that the original Brush "B" type bogies were replaced at Hendon, by almost identical bogies from the Metropolitan stock of spare parts, but hardly any difference is discernible in photographs. They probably had GE58 motors. No further modifications were made to these cars.

When in October 1931, the SouthmeT received on loan, ten similar cars from the London United tramways, but with covered tops and Brill 22E trucks, the South Metropolitan L Type cars and others took their place in store at Fulwell depôt. They never ran in service again.

After London Transport took over they were sold where they stood to Cohens for scrap on 9 May 1934. No. 31 was the last to be broken up in July.

Nos. 30 and 32-34. Built by Electric Railway & Tramway Carriage Works Ltd. (Predecessors of United Electric Car Co. Ltd.) at Preston, in 1902.

Later Type O

Dimensions:— Saloon 23' 6" long, 6' 1" wide over sills.
Overall length 34' 6" (before rebuilding).
Height over trolley plank 10' 1".
Seating 34 inside, 34 outside (before rebuilding).
Half turn reversed staircases.
Dick, Kerr DB 1 form B Controllers.
Two DK 35 Motors of 30 horse power each.
Trucks—Brill 22E bogies (reversed).
Braking—Hand and rheostatic.

A batch of ten large bogie cars built for the Gravesend and Northfleet tramways in 1902, evidently proved too large for that undertaking and between 1904 and 1906, they were offered for sale to other undertakings in the B.E.T. Group at £560 each, by advertisement in the B.E.T. Group magazine. The South Metropolitan Co. accepted one early in 1906 and it took the number 30. It evidently proved suitable to their requirements and another was acquired later in the year. Early in 1907 the SMET enquired whether any more were available, and received the reply that only two were left out of the batch of 10, the others having been disposed of to Swansea (4), and Jarrow (2). The remaining two cars became 33 and 34 in the South Metropolitan fleet.

They were long cars with five window saloons, full length canopies and were the only cars with reversed stairs ever owned by the Company. The saloons were closed by single sliding doors and the internal decor was of Dick, Kerr's standard design. The maple veneer ceilings were divided into four panels with designs in the corners (less elaborate than on the Brush cars). There was a large ceiling support bracket on each window pillar, an ornate lintel board over the door (later covered by a small notice board) and a perforated ventilation board in the top of the door over the window. A mirror formed the left-hand upper panel of the internal bulkhead and when on the South Met. system, there was a circular hole with red glass in the right hand one, the large oil lantern used at Gravesend, having been replaced by a hinged opening vent. There were eight unshaded light bulbs distributed along the edges of the ceiling. The saloon seats were long slatted benches, but the backs were in perforated plywood. Other internal fittings were similar to those on the remainder of the fleet.

Seating on the upper deck was two and two, with a single seat near the head of the stairs at each end. Like other South Metropolitan cars, these seats had solid backs. The Blackwell enclosed spring trolley mast was placed at the centre of the upper deck. Large "two line" tinplate destination boxes were fixed on stanchions above the ends of the upper deck and the deck screens were of close mesh fine wire.

These cars ran on Brill 22E bogies, which unusually for that type were reversed with the pony wheels outwards.

Modifications

Before going into service on the South Metropolitan, only those modifications necessary to make them suitable for working on that system were made. Gravesend used a cumbersome lever operated track brake, these were not required and were removed before the cars went into service on the S.M.E.T. The fixed trolleyhead was replaced by a "Wood's" swivelling head as standard on the South Met. and a wire mesh "dog guard" fixed between the bogies. These were the only modifications made on these cars before the war. Standard South Met. destination blinds were fitted into the existing boxes.

S.M.E.T. No. 30 at Tamworth Road terminus, West Croydon. This car is very little changed from its Gravesend condition and livery on 28 May 1917. Note the connecting curve just under the "Dog guard" had not yet been laid. (Photo O. J. Morris

S.M.E.T. No. 34 as rebuilt and dumped in Fulwell Depôt yard. (Photo Walter Gratwicke

In 1916, sidelamps were fixed under the canopy edge, as with other cars in the fleet. Later the metal destination boxes were replaced by wooden ones in the same positions. The "Leather's Patent Ventilators" between the opening lights projected and were gradually removed.

Rebuilding

In the late 1920s, No. 32 was fitted with lengthened platforms and quarter turn stairs at Hendon. At the same time it received a B.2 trolley mast, hoops over the end of the upper deck, folding platform steps and slatted gates between the bogies instead of the wire cages. The new platforms increased the overall length to 36 feet and the seating had to be re-arranged on the upper deck, reducing it by one.

In 1930, all four cars were sent in turn to Hendon, where in addition to being brought into line with No. 32, they were rebuilt similar to the six "M Type" cars (which see). They received higher dashes, and high metal sheeting round the upper decks and probably long cushioned seats inside. No. 34 retained the wire mesh "dog guards" between the bogies.

However, in October 1931, with the arrival of the London United cars, these four cars followed the L Type into store at Fulwell depôt. Like them, London Transport sold them to Cohens for scrap on 9 May 1934. No. 34 was the last to be broken up in June.

S.M.E.T. No. 19s, de-licensed and in use as breakdown car at Sutton Depôt.

(Photo D. W. K. Jones

Nos. 36-51. Built by Brush Electrical Mechanical Engineering Co. Ltd., at Loughborough, in 1906.   **Later Type M**

Dimensions:— Saloon 16′ 10″. 6′ 1″ wide over sills.
Overall length 28′ 10″.
Height over trolley plank 9′ 10″.
Seating 24 inside, 26 outside (several rebuilt 30 out).
Normal half turn staircases.
B.T-H. B.10 Controllers. Brush Motors.
Truck—Brush (of 21E type) 7′ 6″ wheelbase.
Braking—Hand, rheostatic and later Spencer track brakes.

Although built by Brush themselves, these cars were in most respects shortened versions of Nos. 1-16, with three side windows instead of four. They had all the standard Brush fittings for that date and were mounted on the Brush version of the Brill 21E truck, with three-quarter elliptic springs at the ends. They had the pilot board brackets fixed inside the truck frame instead of outside.

The interior decor was similar to Nos. 1-16. The Brush "Falcon" transfer and the car's number were displayed on the upper left hand panel of the bulkhead and there was the bullseye tail lamp in the right hand panel. Most of this batch had the upper part of the right hand bulkhead window hinged to act as an opening light (opening inwards).

From the Company's accounts, it appears that Nos. 36-43 were delivered in September or October 1906 to Sutton depôt, without track brake equipment, although the price paid, in December, £617 10s. 0d., is said to include them. By the time the rest were ready for delivery, it had been decided that these cars, which turned out to be the most satisfactory of the South Metropolitan fleet, were more suitable for the Crystal Palace route and Nos. 44-51 were delivered to Penge depôt already fitted with Spencer track brakes and regenerative control equipment supplied by J. S. Raworth. They cost £707 each. In due course, Nos. 36-43 received track brakes but not regenerative equipment and as modified were transferred to Penge depôt to replace the radial trucked cars on the Penge service.

In December 1906, automatic cut-outs were fitted to Nos. 44-51 at an extra cost of £10 per car. Another modification, not specified in the accounts, cost £15 8s. 0d. per car. In 1909, it cost £62 17s. 10d. per car to remove the regenerative equipment from Nos. 44-51 and equip them like the other cars.

Nos. 36-51 were easily the fastest cars in the fleet, but had a sort of "rocking horse" motion at speed, pitching from front to rear.

Like Nos. 1-16, they had narrow bodies mounted on standard gauge trucks and consequently had two and one seating on the upper deck, but unlike them the seating was staggered either side of the Brecknell, Munro B.1 type trolley mast which was placed centrally. Folding platform steps were always fitted.

Modifications

Once the regenerative equipment had been removed from Nos. 44-51 and the remainder fitted with track brakes, this batch of cars was left without further alteration until the 1914 war. It is probably that Nos. 36 and 51 were retained at Sutton depôt until after the war, for short workings on the Sutton route, but from 1907, 37-50 were allocated to Penge depôt for the Crystal Palace route.

In 1916, like the rest of the fleet, these cars were fitted with side lamps and were fitted with hoops over the canopies immediately following Nos. 1-16 (none had flat topped hoops).

The writer recalls returning from school one day in 1927, on top of No. 47 and the stanchions and wire screens were loose and moving. He was told that it was the next to go to Hendon for an overhaul. At that time, the Metropolitan tramways were negotiating to acquire three of the ex-Croydon cars which the S.M.E.T. had just obtained, for conversion to Works Cars. They were persuaded to take two Croydon cars and No. 47 instead.

S.M.E.T. No. 45 in original condition except for hoops, driven out of Penge Depôt, by Mr. H. Bennett, the Depôt Engineer for Walter Gratwicke in 1918.

S.M.E.T. No. 41 in Station Road, West Croydon, waiting to run into the terminus. Car in rebuilt condition. (Photo G. N. Southerden

Soon afterwards, No. 42 was sent to Hendon and although externally unchanged, a good deal of work was done to modernize the saloon. The slatted benches were replaced by cushions of the usual UndergrounD Group grey moquette, but the slatted backs were retained. The ceiling was painted white and the central lighting bowl replaced by a plywood disc, with more powerful bulbs in the other positions. As in Nos. 1-16, a single bell cord ran the length of the ceiling. The dark varnish was removed from the interior trim which was revarnished in its natural light oak with some of the more elaborate embellishments removed. One curious alteration was that the opening light in the bulkhead window was replaced by a small metal framed opening light in the saloon door. This sometimes jammed when the door was open, making it impossible to close the door, and was not repeated on any other SouthmeT cars, although a few Metropolitan cars are believed to have been so fitted.

The next car to be sent to Hendon was No. 46, and this was more economically modernized. The ceiling was white and there was moquette on the seats and backs, but it was stuck straight onto the existing benches, to the great discomfort of any passenger who mistook this car for No. 42 and sat down suddenly! In due course the remainder of the class (except 47) had their saloons modernized similarly to No. 46, except that they had cushioned seats and backs. B.T-H. "B.2" trolley masts were fitted, and could be turned through the full circle.

Rebuilding. Nos. 37, 38, 41, 43, 46 & 48 only

Between 7 November 1929 and 13 February 1930, six of these cars were rebuilt, not as extensively as the Sutton cars 1-16 and more like the Gravesend cars. As the saloons had so recently been improved, they were not further altered. The upper decks were widened, but by a very small amount. The stanchions, formerly just over an inch set in from the roof edge were brought right out to the edge and the wire netting screens replaced by metal panelling from roof level to just below the top-rail, and like Nos. 1-16 the destination boxes were fixed just above the top-rail and triangular-section information boards took their place under the canopy edge. The widening of the upper deck was just sufficient to permit their being re-seated with two & two (except adjoining the trolley mast) for 30 passengers. The new seats appeared to be of more solid construction than their predecessors. New higher dashes were fitted at the same time. These concealed the track brake hand wheel and the controllers had to be mounted on blocks, so that the handles could sweep over the dash top-rail. An advertisement board was fixed against the stairs, to replace the adverts pasted onto the dash corner; this was found to make a useful draught screen and was repeated on the rest of the fleet.

The increased weight of metal on the upper deck had an adverse effect on the tendency to pitch and bounce already evident on these cars. Those cars rebuilt were Nos. 37, 38, 41, 43, 46 and 48. At this rebuilding No. 46 received padded seats and backs like the rest. At some time, No. 42 also received padded backs to its already padded seats. No more cars were rebuilt after the six mentioned above.

Nos. 36-46 and 48-51 passed to the London Passenger Transport Board, still working on the Crystal Palace route. Eventually Nos. 36, 39, 40, 44 and 50 were painted in London Transport livery in their original condition. Only No. 48 of the rebuilt cars was repainted and had red panelling round the upper deck.

The others remained in the UndergrounD Group red and white until they were withdrawn with the closure of the Crystal Palace route in February 1936. The deal for their sale to Cohens for scrap had already been concluded on 12 October 1935. So they moved in and broke them up in Penge depot as soon as the route closed. (It had been anticipated that the new trolleybus route Sutton-West Croydon-Crystal Palace would open right through in November 1935.) Nos. 38 and 42 were withdrawn in January 1936 and the rest in February. (No. 47, now M.E.T. Works Car 04 had been broken up at Fulwell in September 1934.)

Nos. 17, 21,   Built by BRUSH ELECTRICAL ENGINEERING Co. Ltd. in 1906
47 & 52   & 1907 for Croydon Corporation.

Type P

Dimensions:—   Saloon 16 ft. 0 in. 6 ft. 2 in. width over sills.
Overall length 28 ft. 0 in.
Height over Trolley plank 9 ft. 10 in.
Seating 22 inside 32 outside.
Normal half turn staircases (extra wide sweep).
Westinghouse 90M Controllers with detachable handles.
Westinghouse 200 motors. 31 horsepower.
Truck—Brill 21E (One on Mountain & Gibson 21EM).
Braking—Hand and Rheostatic.

The S.M.E.T. bought twelve cars from Croydon Corporation in July 1927 as a source of spare parts and to replace the 1902 Milnes cars, some of which were by then considered beyond repair. The Croydon cars came from three batches of 1901, 1906 and 1907, the 1901 cars being the four from that batch that had been heavily rebuilt. The 1906 and 1907 cars were almost identical. However, by the time the S.M.E.T. decided to render these cars suitable for use on their own lines, they had given up the working from Mitcham to Tooting with their own cars and it was found that only four would be required. In the meantime, one of the 1901 cars, No. 13 was sold to the London United Tramways for £60 for use as a rail grinder and numbered 006. The Metropolitan Electric Tramways wished to take three more for use as works cars, but decided to have them on loan instead of purchasing them. They were to have taken Nos. 43, 44 and 69, but as recounted elsewhere, were persuaded to take S.M.E.T. No. 47 instead of 44.

South Metropolitan cars 17, 21 and 47 had been declared beyond economic repair and the four Croydon cars chosen to replace them and to make one addition to the fleet were sent to Hendon for a general overhaul and some slight external alterations to make them resemble South Metropolitan cars as seen by the public. They were returned to Sutton in Underground Group livery, with the destination boxes under the canopies (this necessitated cutting the tops off the stair rails) and hoops over the ends of the upper deck. Thus, they generally resembled the "M" type but had slightly wider and shorter bodies with a more pronounced tumblehome to the rocker panels. The interiors were somewhat more ornate with mirrors etc.

The first two to be put into service now bore the numbers 52 and 53. It is not known for certain which Croydon car took the number 53, but it is known to have retained that number until July 1928 (The Greyhound Racing Bill on the dash corner was found on UndergrounD Group records to have been issued on 13 July, 1928). However, the South Metropolitan Company's accounts state that their Nos. 17 and 21 were to be replaced by Croydon Nos. 64 and 66, valued at £60 each. Croydon No. 67 became 52 and to quote the accounts "Croydon No. 44 was substituted for No. 47", not recognising that one was ever numbered 53. Although Croydon 44 from a different batch than the others, the differences between them were very small indeed and few photographs taken of them. No. 52 was retained as the addition to the fleet.

The writer has not seen a photo of No. 17 and only the following points of difference have been noted on the others. No. 21 was fitted with a Metropolitan B.2 trolley mast but retained its Croydon "Torpedo" side lamps. Its distinguishing feature was a truss bar between the tops of the motor support springs on the truck. No. 47 received a B.2 trolley mast and South Metropolitan side lamps. Its distinguishing feature was a cranked grab rail at the dash corner like No. 19 (evidently a Hendon modification). No. 52 was mounted on a Mountain & Gibson truck and retained its Croydon B.1 trolley mast and side lights. Its distinguishing feature was conical springs beside the axle boxes. Whichever car carried the number 53 for a time was like 52 in most respects except that it was on a Brill truck with parallel sided springs. It can therefore be concluded that the number 53 was carried for a time on the car intended to be 17. (The Corporation "B/1" masts could turn through a full circle, unlike the S.M.E.T. ones.)

As they had the wide sweep "Exhibition" type stairs, these cars retained the extra outer stringer which they had at Croydon. The trucks were slightly longer than those of the M type cars. As they lacked track brakes they could not be used on the Crystal Palace route and were intended for short workings on the Sutton route, which normally required one of them. Four were required on Saturdays for the West Croydon—Red House workings on the Mitcham route.

When Croydon No. 13 passed to the L.U.T. as 006 it retained its upper deck but not the stairs. S.M.E.T. No. 47 became Metropolitan Rail Scrubber No. 04 and had its top deck removed. Likewise Croydon 43 became Metropolitan Breakdown Car 07 and 69 became Salt Car 09, both deprived of their upper decks and stairs.

Croydon Nos. 25, 34, 35, 62 and 63 were not required and were stored in the open at the London United depot at Fulwell, presumably to be canibalized for spare parts as required. They were written off the books in 1931 (valued at £60 each), by which time only three remained, 34, 35 and one other, still in Croydon livery but with the rocker panels painted over a dark colour. 25 and 63 were at Acton.

Although straighter and in better condition than most of the South Metropolitan stock, the P type seem to have seen relatively little service. No. 47 was repainted in the final livery and received an advertisement board against the stairs in addition to the position on the dash (the only car to have both). It survived long enough into London TransporT days to receive the suffix letter "s". Mr. Gratwicke photographed No. 52 at Fulwell in 1932. Nos. 17 and 21 were sold to Cohens for scrap at Penge depôt on the 9 May 1934, No. 52 at Fulwell on the same date and finally 47 at Fulwell on 2 October 1934. With regard to the Works cars loaned to the M.E.T., 04 was sold to Cohens at Hampstead on 13 November 1935, 07 at Mitcham on 14 December 1936 and 09 at Fulwell on 2 October 1934.

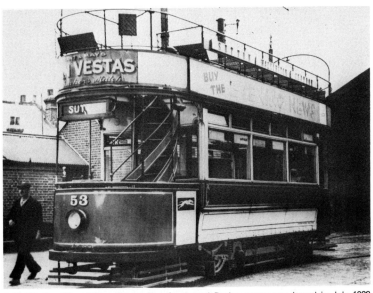

S.M.E.T. No. 53 at Sutton Depôt. The Greyhound Racing poster was issued in July 1928 and it is believed that this car was renumbered 17, soon afterwards (ex-Croydon No. 66).
(Photo S.M.E.T. official

Cars Loaned to the Company

Nos. 145 & 150 Built by BRUSH ELECTRICAL ENGINEERING Co. Ltd. in 1905, for the Metropolitan Electric Tramways Ltd.

Type E

Dimensions:— Saloon 25 ft. 0 in. long. 6 ft. 1 in. wide over sills.
Overall length 33 ft. 10 in. 10 ft. 8 in. high over trolley plank.
Seating 36 in Saloon, single deck.
B.T-H. "B.18" Controllers. G.E. 52 motors.
Truck—Brush 9 ft. 6 in. with Lycett & Conaty radial axles.
Braking—Hand, Rheostatic and "Spencer" track brakes.

The Metropolitan Electric Tramways, with which the S.M.E.T. had become associated, operated two short routes from the Wood Green area to the grounds of Alexandra Palace. Various considerations, including a very low bridge at Wood Green Station on one of them, necessitated single deck cars. Consequently twenty long wheelbase four wheeled single deck cars were ordered to work these two routes. In 1905, the Alexandra Palace was a very popular place of entertainment for North Londoners and no doubt the purchase of 20 cars was justified. However, soon 20 were more than sufficient, six being normally sufficient to work the "Palace" services. They were not suitable for working on the M.E.T.'s main lines; for a time two worked the Southbury Road shuttle service at Enfield and others were used from time to time as breakdown cars.

Four were sold to Auckland, New Zealand in 1907, and at a later date one was transferred to the London United Tramways as a "One Man" car, but on 1 August 1920, it was decided that two others should be loaned to the South Metropolitan tramways to see if they were suitable for the short workings on the Crystal Palace and Sutton routes. Nos. 145 and 150 were despatched to Croydon. Middlesex County Council were able to insist that the coat of arms and lettering be obliterated before they went into service, and that the rental paid for them be increased.

Having track brakes and radial trucks similar to those under S.M.E.T. Nos. 1-16, they were thought suitable for either the Crystal Palace or Sutton routes. (Although most of the M.E.T. "E" type cars had had their trucks altered to the "Warner" radial gear, 145 and 150 were yet to be converted and retained their Lycett & Conaty radial trucks.) They had long "Rattan" cushioned seats in the saloon, six side windows with opening lights above and one window pillar each side thicker than the others, where there was a partition inside dividing the car into two compartments, originally intended for "Smoking" and "Non-Smoking". On Nos. 145 and 150, the door had already been removed, but not the partition. There were roof ventilators over what had been intended as the "Smoking" compartment and double opening doors at the ends of the saloon.

Walter Gratwicke took a number of photos of No. 145 in the yard of Penge depot, but none are known of 150 there. As built these cars had large head lamps on the canopy edge. 145 retained this at one end only! At the other end there was only the small wartime tail lamp near the bottom of the dash.

They were among the first cars in the UndergrounD Group red and white livery to be seen on the S.M.E.T., the Metropolitan always having used those colours.

At the beginning of April 1921, No. 150 was tried on the short workings between the "Robin Hood" and the Crystal Palace, on which it worked for some months. It rarely ventured as far as Selby road, so the only sight the writer normally had of it, was passing in the opposite direction when on his way to school. He did once ride on it on a Saturday afternoon. It was not entirely successful for various reasons; it was slower than the other cars on the route and there was a noticable dip in the road at Low Level Station, but the overhead wires were slightly stretched and did not dip as far as the roadway below, resulting in frequent dewirements of this short poled car. Its shorter platforms and lower capacity put it at a disadvantage on Saturday afternoons when there were events at the Crystal Palace.

Metropolitan E type car No. 145 in yard of Penge Depôt, 1921.   (Photo Walter Gratwicke

No. 145 was put to work on the Sutton-Wallington short workings and then shedded at Sutton. Neither was popular with the staff and their use in service was spasmodic.

The statuary lettering on the solebar was altered to "South Metropolitan Electric Tramways and Lighting Company Limited" and the Metropolitan Co. showed them in their books as leased to the S.M.E.T., the rental charged being the following, £205.0.0d for 1921, £180.0.0d for 1922, £191.7.0d for 1923 and £274.8.4d for 1924, after which payments ceased. They were returned early in 1925.

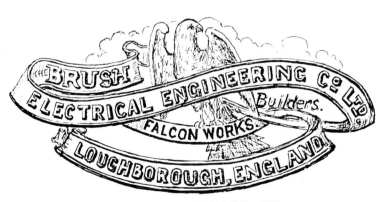

The Brush "Falcon" badge as on the bulkheads of S.M.E.T. Nos. 36-51.
(Traced by G. E. Baddeley

141

Nos. 267, 268, 269, 271, 272, 276, 278, 290, 293 and 299

Built by George F. Milnes & Co., at Hadley, Shropshire in 1902 (for the London United Tramways Ltd.).

Type U

Dimensions:— Saloon 22 ft. long, 6 ft. 0 in. over sills.
Overall length 33 ft. 6 in. Height over roof 16 ft. 0 in.
Seating 30 inside, 39 outside.
Double flight staircases with landings.
Westinghouse type 90 controllers.
Westinghouse 49B motors.
Brill 22E bogies with driving wheels outwards.
Braking—Hand, rheostatic and magnetic track.

For some time, the SouthmeT had been pressing the other two companies in the UndergrounD Group to let them borrow some covered top cars for use on the Mitcham or Sutton routes, in order to increase traffic. The opportunity eventually occurred in 1931. Ten of those which had been top covered were loaned to the South Met. and their nine open top bogie cars put in store at Fulwell depôt of the L.U.T. in their place.

It was the practise of the L.U.T. if the body of one of their covered cars became weak, to remove the top cover and place it on one of the open top cars which had been in store and seen little service in recent years, and then put that into service in its place. The numbers quoted at the top of this page are those of the cars which were working on the SouthmeT at the time of the take over by London Transport and at some time during the period of loan, it seems that No. 299 took the place of 286. They came from the batch 237-300 and the first appeared on the Mitcham route in October 1931.

They were large bogie cars with six "Gothic" pointed windows each side, with ventilation slits above, leading into a roof cavity and clerestorey ceiling with opening lights of white opal glass and two blue dragons on each with their tails intertwined. Over the years, many of these had been replaced by plain glass or covered by notices. There was crossed beading on the ceiling and ornamental capitals on the window pillars. Over the double-opening doors, there were huge lintel boards with ventilation slits which could be closed. Seating in the saloon was in the form of long benches, covered by the ususal grey moquette cushions. Rather primitive top covers had been fitted to many of them around 1911. These conformed to the short canopies and had a door at an angle at the head of the stairs, leaving a triangular aperture which let in draughts. In addition as first covered the two centre windows each side were left un-glazed until the late 1920s, when plain glass windows without sashes were fitted, but could be pushed down in their frames.

These cars had rather tall Blackwell "Dublin" type trolley masts which were retained and passed through a hole in the roof. As this hole was rather larger than necessary, a sort of inverted dustbin lid was fitted round the upper part of the mast to catch any rain water that entered! Two and two wooden seats were fitted on the upper deck, with a single seat beside the trolley mast, hence the total seating of the car remained at 69 even when top covered.

They were mounted on Brill 22E bogies with the driving wheels towards the ends of the car in the conventional fashion. Higher powered motors and magnetic track brakes had been fitted in 1926/27.

The upright stanchion supporting the corner of the roof above the stair landing had three cross braces to the body, which could be used as a ladder to gain access to the roof in the event of trouble with the trolley. Small side lamps projected from the half-canopy and stair landing. There was a destination box on the end screen above the half-canopy, but instead of the usual roller blind, small lettered boards had to be pushed into it from the side nearest the stairs. The box was illuminated from above by two shaded lamps and beside them there was a bracket for a route number plate.

Modifications

As these cars were only on loan to the S.M.E.T., they were not authorized to carry out any modifications on them and the only one noted was the removal of the route number bracket. Henceforth, these cars only showed a number on the side route boards like the company's own cars. Destination boards were made to fit the existing L.U.T. boxes (black on white).

Being still regarded as part of the L.U.T. fleet, they retained their title and fleet numbers, together with a large white triangle on the dash inscribed "Eight Wheel Brakes". Although shedded at Sutton, they were used almost entirely on the Croydon-Mitcham service in Company days.

Disposal

When L.C.C. cars took over the West Croydon-Mitcham service in December 1933, these cars worked on the Sutton route alongside some of the Company's own cars. In due course, several were repainted in London Transport livery, receiving numbers appropriate to their place in the "U" Class. First, No. 269 appeared numbered 2376 painted in the UndergrounD Group's later livery and later Nos. 2382 (276), 2396 (293), and 2401 (299) were noted in the full London Transport red livery, working on the Sutton Route. Only six were at Sutton latterly, 2376 (269), 2382 (276), 2384 (278), 2393 (290), 2396 (293), and 2401 (299). When the Sutton route was converted to trolleybuses in December 1935, they were transferred to Stonebridge Park Depot, and thus worked on all three company's lines in turn. Nos. 2376, 2384 and 2401 later worked from Hendon. They were withdrawn for scrapping in July 1936, when the ex-Metropolitan "Western Area" was converted to trolleybus operation.

Unnumbered Water Car—built by BRUSH ELECTRICAL ENGINEERING Co. Ltd., at Loughborough in 1902.

Dimensions:— Overall length ?
Water tank capacity 2000 gallons.
Brush HD2 type controllers.
Truck—Brush "A" type 5 ft. 6 in. wheelbase.
Motors—Brush 1000A (25 horse power).
Braking—Hand and rheostatic.

When the 15 passenger cars were passed over from the "Croydon District Tramways", this water car came with them to the South Metropolitan system, in 1906.

Ex-London United No. 2401, in London Transport livery (ex-299) waiting to enter Sutton terminal stub when S.M.E.T. No. 2 pulls out. 21 August 1935. (Photo by O. J. Morris

143

According to the late Walter Gratwicke, it closely resembled the car supplied to Middleton Electric tramways and numbered 21, which was illustrated in "The Tramways of South-East Lancashire" on page 53. Namely, a short wheelbase car with a level floor, full length platforms and a cylindrical water tank enclosed in a short body with full length roof covering the platforms and supported by handrails at the corners. There was a slightly shortened "B/1" type trolley mast at the centre of the roof.

Presumably the full length platforms were provided so that street watering or snow sweeping equipment could be fitted according to the season of the year. Later, carborundum track brake blocks could have been fitted for rail grinding.

At the time of transfer the car was valued at £400.

It was said to be painted in an all-over medium green livery, with presumably the B.E.T. magnet and wheel badge on the side.

It was shedded at Sutton and does not appear to have seen a great deal of service. It disappeared from the South Metropolitan stock list not long before the company was absorbed into the UndergrounD Group. It is assumed that it passed to another undertaking in the B.E.T. Group.

After this the South Metropolitan tramways had no regular watering car, but from time to time, car No. 36 was taken out of service, fitted with carborundum blocks on the track brakes and barrels of water on the platforms. No. 36 was a good choice of car as it was suitable for use anywhere on the system. The writer saw it thus equipped at Selby Road around 1930.

After 1927, No. 19 was kept as a breakdown car at Sutton depôt. Welding equipment, etc., was borrowed from the L.U.T.

There was also a flat truck which could be towed by any of the passenger cars.

General Note on South Metropolitan Cars

Under the Defence Regulations of 1916, it became compulsary on tramcars working in the London area to dim the headlights and fit side lamps. (The latter seem to have been in general use on British trams only in London and Sheffield.) The plain glass in the head lamps were replaced by frosted glass and side lamps were fitted in small wooden boxes under the canopy edge of the single truck cars and near the top of the dash of the bogie cars (Type L). After the war, those on the four wheelers were replaced by rather neater small metal containers, not as elaborate as those used by the Corporation, but like them, the one nearest the stairs had a red bulb behind the white one, for use as a tail lamp (in circuit with the head lamp at the opposite end of the car).

The platform occupied by the driver was closed by a metal chain. Unlike those on the Corporation cars, it was not leather covered and clanged loudly against the grab rail as the car proceeded.

In the late 1920s, the loops at the bottom of the stair hand rails were removed and the holes left in the stanchions filled with pieces of wood shaped like champagne bottle corks.

Seat covers for the upper deck (a square of canvas fixed to the back of a seat which could be hooked over the next seat in front) were purchased for Nos. 36-51 in 1926 at £6-1-0d per car. In 1929, they were purchased for the rest of the fleet at £7-3-6d per car. (Inflation!)

By 1929, the whole of the operating fleet had B.T-H. B.2 type trolley masts which could be turned through the full circle and it was no longer necessary to indicate which way the trolley had to be turned. Trolley ropes were always kept tied.

After the war, small plain notice boards were fixed covering the elaborate lintel boards over the saloon doors. They usually carried a list of "First & Last Cars" on each route. Just below this and to the right there was a small metal container for folder maps, inscribed "Please take one", often covering the "No" of "No Smoking or Spitting Allowed". Below there was a small piece of metal with grooves cut in it for testing the thickness of counterfeit coins.

OTHER CARS WHICH WORKED IN CROYDON

It is not proposed to describe these in great detail, as most are now described in other works, dealing with the undertakings to which they belonged.

L.C.C. Class E.   Nos. 402-551 & 602-751. Built in 1906.

These were the first L.C.C. cars built with totally enclosed upper decks. They had Hurst, Nelson four windowed bodies, direct quarter turn stairs and both decks were of the same length, so that the front of the dash was level with the front of the upper deck. They were mounted on Mountain & Gibson maximum traction bogies. By the time they came to run through to Croydon on route 30, they had been painted red and given 2 & 1 cushioned seats in the lower deck, seating 71 passengers in all.

It was mainly cars from the 402-551 batch that worked on route 30, as nearly all of them had trolley poles; many of the 602-751 batch which worked in North London, were for conduit only. Several of those working on route 30, had the three signal lamps removed from the destination boxes to make room for three line blinds instead of two.

L.C.C. Class E/1.   Nos. 752-1426 & 1477-1676. First series 1907-1912.
                              Nos. 1727-1851.   Second series 1922.
                              Nos. 552-601.   Third series 1930.

These were an improved version of the E class, with the saloon slightly longer and double width corner pillars. As the upper deck was the same length as on the E class, the front of the dash was just beyond the front of the canopy and upper deck. When reseated and painted red, the capacity was 73 seated passengers. Like the E class, the first series had lifting platform steps, peculiar to the L.C.C. When a handle beside the brake staff was pulled up. the step lifted up by about six inches but did not fold. The majority had a single trolley pole, but a few had two. They had the change over switch for conduit/trolley operation under the stairs at one end only.

The second series had two trolley poles and folding platform steps (still operated by a handle). They also had side lifeguards to the platforms, those on the near side (rear) being attached to the backs of the folding steps. It was on the designs of this batch that the Croydon cars were based. They had change-over switches at both ends.

The third series were new bodies mounted on the trucks and with the motors and controllers from the former single deck Subway cars. The lower saloons were of timber construction and differed from the second series only in having a double width pillar between the centre windows as well as at the ends. Although similar in appearance to the earlier cars, the upper decks were of all metal construction and they had large route number stencils like the Croydon cars and some had three line destination boxes. As they retained the motors intended for single deck cars, they were rather slow. Nos. 582-584 were transferred from Leyton to Thornton Heath Depôt in October 1936, to work on route 30 and 552-556 followed.

E/1 class cars of the first and second series worked on route 16/18 from Telford Avenue depot, serving Croydon from 1926 onwards. Latterly most of the second series were transferred to Clapham Depot. The ex-L.C.C. cars "rehabilitated" were in all respects similar to the ex-Croydon ones already described. One of the prototypes, No. 1001 was shedded at Thornton Heath for a time, around 1935. The others rarely worked to Croydon except during the period when West Norwood Depôt had to supply two cars on route 16/18.

L.C.C. Class E/3.   Nos. 160 & 1904-2003 built in 1931.
                              Nos. 161-210 built in 1932 on behalf of Leyton
                              Corporation.

These were an improved version of the E/1 Class (an E/2 class failed to materialize). They had all metal bodies, with no tumble-home and the upper decks were like those of the third series E/1s. They had turn-over cushion seats on both decks from the start, seating 74. The bogies were similar to those of the E/1s but more robust. They always had body mounted plough carriers with change-over switches under the stairs at both ends.

No. 160 was intended to have been an HR/2 class car on equal wheel bogies but the bogies supplied with it were used for the experimental car No. 1. As it lacked trolley poles, it could never work through to Croydon. It was mounted on a spare pair of E/3 bogies.

Nos. 1904-2003 were delivered without vestibule windscreens, but received metal framed windscreens after a few months. (Several damaged during the war had them replaced by standard timber framed screens.) Nos. 161-210 were delivered already fitted with metal framed screens and were nominally the property of Leyton Corporation, whose tramways were then worked by the L.C.C. Later they were used indiscriminately with the others.

In December 1939, Nos. 1904-1921 were transferred from Hackney depôt to Thornton Heath depôt to take over the Thornton Heath branch line from the elderly E/1 class cars which had replaced the Croydon old bogie cars, thus giving the typical suburban, but profitable route, rather more luxeury than might have been expected. In fact, they and the ex-Croydon E/1s were worked indiscriminately on routes 16/18 and 42. 197 was at Thornton Heath early in 1940.

Ex-Walthamstow Corporation Nos. 2042-2053 built in 1927.
Nos. 2054-2061 built in 1932.

Nos. 2042-2053 were built by Hurst, Nelson for Walthamstow Corporation immediately prior to those for Croydon and were almost identical. The only noticable differences were that although the upper decks were shorter than the lower decks (like the L.C.C. & Croydon cars), the canopy bends were not and projected. They had large controllers and lower dashes than the Croydon cars.

The second batch 2054-2061 were built by Brush and were similar to the first batch but were delivered with metal framed windscreens and plough carriers on the underframe. Nos. 2048 were transferred to Telford Avenue depôt in September 1939 and 2049-2061 in November. In power and acceleration they were considered comparable with the Feltham class cars. In November 1942, 2050 and 2061 were loaned to Thornton Heath depot for three months, while 2044 and 2051 were war casualties in August 1944. All Walthamstow cars left Telford Avenue Depot for New Cross on 30 September 1950.

L.C.C.   No. 1. Built 1932.

This car was a prototype designed and built at Charlton Works. As already recounted it had the equal wheel bogies intended for No. 160 and four motors. The metal body had a domed roof, separate cabs for the driver, platform doors, folding steps and luxurious internal appointments. It had two trolley poles and underframe mounted plough carrier.

As built it was painted dark navy blue and ivory, in a streamlined style with very light grey trucks and life guards. It had air brakes and seated 66 passengers in considerable comfort. It was originally shedded at Holloway Depôt.

In March 1938, No. 1 was painted red and decked out with the usual advertisements. It was then transferred to Telford Avenue depôt, from which it made the famous Waltham Cross-Purley run on Sunday 15 May, after which it worked regularly on route 16/18. It was stored at the back of Telford Avenue depôt during the war, but overhauled and put back into service again afterwards.

It was sold to Leeds Corporation in April 1951, to replace one of the two Feltham type cars destroyed in a fire in October 1950. When Leeds trams were abandoned, it was displayed on the British Transport Museum at Clapham and has since been moved to the Tramway Museum at Crich, where it awaits proper restoration.

Ex-Metropolitan   Nos. 2066-2119 built in 1930-31.   **Type UCC**
Ex-London United   Nos. 2120-2165 built in 1930-31.

These were the famous "Feltham" type cars built by the Union Construction Company at Feltham, Middlesex.

They were long cars with 6½ side windows, extended driver's cabs which were slightly raised above the level of the saloon floor and domed roofs. They had double folding doors at the rear and a single exit door near the front. They had two trolley poles and were mounted on maximum traction bogies with roller bearing axle boxes (except No. 2165). There was a two line inset destination box in front with a small route number box either side of it, with inset side lamps below.

The Metropolitan and London United Felthams looked identical but had different electrical equipments. As delivered and running in Company service, only the Metropolitan Felthams were equipped to run on the conduit, with a plough carrier on the underframe between the bogies and a change-over switch inside the driver's cab at one end only.

The Uxbridge route on which the London United Felthams worked was converted to trolleybus operation on 15 November 1936 and the 46 Felthams, now fitted with plough carriers were transferred to Telford Avenue depôt from which they regularly worked on route 16/18 and others.

The L.U.T. Felthams were followed by the ex-Metropolitan Felthams to Telford Avenue, early in 1938. They already had conduit gear and did not require modification.

Only two Felthams were actual war casualties, 2109 and 2113, but 2067, 2091, 2122, 2130, 2163 and 2165 were scrapped as the result of post-war accidents, while 2144 and 2162 were burned out at Brixton Hill on 18 November 1950. As overhauled the rest lost their dash mounted stop lights and off-side route numbers. The remaining 90 were sold to Leeds as they could be spared during 1950/51.

Ex-Metropolitan   No. 2167 built in 1929.

This was the only prototype for the Felthams to survive and be tranferred to Telford Avenue. The most obvious way in which it differed from the production batch, was that the cabs were not raised. It was broken up at Purley in November 1949, for lack of spare parts.

Feltham type car No. 2159, at Coombe Road crossing, South Croydon. Either side of this crossing were Croydon's only centre posts.   (Photo D. A. Thompson

LIVERIES

Croydon Corporation Tramways

(a) 1901-1927

The colours adopted for the first delivery of cars to Croydon Corporation, were officially described as "Munich Lake & Ivory". Munich Lake was a name favoured by Milnes for a dark chocolate, with little or no trace of red in it, probably made up from a mixture of black and yellow. The ivory was quite a pale shade. Munich Lake was applied to the waist panels, dashes, stair stringers, cantrails and the corresponding positions on the bulkheads. The main side panels of the decency boards on the upper decks were also Munich Lake edged ivory. The rocker panels and window frames together with the corresponding parts of the end bulkheads were ivory also the decency panels over the canopies.

The Munich Lake parts were lined out with a double gold line, divided into three separate panels on the waist panel. At first this lining had plain square corners, but on some cars later the inner line had elaborate scroll-like corners and some did not have the three separate panels. The rocker panels had a thick black line with square corners and a thin orange coloured inner line. The title "Croydon Corporation Tramways" and the number on the dash were gold shaded blue on silver. There was a single black line round the ivory parts on the upper deck.

Trucks, lifeguard gates and trays (except possibly the "Providence" lifeguards), platform bearers and platform step risers, stair risers, trolley masts, destination boxes and the interior of the dash and upper deck panels were painted a rich deep crimson colour and varnished. The upper deck seats were painted the same colour and their frames were black. Controllers dumb-irons, stair kick-plates and all hand rails (except where polished brass), were black. (A few cars had black sills.)

There were few modifications before 1927, but after advertisements were accepted in 1906, they did not normally fill every space on the upper deck and any empty spaces, whether main side or over the canopies would be painted Munich Lake with ivory edging. At first cars Nos. 1-35 had the B.E.T.'s blue and silver "Magnet & Wheel" badge on the bulkhead panel. Not long before the 1914-18 War, when cars were repainted, the shading to the external numerals was changed from blue on silver to red on silver as that was thought to go better with the coat of arms which was partly red on gold and silver. The shading to the lettering was changed at the same time. Robert Kearsley paint was used.

The Manager's name "Thomas Boyce Goodyer" appeared in script letters at the bottom right-hand corner of the rocker panel, with until 1906, the title "British Electric Traction Company Limited Lessees" in the left-hand corner.

Floors of both decks and of the platforms and steps were the usual grey.

(b) 1927-1928

The first batch of modern bogie cars was delivered late in 1927, painted in a dark red and ivory livery and a few of the older cars were repainted in that livery. The red was a rich carmine, dark but with no trace of brown, known as "Port Wine" red, was applied in the same places as the Munich Lake had been. The ivory was as before. There was a single black line with triple Greek key patterns in the corners on the waist panels. There was also a single black line on the dashes, stair stringers and rocker panels. The title "Croydon Corporation Tramways" appeared in gold letters shaded red on silver as before, with the manager's full name in small Roman letters in the right-hand corner.

Handrails, channel steel solebars and the interior of the dash were black, with class letters in small white figures in the lower right-hand corner of the solebar. (E/1 for modern bogie cars, B/1 for the old bogie cars and W/1 for the four wheelers). "A End" and "B End" was painted inside the dash. There was black edging between panels and on the upper deck decency panels. Collision fenders and controllers remained black.

Trucks, lifeguards, platform bearers, destination boxes and upper deck window sashes were oxide brown.

Cars included in this livery were Nos. 31-40, new bogie cars, 5 and 17 four wheelers (renumbered) and several of the old bogie cars.

(c) 1928-1933

The second batch of new bogie cars Nos. 41-55 were delivered in a similar livery, but the ivory was replaced by medium pearl grey. (This was a definite grey and not off white or the ivory gone dirty!) The black lining on the rocker panel was omitted, but the gold shaded lettering retained. All other features remained as in livery (b).

This livery was adopted for the old bogie cars as top covered and in due course applied to the rest of the fleet. All the old cars were renumbered concurrently with being painted red. In 1933, when London Transport took over the whole fleet was red and grey.

Works Car

The works car owned by the B.E.T. was said to have been painted a medium green; it was transferred to the South Metropolitan system in July 1906.

The replacement car acquired in 1907, was painted all over Munich Lake with gold lining and Croydon Corporation Tramways in small gold letters low down at the right-hand end each side. Presumably truck, collision fenders, life guards and trolley masts were in the usual colours.

When rebuilt as a welding car in 1916, it was painted light grey, with C.C.T. in a dark colour on the body side. There was a coat of arms on the dash where the head lamp should have been and a thin black line round the edge of the dash. This car was not numbered by the Corporation.

London Transport numbered it 056, fitted head lamps and painted it plain grey, with black truck, lifeguards, collision fenders, handrails etc. The number was in small unshaded gold figures, finely edged in black.

Croydon Coat of Arms

Croydon Corporation trams displayed the correct coat of arms for the County Borough of Croydon, as described below in non-heraldic language:—

The shield was divided into four quarters. The upper left quarter was silver with three black birds. Upper right was gold with three black daggers. Lower left was gold with a blue cross and lower right an "embattled wall" in red on silver. The four quarters were separated by double red rules or "frets". Above the shield, there was a silver helmet looking to the left, surmounted by the crest, a silver ball with blue wavy lines between two gold cornucopias. The mantle protruding either side of the helmet was red and silver and the motto, below, "Sanitate Crescamus" on a pink ribbon.

The arms of the new London Borough of Croydon are quite different, based only on the blue "Whitgift Cross" of the third quarter.

South Metropolitan Electric Tramways

The official livery first adopted was described as "Brunswick Green and cream". It was in fact a dark shade of holly green and pale ivory similar to the shade adopted by the Corporation. Waist panels, dashes, stair stringers, cantrails and the corresponding positions on the bulkhead were green. The rocker panels, window frames and decency panels round the upper deck were ivory, likewise the corresponding positions on the bulkhead and probably the platform ceilings. The interior of the dash, stair risers and the interior of the upper deck panelling are believed to have been painted light brown. Destination boxes and the opening light frames were in natural varnished unpainted wood.

The waist panels and dashes had a thick gold line with square corners and a thin inner line with a scroll pattern in each corner. There was also gold lining on the stair stringers and cantrail. The rocker panel had a thick black or sepia line and a thin orange inner line, both with square corners. There was the usual B.E.T. ′'Magnet & Wheel" badge with the full title round the edge in the centre of the waist panel, but unlike the "Croydon & District" badge, which was in the usual silver on blue, the South Metropolitan cars had the badge in black on gold. The full title of the company appeared on the rocker panel, taking up two lines on the single truck cars. It was in sans-serif capitals with blue on silver shading to the left. The numerals on the dash were in similar style. The Manager's name appeared in small script letters at the bottom right-hand corner of the rocker panel.

Trucks, platform bearers, lifeguards and the trolley mast were in oxide brown. Fenders, controllers, step kick plates, handrails and the wire mesh round the upper deck were black. Upper deck seats were natural wood, as was the strip round the top of the dash. There was some black edging.

Most cars retained this livery until after the 1914-18 War and Merton Atkins photographed No. 38 on 3 June 1923, noting that it remained in the full green livery until some time in 1924 and was the last car to do so. Some of the ex-Croydon & District cars stayed in the chocolate livery for a very long time, with only the number changed and the coat of arms replaced by the "Magnet & Wheel". On the same day as he photographed No. 38, Merton Atkins also photographed bogie car No. 27 still in chocolate and ivory and ex-Gravesend No. 30 in that undertaking's reddish brown and primrose, still with "Gravesend & Northfleet Electric Tramways" inscribed on the magnet. Probably, these cars were never painted green.

(b) 1916-1921

Any cars in urgent need of repainting, including Nos. 8 and 18, were repainted green and ivory as before, but with simpler lining with plain corners and without the "Magnet & Wheel" or lettering.

(c) 1921-1929

From about 1921, the company commenced painting cars in the UndergrounD Groups's red and broken white livery. The red was a very bright shade, signal red, probably on a white undercoat. "Broken White" was white to which a suspicion of grey had been added to counteract the yellowing effect of varnish. The red was applied where the green had been and the white where it had been ivory. The hoops over the ends of the upper deck, first used in 1916 were always white. Black parts were collision fenders, controllers, hand rails and wire mesh screens as before. Trucks, lifeguards, platform bearers, and trolley masts were still oxide brown, a rather dull shade, while destination boxes and dash interiors were light yellowish brown (stone colour), also the top-rail of the dash. Stair risers and the interior of the upper deck were grey.

There was still gold lining on the red parts. Corner designs varied and a dagger design was the most common. Numerals were in gold edged white and shaded black. There was a black outer line and a red inner line on the rocker panel, with statutory lettering in black. White panelling on the upper deck was edged black.

Upper deck seats were light brown with oxide frames.

(d) 1929-1933

The red and white livery was retained but a simpler style adopted. The area of white was increased to include the cantrail, the upper part of the bulkheads, handrails and the wire mesh screens of the upper deck. There was a single black line on the red dash and waist panels, with square corners. There was a single red line on the rocker panels and no other lining on the cars. On the MetropolitaN and London UniteD cars, the stair string became white, but not on the SouthmeT. The fleet title "SouthmeT" was adopted with this livery.

A number of cars appeared after overhaul bearing a compromise between liveries (c) and (d). Notably, some had yellow lining on the red parts instead of black. Most of the London United cars on loan had this feature. Rebuilt cars were painted in special liveries, see below:—

(e) Rebuilt cars 1929-1933

When cars Nos. 1-16 were rebuilt, they retained the white window frames, upper deck panelling, upper parts of the bulkhead and hand-rails. From just below the windows, down to and including the sole-bars were red, also the dashes. There was no lining, but black metal bands just over one inch deep below the windows and extended round the dash. There was another band at solebar level, also extending round the dash. Three similar bands extended right round the upper deck. Statutory lettering was in white. The car's number and type of braking were written in white on the controller (this was extended to the rest of the fleet with "No. 1 End" and "No. 2 End" inside the dash).

The destination boxes, trolley masts and interior of the upper deck were painted an attractive shade of dark green. Other cars partly rebuilt, had the green parts on the upper deck, but retained the ordinary 1929 livery for the rest of the car. All had retained the oxide brown trucks and lifeguards.

(f) London Transport—1933-1935

A number of cars were repainted in the Hendon version of the London Transport livery, with white window frames and cantrails, red below the windows, dashes and upper deck panelling. Trucks, lifeguards, handrails, upper deck wire mesh and trolley masts were black. There was a single yellow line round the dash and the large gold numerals with black shading were retained on all ex-SouthmeT cars.

Several of the J Type cars (Nos. 1-16) were repainted in this livery.

On the Crystal Palace route Nos. 36, 39, 40, 44 and 50 were painted in London Transport Livery with red rocker panels and black wire mesh deck screens. Only one of the rebuilt cars were repainted thus, No. 48 with red panelling round the upper deck where the wire screens had been. It looked quite revolting. "London TransporT" appeared in gold letters on the waist panel of all cars, from May 1934, irrespective of whether they were repainted in L.T. livery or not. No SouthmeT car was renumbered and all retained the large gold figures, shaded black, with the suffix "s" to the end. (it is believed that numbers in the 2000 series were allocated at one stage, but never applied to the cars).

Of the ex-Croydon Corporation cars transferred, Nos. 2 and 3 were repainted in livery (d) even with the white stair stringers and the numbers 346 and 347, in very small unshaded numerals. No. 1 was repainted slightly later in livery (f), but that too had white stair stringers. It became 345.

As already mentioned most of the ex-L.U.T. cars arrived on SouthmeT metals in a compromise livery, something between (c) and (d). Nos. 269 and 272 were at some stage repainted in livery (d). Later most were repainted in London Transport livery (f)

Of course the cars which ran through Mitcham from 1926 onwards were in standard L.C.C. livery and later in London Transport (Charlton) livery.

The separate "Charlton" and "Hendon" practices persisted, while Hendon continued to overhaul ex-Company cars and it is doubtful whether any ex-Metropolitan or London United standard cars (except Felthams) ever appeared with other than off-white window frames and single line route boards.

In the meantime. Charlton was developing a distinctive London Transport style for trams, based more on the L.C.C. style. Instead of "off-white", trams, trolleybuses and Underground Trains had the window frames and cantrails (both decks on trams) painted a rich cream and the rest of the bodywork was bright red. There was black edging between panels, but no lining except a yellow line round the dash, on which the car's number appeared in small black edged but gold figures. The title and address of the undertaking appeared in small black letters on the left-hand corner of the rocker panel and "London TransporT" in gold letters on the waist panel of course in Johnston type.

The interior of the dash, collision fenders and handrails were black, but when the L.C.C. built the new No. 1, they evidently acquired a large quantity of light grey paint for its trucks. London Transport continued to paint trucks and lifeguards of cars overhauled at Charlton, in this light grey until it was used up, then black was adopted and retained throughout the remaining life of the trams. Even the Felthams were painted in this livery when overhauled at Charlton and of course ex-Croydon 375-399.

Croydon Corporation Tramways—Staff Uniforms

The horse tram crews were not provided with uniforms, but drivers normally wore bowler hats and leather aprons, to protect their clothing when walking the horses round the car and from rubbing against the dash of the car.

At first when the Croydon Tramways were electrified and worked by the British Electric Traction Co., they provided and kitted out the staff. Drivers and conductors wore blue serge suits, with red piping on the collar, cap and trouser leg. The top button of the jacket was undone, showing a white shirt and black tie. Drivers often wore white chokers (scarves). The brass cap badges were in the form of the B.E.T. "Magnet & Wheel" device, which also appeared on the brass jacket buttons. White cap covers were worn in the summer. The Croydon staff paraded in front of one of the bogie cars in Thornton Heath depôt yard, formed the subject of an advertisement for H. Lotery & Co., for many years.

Inspectors wore similar uniforms, made of better quality material and without red piping.

When the Corporation took over operation in June 1906, a new set of uniforms was ordered. They were generally similar to the above, but Mr. Goodyer designed a new cap badge, comprising the coat of arms of Croydon within a wreath and executed in brass. The coat of arms was embossed on the buttons and inspectors had cloth cap badges, with gold thread and the shield in its correct colours. In one feature, Croydon was almost unique; throughout the era of Corporation ownership, drivers continued to wear the black leather aprons, inherited from the horse tramways and conductors often wore black leather leggings. Conductor's tunics had leather cuffs and drivers were issued with heavy overcoats for winter use. Unlike the L.C.C., goggles were not an issue.

In 1917, Motormen and Conductors were issued with new caps, with yellow plaited straw tops. These were covered by black waterproof covers in the winter. With these caps, the large brass badges disappeared and embossed buttons were worn in their place. Tunics were worn with one more button undone exposing more of the shirt. These uniforms were retained until after 1933.

Because of the very exposed platforms of the old bogie cars, drivers of these vehicles were issued with voluminous oiled waterproof capes and "Sou'wester" hats for use in inclement weather. All drivers had heavy leather gauntlets and conductors carried cash pouches and Bell punches on leather harnesses.

South Metropolitan Tramways—Staff Uniforms

Throughout the period that the B.E.T. controlled the South Metropolitan Company, the uniforms of their staff did not differ from those issued to Croydon staff when under B.E.T. management. They retained the "Magnet & Wheel" cap badges, but additionally wore brass collar dogs in the form of the letters SMET. Some motormen on the Crystal Palace route even wore black leather aprons, perhaps purchased second-hand from Corporation staff.

When the UndergrounD Group took control, the cut of the uniform was slightly different, but the red piping remained and a cap badge in the form of a dark blue and silver "Bar & Circle" with "TramwayS" written across the bar was used by all three companies. The collar dogs remained. In 1930, experiments were made with different shaped white plastic or celluloid strips let into the cuffs of conductor's jackets for signalling in traffic. Eventually a triangle was adopted. The UndergrounD Group had a liking for large men, and SMET staff were generally a better physique than the Corporation counterparts.

Drivers had double breasted overcoats for winter wear and inspectors wore similar overcoats, with plain buttons and of a better quality material. They had SMET collar dogs and small silver cap badges. As with the Corporation, inspector's uniforms did not have red piping. Drivers and conductors wore white cap covers from 1 May to 1 October each year.

London's tramways all employed women conductors during both world wars and in 1916, both Croydon Corporation and the S.M.E.T. took on women conductors dressed in large floppy hats, jackets and long skirts.

London Transport—Staff Uniforms

When London Transport took over in July 1933, the different uniforms worn by staff of the various undertakings taken over, were gradually replaced by UndergrounD style uniforms, even to the white cap covers and the dates beween which they had to be worn. The "Bar & Circle" cap badge was retained, but with "London TransporT" on the bar and in different colours for each of the services— that for trams and trolleybuses was silver on red. In the case of inspectors, the circle was flanked by "Couchant" griffins, in gold for senior inspectors and silver for junior inspectors.

At different stages during the war, women conductors were issued with blue serge uniforms with skirts and soft caps or light-weight grey uniforms with a choice of skirts or trousers and soft peaked caps or berets. The grey uniforms continued in use after the war, as women conductors were not dispensed with as they were immediately after the 1914-1918 War.

Metropolitan Stage Carriage Badges

Police authorities throughout the country have always insisted that bus drivers and conductors should be licenced by them and wear some sort of badge to prove it. In the London area alone, the Public Carriage Office, which is controlled by the Police, insisted that tram drivers and conductors must be similarly licenced.

The "Badge" issued on an applicant's credentials being checked, consisted of an oval enamelled iron plate about 5 in. by 3½ in. Originally with a crown and black or white lettering on a solid colour, blue for tram drivers and brown for conductors (buses had red and green respectively). The badges had a number in the centre and had to be returned at the termination of their validity. Later the crown was omitted and the centre part coloured white, with the edges coloured as before. In that style, the inscription round the edge read "Public Service Vehicle—Driver", etc. These heavy metal badges were worn on a leather thong fixed to one of the buttons of the jacket.

From the beginning of 1935, the metal badges were replaced by smaller plastic ones, circular in shape and worn in the buttonhole. The colours and information on them were as before. Trolleybuses counted as trams.

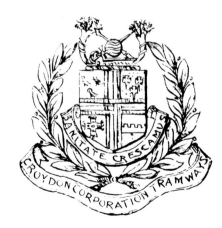

The original drawings by Mr. Goodyer for button and cap badge.

153

Trackwork

Little is known about the rails supplied for the first opening of horse tramways in Croydon in 1878. They were probably of the light cast iron type, favoured in the early days. It is known that the rails used for the 1881 extensions, were 66 lbs. per yard steel rail, 5½ inches high 1 5/8 inch running surface, one inch groove and half inch flange on top. In section, they resembled the later electric tram rails. Similar rails were used by the Croydon & Norwood Co. and evidently thought suitable for steam traction. The short connecting line between North End and the High Street had 75 lbs. to the yard rolled steel rails, which survived electrification.

For electrification in 1901, 7 inch high rails weighing 95½ lbs. per yard were supplied by Walter Scott Ltd., of Leeds, with "Phoenix" joints held by 2 foot fishplates. Pointwork was supplied by Askham Bros. & Wilson Ltd., of Sheffield (later, from 1906 Edgar Allen & Co.) There were movable tongues in both rails. The old horse tram rails were cut up and used as sleepers (several were dug up in George Street recently). The track was laid on a concrete foundation 6 inches deep. Most of the road surface was made up of wood blocks, but at George Street corner and other places of considerable traffic, basaltic lava setts were used, as they were found to be less slippery than granite.

For later extensions Hadfield's and Lorain pointwork was used.

In 1923/24, the main line from Norbury to Purley was relaid with heavier rails suitable for the L.C.C. covered top cars, which weighed more than any of the Corporation's own cars.

The track for the South Metropolitan Company was laid by Brush, Dick, Kerr Ltd. and William Griffiths Ltd. The rails were supplied by the North Eastern Steel Co. Ltd., of Middlesbrough, Walter Scott Ltd. and Charles Owen Ltd. They were in 45 ft. lengths weighing 95 lbs. per yard and similar to those supplied to the Corporation. There were Lahmeyer's "Neptune" bonds between the rails and mild steel plates under the joints on the Penge section. Again there was a six inch bed of concrete and most of the paving was in wood blocks. Both systems were laid to standard gauge.

Electrical Installations

As the whole system was planned and constructed by British Thomson-Houston Ltd., of Rugby, it is impossible to separate the Corporation and South Metropolitan supply systems. The Corporation already had a Power Station in Factory Lane, Pitlake, off the Mitcham Road. It was equipped by B.T-H., who installed additional equipment to feed the trams. This comprised three direct current 500 volt, 300 kw generators, with Bellis steam engines, to which were added in 1906, a Dick, Kerr 1,000 kw set. This supplied to the whole of the Corporation system through three sub-stations. It also supplied the South Metropolitan lines within the Borough of Croydon, there being separate switch-boards for the Corporation and the Company.

The Company's lines in Penge were fed from the Beckenham Council Power Station in Churchfields Road. The parts of the Sutton and Tooting routes outside Croydon were fed from the Company's own Power Station in Langley Road, Sutton, with two turbo-generators of 250 kw supplied by C. A. Parsons Ltd.

Included in the original contract were B.T-H. "C" type section feeder cabinets of plain design, to be placed on the pavement alongside traction posts. They had small knobs on top and the B.T-H. monogram low down on the door. This pattern continued to be used by the South Metropolitan Company.

After 1906, the Corporation used similar cabinets, with a smaller knob on top and the coat of arms on the upper part of the door, instead of the B.T-H. monogram. There were two different versions of the coat of arms. Several of these cabinets still exist in Croydon, in locations away from the former tramways and are presumably used in connection with street lighting.

As the system was originally laid out, Croydon Corporation used only traction posts with bracket suspension, with the short bracket "open sky" arrangement between Norbury and West Croydon and brackets of varying length for the rest. The scrollwork supporting the bracket arms was slightly more ornate than usual and the "whorl" in the centre curved in the opposite direction to most others. They were supplied by James Russell & Sons of Wednesbury, but in Great Britain, only used by Hull and Croydon. They had fluted bases bearing the coat of arms and ball and spike finials, the spike was very tall and slender. The Corporation insisted that identical posts were used on the running lines of that part of the South Metropolitan system that lay within the Borough of Croydon. Simpler scrollwork was used on the depot approach in Aurelia Road. There was some bracket suspension on the Sutton route in Wallington, using scrollwork of the Greenwood and Batley design, like many other British systems. For the most part, the South Metropolitan Company used span wire with traction posts on both sides of the road, with massive octagonal section bases, short cross-arms with a little scrollwork and "wreath & spear" finials.

When the Corporation relaid their track on the main line in the 1920s, the L.C.C. insisted on span-wire overhead layout. The new traction poles retained the fluted bases and had small ball shaped finials, but were otherwise unadorned. In the same period the South Metropolitan dispensed with much of the scrollwork and substituted plain turned wood, ball or cone shaped finials. London Transport used plain concrete bases cast on the spot and finials in the form of a pressed steel ball for both trams and trolleybuses. Traction poles in the Croydon area were always painted dark green. The Corporation ones faded to a bluish shade.

Both undertakings used ordinary "Wood's" swivel trolley heads.

Unusual features included, after 1925, centre posts either side of the Coombe Road crossing in South Croydon. They remained carrying traffic lights long after the trams had disappeared. A little further down, the post on a traffic island in front of the "Swan & Sugar Loaf" was remarkable for the number of appendages it carried. It formed a vent for the toilet under the island and had a suitable cowl on top, a toilet sign, an inn sign, a street lamp on a bracket, a tram stop sign and at one time a car park sign. Most remarkably, the pole is still standing, complete with scroll work and many of the above appendages.

Before the one way working at Spurgeon's Bridge was given up, the two wires crossed over each other then ran parallel for a short distance before diverging. There was an additional wire between Oakfield Road and West Croydon Station and the presence of a trolley on that wire, automatically set the points for Station Road. Although at one time there were Turner's automatic points at Thornton Heath Pond, latterly the pointsman there was expected to perform gymnastics, pulling the point lever with one hand and a cord for the overhead points with the other. London transport provided a canvas tent for him, replacing a small hut.

Signs and Notices

Originally, stops on the Corporation system were indicated by coloured bands round the traction posts, white for a fixed stop and white and red for a request stop. Soon after the Corporation took over operation themselves small shields fixed high up on and partly wrapped round the posts were used. From 1926, when through running with the L.C.C. commenced, their practices had to be adopted, with flag type signs about one foot square fixed just above head level on the posts. They were red or blue with white and black lettering.

Notices inside the car, prohibiting smoking or spitting were in gold Roman letters about one inch high with very dark blue shading, back shaded light blue on silver. The car's number on the bulkhead was in similar style as were the notices on the upper deck. On the back of the destination box, there was written "Smokers are requested to occupy the rear seats" and "Spitting Prohibited" appeared near the top of the trolley mast. "When travelling in Direction of Arrow" ⟶ "Pull cord this side" appeared just above the windows of the saloon on the older cars. Faretables were pasted onto the offside bulkhead windows, and were in the traditional municipal style, with the coat of arms at the top and lettering of ever

155

decreasing size from top to bottom. They were printed in black and white, but at one stage, a map of the system was faintly printed in colour as a background. Sometimes, notices in red and blue on white card were hung in the windows.

When the cars were repainted in the new livery in the late 1920s, the gold lettering inside, was usually replaced by plain black and on the through route, Corporation type fare tables were replaced by L.C.C. graphic type tables in blue and red on creamy white paper.

The South Metropolitan Company originally used shield shaped stop signs like the Corporation, but when they came into the UndergrounD Group, they used cream coloured flag type enamelled iron signs with black lettering and curved tops to take the bar and circle device.

Owing to the varied origins of the cars and alterations made on acquisition, the lettering inside South Metropolitan cars was rather a jumble of styles. Those prohibiting smoking and spitting were originally in gold shaded blue, like the Corporation; others were in plain black Roman capitals and the Metropolitan Stage Carriage and capacity notices were traditionally in script. Fleet numbers on the bulkhead were gold shaded black.

After the UndergrounD Group took over, it was decreed in 1916, by Frank Pick, that all notices of any sort must be Johnston's sans serif capitals, which had been specially designed at his behest. From then on, any car that was completely stripped down, had to have all lettering renewed in that style usually in plain black, but sometimes in white on a dark colour. The Johnston alphabet has been retained by London Transport to this day and even includes fleet numbers. They have retained the copyright.

Street Furniture

Traction poles, feeder cabinets and stop signs have already been mentioned. The Corporation provided large glazed and illuminated signs, with lists of principal stopping places at several places in the centre of the town and fixed to traction posts. They did not provide any shelters. As mentioned in the main text, the Company provided shelters at the Crystal Palace and at the "Blue House", Mitcham. There was an inspector's sentry box at the "Robin Hood".

CAUTION

Passengers must remain seated whilst the car is passing under railway bridges

RIDING ON PLATFORM PROHIBITED. WAIT UNTIL THE CAR STOPS.

NO DOGS ALLOWED ON LOWER DECK.

L.C.C.-type stop sign used latterly by Croydon (blue for compulsory and red for request stops). The other illustrations are of enamelled iron notices on S.M.E.T. cars.

156

CHAPTER EIGHT

FARES AND TICKETS by A. W. McCall

With both Croydon and the South Metropolitan Electric Tramways operating routes on their own as well as jointly, plus the incursion into the field at a later date by the London County Council, has always involved the area in a somewhat complicated structure of fares and tickets.

The Corporation, on the Norbury—Purley main line, plus the Thornton Heath and Addiscombe branches and the South Metropolitan on the Tooting and Sutton routes, were self-contained, but on the Penge and Crystal Palace (High Level) routes, the two systems were more or less merged. It is perhaps best, therefore, to deal with the subject in three parts as follows:—

(1) The routes solely operated by the Corporation.
(2) The routes solely operated by the South Metropolitan.
(3) The joint working across the boundary at Selby Road.

First of all, however, the fare and ticket system used on the horse lines of the Croydon Tramways Company must be considered.

CROYDON TRAMWAYS COMPANY

In common with the majority of horse tram routes, the fare scale used by this company was very simple. An all-the-way fare of twopence with a penny stage to or from an approximately halfway point applied to the Addiscombe, Norwood and Thornton Heath routes, whilst a penny maximum was imposed between Croydon High Street and "The Red Deer", South Croydon. During the period when through cars were operating, the following fare table applied:—

South Norwood (Portland Road)	—	"Gloucester Tavern"*	1d.
Selhurst Station	—	Crown Hill	1d.
"Gloucester Tavern"	—	East Croydon Station	1d.
East Croydon Station	—	Addiscombe (The Alma)	1d.
South Norwood (Portland Road)	—	Crown Hill	2d.
Selhurst Station	—	East Croydon Station	2d.
"Gloucester Tavern"	—	Addiscombe (The Alma)	2d.
South Norwood (Portland Road)	—	Addiscombe (The Alma)	3d.

Shortly after the Corporation acquired the system in 1899, the following fares were in operation:—

Thornton Heath—South Croydon (Red Deer) Section:—				*Distance:—*
Thornton Heath Terminus	—	Thornton Heath Pond	1d.	One Mile
Thornton Heath Station	—	Stanley Road	1d.	One Mile
Thornton Heath Pond	—	West Croydon Station	1d.	1⅛ miles
Stanley Road	—	"The Greyhound"	1d.	1⅛ miles
West Croydon Station	—	"Swan & Sugar Loaf"	1d.	One Mile
"The Greyhound"	—	"The Red Deer"	1d.	1¼ miles
Thornton Heath Terminus	—	"The Greyhound"	2d.	2½ miles
Thornton Heath Pond	—	"The Red Deer"	2d.	2¾ miles
Thornton Heath Terminus	—	"The Red Deer"	3d.	3¾ miles

Norwood Junction—Addiscombe Section:—				
Norwood Junction (Portland Road)	—	"Gloucester Tavern"	1d.	1 18 miles
Selhurst Station	—	Crown Hill	1d.	1½ miles
"Gloucester Tavern"	—	East Croydon Station	1d.	1⅜ miles
West Croydon Station	—	Ashburton Road	1d.	1¾ miles
Norwood Junction (Portland Road)	—	Crown Hill	2d.	2⅜ miles
Selhurst Station	—	East Croydon Station	2d.	1¾ miles
"Gloucester Tavern"	—	Ashburton Road	2d.	2½ miles
Norwood Junction (Portland Road)	—	Ashburton Road	3d.	4⅜ miles

* In electric tram days "The Gloucester Tavern" was always known as "The Gloster". Its name reverted to "Gloucester" when rebuilt after the 1941 blitz.

Croydon horse tram ticket, and early Corporation electric tram tickets.
(Omnibus Society Collection. Courtesy R. J. Durrant

In the early days of operation, the tickets in use were the fore-runners of the Bell Punch type, although the punch itself had not yet been invented. Early issues had the stages printed diagonally across the corners, the ticket being perforated below each farestage. Issue of the ticket was indicated by the appropriate corner being torn off before the ticket was handed to the passenger. During the later 1890's the Bell type punch was used instead of tearing the corner, and, following the experimental period in which these punches were used, the more standard type of ticket with stage names along the edges came into use. Punches were hired from the Ticket Punch & Register Co. Ltd. Tickets were of the usual thin card.

CROYDON CORPORATION TRAMWAYS

When the Croydon Tramways Company was taken over by the Corporation and leased to the British Electric Traction Company, no alteration in fares took place whilst the horse cars were still operating, but, with the introduction of electric traction and the extension to Norbury, a complete revision of fares took place. The first faretable of this period was:—

```
Norbury Terminus
—  Thornton Heath Terminus
1  1    Thornton Heath Pond
1  1   1    West Croydon Station
2  1   1   1    "The Greyhound"
2  2   1   1   1    "The Swan"
3  2   2   1   1   1    "The Red Deer"
4  3   3   2   2   2   1    Purley
```

A penny Workman's Single ticket was available up to 7.30 a.m. on any journey to or from "The Greyhound". At the same time, the maximum fare on the Addiscombe and Norwood branches was reduced to one penny, and transfer fares were inaugurated, these being the first of what was to become a most comprehensive facility. These early transfers were between Thornton Heath High Street and Norbury (change at Thornton Heath Pond); Norwood and "The Greyhound" (change at West Croydon Station); West Croydon Station or "The Swan and Sugar Loaf" and Addiscombe Station (change at Crown Hill). All the transfers were at one penny. Even cheaper fares came into operation during 1903, when the through fare from Norbury to Purley was reduced to threepence, with a corresponding reduction in the fare between Norbury and South Croydon (Red Deer) from threepence to twopence.

The Corporation followed the same colour scheme for tickets as its Company predecessors, namely, 1d. White; 2d. Magenta and 3d. Blue for the single tickets. In addition, there was a 1d. Workman Single (Primrose); 1d. Transfer (White) and 1d. Transfer Exchange Ticket (Pink). With the exception of the title, all these tickets were identical with those issued by the Company. All transfer tickets were collected on the second car and an Exchange Ticket issued in lieu.

With the exception of the introduction of a twopenny Workman Return, which was available to and from "The Greyhound" (as was the 1d. Workman Single ticket), no other fare alteration took place until the takeover of operation by the Corporation itself. The fare on the Addiscombe and Norwood routes remained at one penny from Crown Hill to Addiscombe and between West Croydon and Norwood (Selby Road). On the main line, 1½d. and 2½d. fares were introduced as follows:—

1½d. Fares:—Norbury Terminus and "The Greyhound"
     Warwick Road and "The Swan and Sugar Loaf"
     Broad Green   and "The Windsor Castle"
     West Croydon Stn. and "The Royal Oak"
     "The Greyhound" and Purley Terminus

2½d. Fares:—Norbury Terminus and "The Royal Oak"
     Warwick Road and Purley Terminus
     Thornton Heath Terminus and Purley.

The scope of the transfer facility was considerably widened at this time, 1½d. transfers being added, together with a number of additional one penny ones, including one that was unique in that it involved the use of three tramcars. This was a penny fare between East Croydon Station and "The Gloster" on the Norwood Route, with change points at Crown Hill and West Croydon Station. A special two-coupon ticket, blue in colour, was used for this transfer. It was punched on issue in the top coupon on the right or left, according to the direction of travel. Handed intact to the conductor of the second car, he then punched the lower coupon, tearing off and retaining the first coupon to account for the punch registration. On the third car, the lower coupon was retained and an Exchange Ticket issed in lieu. All other transfer tickets were of the full geographical type of layout at first, including the boarding, transfer and alighting points, with the Exchange tickets being a replica of the Transfer ticket concerned. Later the transfer point was left out, and in a later form still, only the destination of the passenger was indicated. Whilst in this stage, an instruction book was issued to all conductors and inspectors, containing full details of all transfer fares available, where they were to be issued, and at which points they were to be accepted. Also in the book was the following instruction, set in heavy type:—

"Conductors must call out all transfer points, and every line that can be transferred to at each point, and also speak loudly enough so that passengers in every part of the car can hear and understand every word said".

The full list of transfers available was:—

Change at Thornton Heath Pond

Norbury Terminus	and Thornton Heath Terminus	1d.

Change at West Croydon Station

Broad Green	and "The Gloster"	1d.
Selby Road	and "The Greyhound"	1d.
Portland Road (Norwood)	and "The Swan and Sugar Loaf" ..	1½d.
Selhurst Station	and South Croydon ("Red Deer")	1½d.
"The Gloster"	and "The Windsor Castle"	1½d.
"The Gloster"	and "The Swan and Sugar Loaf" ..	1d.

Change at West Croydon and Crown Hill

"The Gloster"	and East Croydon Station	1d.

Change at Crown Hill

Warwick Road (Norbury)	and East Croydon Station	1½d.
Thornton Heath Terminus	and East Croydon Station	1½d.
Thornton Heath Pond	and East Croydon Station	1d.
Thornton Heath Pond	and Addiscombe Terminus	1½d.
West Croydon Station	and Adsdiscombe Terminus	1d.
Addiscombe Terminus	and "The Swan and Sugar Loaf" ..	1d.
Addiscombe Terminus	and South Croydon ("Red Deer")	1½d.

Apart from the double transfer ticket mentioned earlier, all transfer tickets bore an overprinted code letter to indicate the day of issue, but in later days this was replaced by a skeleton overprint letter "T" instead of the day code. The colours used for the Transfer tickets were 1d. Buff and 1½d. Green, and for the appropriate Exchange tickets, 1d. Pink and 1½d. Grey.

From 31 July 1909 through fares were instituted between the Croydon cars and the London County Council trams at Norbury, the fare point from which they were issued in the Croydon area being Warwick Road, which had by that time become a fare stage in the regular Croydon Farescale, and transfers were issued at one penny to Greyhound Lane (Streatham Common), 1½d. to Streatham Hill Station and 2d. to New Park Road (Brixton Hill). All the fares quoted were the appropriate fare from Norbury on the L.C.C. system, plus a halfpenny.

Later Croydon Corporation and Croydon/L.C.C. through tickets.
(Omnibus Society Collection. Courtesy R. J. Durrant

When a Croydon ticket was accepted on an L.C.C. car, the conductor retained it, issuing a normal single fare ticket for the L.C.C. portion of the journey, the Croydon ticket being counted as cash for its face value less one halfpenny. When an L.C.C. ticket was accepted on a Croydon car, it was retained, and a special Exchange Ticket, sage in colour, and available only between Norbury and Warwick Road, was issued. For the 1d. and 1½d. Transfer fares from the Croydon area, the appropriate stage was included at the bottom of the Ordinary Transfer tickets, but, as no 2d. transfer fare then existed in the Croydon area, special provision was made for the relative section at the foot of the 2d. Ordinary Single ticket. These Croydon—L.C.C. Transfer fares remained in force until 18 June 1918, when they were withdrawn in the spate of economies.

Up to 1917, there had been no reduced fares for children, but, in the early part of that year, the Council asked the Tramways Committee to consider reduced fares for children travelling some distance to school. "The Electric Railway and Tramway Journal" in its issue dated 20 April 1917 stated that the Tramways Committee had reported back to the Council that they were against the reduced fares at that time. Upon hearing this, the Council referred the matter back for reconsideration, but without success, as the "Journal" in its issue dated 11 May 1917, stated that the Croydon Town Council have adopted the Tramway Committee recommendation that half-fares for children be not adopted. The issue for 19 October 1917 reports that the Tramways Committee have authorised the Manager to put into service any additional early morning cars to Purley, which he may deem advisable. They also agreed to the issue of twopenny Return tickets issued up to 7.30 a.m. only, but available for return on any car at any time of the day of issue. These tickets were only available over certain farestages.

Other than the item mentioned above, the actual war period did not cause much alteration to fares, but following its conclusion, gradually the former cheap farescale increased, mainly by the inclusion of additional farestages, thus lessening the distance travelled for the fare charged. Two were introduced in September 1918, these being Bensham Lane Fire Station on the Thornton Heath route and Broad Green on the main road, thus increasing the through fare to Purley on both sections to fourpence.

During 1919, further additional farestages were brought in at Mayday Road and Haling Park Road, with a corresponding rise in the through fare from 4d. to 5d. The penny through fare from Crown Hill to Addiscombe and between West Croydon and Selby Road (Norwood) was also increased to 2d., and several intermediate stages were introduced on both routes. These alterations caused the introduction of two separate penny tickets, both coloured white. That for the Thornton Heath and Norbury to Purley route was headed "MAIN" under the fare value box, whilst the combined penny ticket used on the Addiscombe and Norwood routes carried the word "BRANCH" under the fare value box. In July 1920 five new farestages came forth:—Pollards Hill North on the Norbury route; Thornton Heath Clock Tower on the Thornton Heath route with Coombe Street, Drovers Road and Purley Park Road on the Purley section, this bringing the through fare from Norbury up to sixpence. 1½d. and 2½d. sections were introduced as well during some of these alterations, but the penny minimum fare was retained, sometimes for one stage only.

Workmen's fares had also increased during this period, and on the Main Line were as follows:—
Norbury to Thornton Heath Pond, 1d. Single; Croydon (The Greyhound), 1½d. Single, 3d. Return; South Croydon (The Red Deer), 2d. Single and Purley, 3d. Single, 6d. Return.

Until the last increase of farestages were brought in, there had been sufficient room on the standard-sized ticket for the fares to be set out in "fareboard" style, with the stage of availability shown opposite the stage boarded. Without making a longer ticket however, the increase in the number of stages prevented a continuation of this form of layout, so subsequently, the stages were laid out in purely geographical form down each edge of the ticket, the punch hole then indicating only the point to which the ticket was available. Tickets of this style, although denoting the various stage points, do not give any specific information regarding the fare structure, and thus, with the frequency with which alterations were being made during the years following the end of the war, it is difficult to obtain a complete picture of all the various fare scales. At some time during this period, a stage was introduced at Ederline Avenue in place of Pollards Hill North also at Winterbourne Road in place of Warwick Road in order to make the distances between stages more even.

Transfer fares had, of course, also increased in price during this period.

Norbury Station	and Bensham Lane Fire Station	2d.
Norbury Station	and Thornton Heath Terminus	3d.
West Croydon Station	and Addiscombe Terminus	2d.
East Croydon Station	and "The Swan and Sugar Loaf" ..	1d.
East Croydon Station	and Broad Green	1d.
East Croydon Station	and Mayday Road	2d.
Addiscombe Terminus	and "The Swan" or Broad Green ..	3d.

Although an attempt was made in 1917 to provide half-fares for children travelling to school, it was not until January 1921, that a scheme was introduced on the Corporation tram services, by which, on production of a registration card proving the child to be a scholar in the Borough, half the ordinary fare would be charged. Incidentally, the child had to pay sixpence for the registration card, and the facility was only applicable for journeys to and from school. This scheme was later rationalised to a standard charge of half the ordinary adult fare, excluding fractions of a penny, for any child at any time.

The first decrease of fares after the post-war series of increases was introduced on 10 February 1922, when the 1½d. and 2½d. fares were reduced to 1d. and 2d. respectively, although the through fare from Norbury to Purley remained at sixpence. On 1 January 1923, an agreement was implemented by the Corporation with the then highly competitive omnibus proprietors, the London General Omnibus Company Ltd. & Thomas Tilling Ltd., a standardisation of fares on both forms of transport resulting. Previously, there had been no co-ordination of any sort, but from this date, the following fare scale applied to both:—

Two stages for 1d.; 4 stages for 2d.; 6 stages for 3d.; 8 stages for 4d.; 10 stages for 5d. (Norbury Station—Purley). Children's fares were:—four stages for 1d.; 8 stages for 2d. and 10 stages for 3d.

The number of farestages on the Norbury—Purley route were reduced from fifteen to ten, whilst the number on the Thornton Heath route came down from thirteen to ten. The Workman Single fares had disappeared by this time, and a new scale of Workman Return Fares applied, with a minimum charge of two-pence return for a 2d. Ordinary Single fare.

These Workman fares, together with the revised transfer fares quoted below·were not available on the buses at that time, however.

CA 566 500 19-9-33

CROYDON CORPORATION TRAMWAYS
FARE LIST

TO OR   **FROM**

1d.

TO OR	FROM
Norbury and Warwick Road	"Swan" and "Royal Oak"
Tylecroft Rd. and Brigstock Rd. (LONDON ROAD)	"Red Deer" and Purley
Warwick Road and Mayday Road	W. Croydon Stn. and Selhurst Stn.
T.H. Terminus and Mayday Road	"Glo'ster" and Portland Road
Brigstock Rd. (LONDON ROAD) and W. Croydon	Selhurst Station and Selby Road
Mayday Road and "Greyhound"	Station Road (NORWOOD JUNCTION) & "Robin Hood"
West Croydon Station and "Swan"	Selby Road and "Pawleyne Arms"
"Greyhound" and "Red Deer"	"Robin Hood" and Penge

TRANSFER TICKETS ARE ISSUED TO OR FROM

Thornton Heath Clock and Warwick Road (B)	* St. James' Road and East Croydon Station (A)
" Greyhound " and " Glo'ster " (C)	St. James' Road and " Glo'ster " (C)
*" Swan " and East Croydon Station (A)	West Croydon Station and " Leslie Arms " (A)
	Thicket Road and " Pawleyne Arms " (D)

2d.

Norbury and Mayday Road	West Croydon Stn. and "Royal Oak"
Tylecroft Road & West Croydon Stn.	"Greyhound" and Purley
Warwick Road and "Greyhound"	West Croydon Stn. and Selby Road
T.H. Terminus and "Greyhound"	"Glo'ster" and "Robin Hood"
Brigstock Road (LONDON ROAD) and "Swan"	Selhurst Stn. and "Pawleyne Arms"
Mayday Road and "Red Deer"	Station Road (Norwood) and Penge

TRANSFER TICKETS ARE ISSUED TO OR FROM

Thornton Heath Terminus & Norbury (Hermitage Bridge) (B)	*" Swan " and Bingham Road (A)
" Red Deer " and " Glo'ster " (C)	* St. James' Road and Bingham Road (A)
" Swan " and Selhurst Station (C)	St. James' Road and Portland Road (A)
" Greyhound " and Portland Road (C)	Brigstock Road (LONDON ROAD) and " Leslie Arms " (A)
*" Red Deer " and Addiscombe Station (A)	* Fire Station (T.H.) and East Croydon Station (A)
	High Level and Penge (D)

3d.

Norbury and "Greyhound"	Brigstock Road (LONDON ROAD) and "Royal Oak"
Tylecroft Road and "Swan"	Mayday Road and Purley
Warwick Road and "Red Deer"	West Croydon Station and "Pawleyne Arms"
	"Glo'ster" and Penge

Transfer Stage :—Thornton Heath Terminus and " Red Deer " (B)

4d.

Norbury and " Red Deer "	Warwick Road and Purley.
Tylecroft Road and " Royal Oak "	West Croydon Station and Penge

Transfer Stage :—Thornton Heath Terminus and Purley (B)

5d.

Norbury and Purley - - - - - - - - - -

CHEAP MID-DAY FARES on all cars leaving following points between 10 a.m. and 4 p.m. Mondays to Fridays inclusive. Public Holidays excepted :—

2d.

Norbury & Purley	Thornton Heath & Purley (transfer stage B)
Selby Road & Norbury (transfer stage C)	Selby Road & Purley (transfer stage C)

CHILDREN'S FARES
Children under five years of age, one only per fare-paying passenger, may travel free, if not occupying seats to the exclusion of paying passengers. Children over 5 years of age MUST in all cases be paid for.

The following Reduced Fares are available for Children between the ages of 5 and 14 years :—

Ordinary Fares, 1d. and 2d., Children's Fare, 1d. ; Ordinary Fares, 3d. and 4d., Children's Fare 2d ; Ordinary Fare, 5d. ; Children's Fare, 3d.

Upon production of a Registration Card (obtainable at Tramways Offices), the above Reduced Fares will also be available for Scholars under 18 years of age, WHEN TRAVELLING TO OR FROM SCHOOL as follows :—MONDAY to FRIDAY inclusive between 8 a.m. and 5.30 p.m. ; SATURDAY between 8 a.m. and 1.30 p.m

CHANGE—A*—At Crown Hill, to or from Omnibus. B –At Thornton Heath Pond. C –At Station Road, West Croydon. D –At Anerley Road.
Transfer Tickets are NOT Transferable between Passengers, and are available on day of issue only for one Through Journey between the points from and to which such Tickets are issued, by the next available Car. Accommodation is not guaranteed in a second Car for a person taking a Transfer Ticket, and no responsibility will be accepted in case there is no such Accommodation.

DOGS (Small) which must either be carried, or be on leash, are allowed on the OUTSIDE of Cars only.
LUGGAGE other than personal and in charge of passengers must be paid for at the rate of Ordinary Fare per package, with a maximum of 2d

WORKPEOPLE'S RETURN FARES UP TO 7.30 A.M.
(Return Tickets available on any Car during day of issue)

2d. RETURN

Norbury and Mayday Road	Mayday Road and " Red Deer "
Warwick Road and " Greyhound "	West Croydon Station and " Royal Oak "
Thornton Heath Terminus and West Croydon Station	" Swan " and Purley
Brigstock Road (London Road) and " Swan "	West Croydon Station and Selby Road
	Selby Road and Penge

3d. RETURN

Norbury and Thornton Heath Terminus	Brigstock Road (London Road) & " Red Deer "
Norbury and " Greyhound "	West Croydon Station and Purley
Thornton Heath Terminus and " Greyhound "	

4d. RETURN

Norbury and " Red Deer "	Brigstock Road (London Road) and Purley
Thornton Heath Terminus and " Royal Oak "	

5d. RETURN

Norbury and Purley	Selby Road and Purley
Thornton Heath Terminus and Purley	

1/- ALL-DAY TICKETS : Available on day of issue only, for passenger to whom issued for unlimited travel on all cars in Croydon Corporation Tramways area (i.e., to Purley, Thornton Heath or South Norwood (Selby Rd.)) ; within the County of London (between Manor House and Amhurst Park on Service 53 only) ; Leyton ; between Merton or Summerstown and Wimbledon Hill, and in East Ham, West Ham and Walthamstow. (Not available in M.E.T. or S.M.E.T. areas, nor on Bexley U.D.C. cars.) Not transferable.

6d. EVENING TOURIST TICKETS : Issued after 6 p.m. daily (including Sundays and Public Holidays) for travel free, if not used within the same area as for the 1/- All-Day Ticket. Not transferable.

6d. ALL-DAY (CHILD) TICKETS : Available on day of issue to children under 14 years of age on same routes as the 1/- All-Day Tickets, on Saturdays, Sundays, and on school holidays as announced from time to time. Not transferable.

PREPAID TICKETS, obtainable at the Tramways Offices, Thornton Heath, are issued in Multiples of 25 at their Face Value of 1d.
Passengers are respectfully requested to observe that the Conductor punches in their presence a Ticket representing the value of the Fare paid and the section to be Travelled over.

Tramways Offices, Thornton Heath. *May*, 1933

(Courtesy G. D. Morgan)

Transfer Fares

Warwick Road and Thornton Heath Clock Tower	1d.
Broad Green and East Croydon Station	1d.
Broad Green and "The Gloster"	1d.
"The Swan and Sugar Loaf" and East Croydon Station	1d.
"The Swan and Sugar Loaf" and "The Gloster"	1d.
"The Greyhound" and Portland Road (South Norwood)	2d.
Bensham Lane Fire Station and East Croydon Station	2d.
Thornton Heath Pond and "The Leslie Arms"	2d.
Broad Green and Addiscombe Terminus	2d.
"The Swan and Sugar Loaf" and Bingham Road	2d.
"The Swan and Sugar Loaf" and Portland Road (Norwood)	2d.
"The Red Deer" and Addiscombe Terminus	2d.
"The Red Deer" and Selhurst Station	2d.

An innovation in the way of fares in the Croydon area was the experimental introduction in the summer of 1924 of a 2d. All-the-Way fare during the middle hours of the day (between 10 a.m. and 4 p.m.) on Mondays to Fridays. This was available as a direct fare from Norbury or Thornton Heath to Purley or as a Transfer fare from Selby Road (Norwood) to Purley or Norbury by changing cars at West Croydon. This fare was retained until the end of the Summer, when it was withdrawn. It returned as a permanent facility on 5 January 1925, and at the same time, a penny fare was introduced between Norbury, Thornton Heath or Purley to "The Greyhound" and from Selby Road to West Croydon and Addiscombe to Crown Hill. A review of these fares was taken in September 1927, present mid-day fares be discontinued from 30 September 1927. In their report, the Committee proposed to substitute a limited number of cheap twopenny fares within the Borough. They informed the Council that the L.G.O.C. and most of the proprietors of the independent buses operating within the Borough have agreed to abolish cheap mid-day fares if the Croydon Council did so. "The Electric Railway and Tramway Journal" in its issue dated 7 October 1927 reports that, at a meeting held on Monday 3 October, the Croydon Council decided by a large majority to abolish cheap mid-day penny fares upon their tramways. It was stated that they have been in operation for over 2½ years and that they were the cause of the larger part of the loss of £4,500 a year in receipts. It was also revealed that the loss of the Croydon Tramway undertaking for the year ended 31 March 1927 was £66,388. The last day of issue of the penny cheap mid-day fare was Friday, 7 October 1927.

At some time during 1927, there was an adjustment of fares on the Thornton Heath route. Although Bensham Lane Fire Station was retained as a farestage, it only applied to the penny fare to and from Mayday Road. The fare from Thornton Heath Terminus to "The Greyhound" was reduced to 2d., that to the "Red Deer" to 3d., and the through fare to Purley to 4d. The Workman fares on this route remained unchanged, however.

From 7 February 1926, when through operation to London commenced, completely revised tickets came into operation over the whole Corporation tramway system. Hitherto, several issues of penny and twopenny tickets had been required to cover all routes and transfers, each value carrying under the fare value imprint its designation, such as "Main" for Norbury and Thornton Heath to Purley only, "Branch" for Selhurst and Addiscombe only, "Local" for tickets applicable to all non-joint lines in the Croydon area, or in some cases, a combination of these designations. With the curtailment of the Thornton Heath route at "The Greyhound" and the separation of the Norbury route, the number of tickets was reduced considerably. Formerly, the full range had been 1d. to 5d. Ordinary Single; 2d. to 5d. Workman Returns and 1d. and 2d. Transfer Tickets. Of these values, only the singles from 1d. to 4d. remained, together with the 2d. Workman Return, all other values being covered by the special issues only on the joint route with the L.C.C. Separate Transfer tickets were also withdrawn, as space was available for the stages concerned to be placed at the top of the Ordinary Single tickets, this system conforming with the practice used on the L.C.C. system, whose conductors would have to accept Croydon local transfers on their cars when passing through Croydon on their way to and from Purley. Conductors were issued with cancelling punches very similar to those already in use on the L.C.C. cars for cancelling transfer and return tickets, and in consequence the Exchange tickets issued for transfers in the Croydon area were also withdrawn.

Except on the joint route to London, no special tickets were issued for Children's half-fares in the Croydon area, and Ordinary Single Tickets punched in the appropriate farestage sufficing.

As the Thornton Heath route had now been curtailed at "The Greyhound", in order that intending passengers from Thornton Heath requiring to travel beyond that point should not suffer a fare increase by the withdrawal of the through facility, new transfer fares at threepence single to "The Red Deer" and fourpence to Purley were introduced, passengers changing cars at Thornton Heath Pond. A new twopenny Cheap Mid-day Fare Transfer from Thornton Heath Terminus to Purley was also brought into operation at the same time. New Workman Return Transfers from Thornton Heath Terminus were also introduced at the same time, these being threepence return to Norbury; fourpence return to "The Royal Oak" and fivepence to Purley.

The titled tickets remained in use on the local routes until after the Addiscombe route was withdrawn on 28 March 1927, when they were gradually replaced by a new set of tickets in the standard colours described in a previous paragraph. The penny and twopenny values carried the farestages from Thornton Heath Terminus through to Purley, despite the fact that the route now terminated at "The Greyhound", and in the box carrying the fare value, bore the initials "T.H." in the right-hand corner, which indicated they were for use on the Thornton Heath route. The threepenny and fourpenny values still carried the "Local" title, and in addition to the full stages to Purley, carried the stages for the transfers at Thornton Heath Pond, and the through threepenny and fourpenny fares over the South Metropolitan lines to Penge. Local penny and twopenny fares on the Penge and Crystal Palace routes in the Corporation area were covered by the issue of tickets entitled "1d. NORWOOD" (Colour as described in the Bell Punch official colour chart—cedar) and "2d. NORWOOD" (Colour Blue), which carried the through and transfer destinations on each ticket.

Prepaid tickets—1d. (Green) and 2d. (Lilac) bearing the title "DEPARTMENTAL" were issued to the staff of other Corporation departments for use on journeys in connection with Corporation business, and there was also a yellow 1d. value which simply stated "Good for 1d. Stage" and which may have been sold to the public. The Departmental tickets carried the name of the Borough Accountant, whilst the yellow one bore a facsimile of the signature of the Tramways Manager, T. B. Goodyer. These yellow tickets also carried the inscription "To be given in Exchange for another ticket of equal value". Folding passes of two types were issued to tramway officials and clerical staff. The first type was available on all routes and was issued to tramway officials, including certain operating officials of the L.C.C. Tramways. The second type was issued to the clerical staff of the Tramways Department, and was available between specific farestages when on duty. Both types were reissued annually. There was a card pass issued monthly to unemployed allotment holders, enabling them to travel between their homes and the allotments at Biggin Hill (Norbury) or Purley Way. These passes were also available on South Metropolitan cars on the Sutton route to enable those with allotments at Purley Way to reach that point. They were not available between 8 and 9.30 a.m. or from 5 p.m. to 7 p.m., and in no case later than one hour after lighting-up time. Uniform staff travelled free to and from duty, whilst depôt staff were issued with a numbered wrist badge. Surprisingly, Corporation officials of departments other than the Tramways were not granted free passes, neither were Council members or old age pensioners. Blind persons carried a free pass which carried a photograph of the holder.

On the new joint route to London, all cars worked by Croydon had their own tickets, supplied by the Corporation, but in fact being as near a copy of the L.C.C. style as the printers (Bell Punch) could achieve. They also adopted the same colours as the L.C.C. for these tickets, and had the distinguishing feature of having the colour overprinted on white card, along each edge, thus giving the appearance of a white central stripe. The colours were an extremely good match, except perhaps for the eightpenny value. The values introduced were 1d. White; 2d. Pink; 3d. Blue; 4d. Green; 5d. Brown; 6d. Yellow; 7d. Bright Salmon and 8d. Grey. Normally, only 1d. to 5d. Ordinary Single values were carried, the higher values being brought out for issue on Sundays and Bank Holidays, also on other days of heavier through traffic and also when traffic censuses were carried out. Workman Return tickets of values from twopence to eighpence in the same colourings were issued, the sevenpenny value being unlike the rest of the set in the fact that it was in an all-over colour of salmon, instead of striped. To distinguish them from the ordinary return tickets issued in the L.C.C. area, a red diagonal stripe was over-printed on all values, except the sevenpenny, which carried a blue diagonal stripe. Ordinary return tickets at 5d., 6d. and 8d. were carried for issue in the L.C.C. area, these being in the same colours as the single tickets of the same value, and bore a large skeleton "R" overprint.

Cheap Mid-day Fare tickets for one penny and twopence Adult Single and 1d. Child Single were also provided and used for the Cheap fares in the London and Croydon areas, all of these bearing the very characteristic L.C.C. overprints, as did the Children's Single tickets, which were issued in values from one penny to fourpence. Once again, the threepenny and fourpenny values only appeared in the ticket boxes on Sundays, days of heavy traffic and during traffic censuses.

Although the Ordinary Single tickets used on the L.C.C. cars all carried value overprints, those issued by Croydon Corporation did not, having the fare value printed in the text, in a box at the top of the ticket which carried the relevant fare value plus the service numbers 16—18. Another difference between the L.C.C. tickets and those of the Corporation was the stage numbers 1—24 included on the L.C.C. Single tickets from 1d. to 4d.; 1d. Child Single; 1d. Cheap Mid-day Adult Single and 2d. Workman Return tickets.

Croydon Corporation had never issued Ordinary Return Tickets in its own area, but as mentioned in a previous paragraph, these were issued in the L.C.C. area, whilst twopenny Child Ordinary Singles, plus 2d. Adult and 1d. Child Cheap Mid-day tickets were also required to cover the complex system of transfers the L.C.C. operated at that time throughout their area. These L.C.C. transfer fares gave rise to a number of headaches in the ticket office of the Croydon Corporation, as for example, the extension of the L.C.C. tramways through the Downham Estate to Grove Park, together with the introduction of double-deck tramcars through the Kingsway Subway, although miles away from their own scenes of operation, nevertheless meant a revision of 5d. Ordinary Single; 2d. Child; 2d. Adult and 1d. Child Mid-day; 4d. and 6d. Workman Returns and all values of Ordinary Returns, all of which had some transfer sections not only applicable to the Grove Park route, but through the Kingsway Subway to Southampton Row, Farringdon Road, Angel (Islington) and Cross Street (Upper Street) on Routes 33 and 35 (LCC) and Goswell Road and City Road (Old Street) on Route 31. In addition, the L.C.C. was constantly introducing new transfers in its Southern Division, all of which meant constant reprinting of various values of ticket, and which meant constant expense to the Corporation, whom, unlike the L.C.C. did not possess its own printing works. The writer, who was around at the time all this happened, often wondered why Croydon Corporation did not do the same as Walthamstow Council did in the end, and that was to insist that the L.C.C. supplied the necessary tickets if they kept adding transfers.

During the early years of through running a close touch was kept on the amount of through traffic, partly of course, as a matter of interest, but also to ensure that a fair distribution of traffic receipts was being made to each operator, and to be able to compute this accurately, for a while in 1928, both operators produced one penny and twopenny tickets headed "LONDON" and "CROYDON" respectively, each carrying the stages applicable to the area concerned—the Croydon tickets also carrying the necessary transfer sections. Several overlap tickets were provided. Special overlap tickets were provided to cover fares which crossed the boundary at Norbury, including a penny one for the Greyhound Lane—Tylecroft Road stage and twopenny values for use on the Streatham (Telford Avenue)—Warwick Road and Streatham Library—Thornton Heath Pond stages. A separate issue of the twopenny Adult Cheap Mid-day Fare ticket for the Croydon area was also issued.

The withdrawal of the Addiscombe branch and its substitution by L.G.O.C. buses, made very little difference to either fares or tickets of the Corporation, except the eventual deletion of the stages concerned from the tickets as existing stocks became exhausted. The fares adopted by the buses were those previously in force on the trams, including the transfer fares, but with the exception of the twopenny Workman Return between Addiscombe Terminus and Crown Hill, which was withdrawn.

The buses issued their own tickets on Routes 178, 179 and 197, with the transfer fares printed on the reverse side of each value, and they were accepted and cancelled on the trams in the normal manner. The changeover did have one effect however. Hitherto, although fares had been equated between the buses already operating on existing routes and the trams, no inter-facility of transfer had been permitted. With the introduction of the buses replacing the Addiscombe trams, the issue and acceptance of transfer tickets by the remaining "General" and Thos. Tilling bus routes came about. It had been agreed that, on the three routes directly replacing the trams, such receipts as may accrue from the sale of a transfer ticket should be the prerogative of the issuing operator, and as a consequence, no special accounting check had to be made.

This agreement however, did not apply to tickets issued on the other bus routes. Therefore, the L.G.O.C. prepared special duplex tickets covering the transfer fares for the Croydon area, whereby one half, punched as a replica of the half handed to the passenger, could be returned to the office and used to ascertain accurate totals of receipts. It is to be presumed that Croydon Corporation and the L.C.C. Tramways were willing to accept the bus companies figures, as they made no adjustment to their methods of issuing transfers or accounting for them. An examination of one of the Duplex tickets issued by the L.G.O.C. reveals that it only covers the transfers available by changing vehicles at "The Greyhound", Croydon, and not those available at West Croydon or Thornton Heath Pond. They remained in issue until 1 November 1934. A peculiarity of the time was that, despite the fact the buses formerly operated by London General Country Services Limited had now become the responsibility of the L.P.T.B., the transfers issueable to and from "The Red Deer" and "Swan and Sugar Loaf" were neither issued or accepted on the Country Buses.

From 28 May 1932, the L.C.C. 1/- All-Day Ticket, which had been gradually extending its area beyond the original confines of the County of London, took into its limits the whole of the Croydon system, that is, from Norbury to Purley; to Thornton Heath Terminus and between West Croydon and Selby Road (Norwood). These limits also applied to the sixpenny Evening Tourist Ticket (which was then a cheap evening version of the 1/- All-Day), and the sixpenny Child All-Day (available on Saturdays and Sundays only). Although these tickets were issued as well as accepted on all Croydon Corporation cars and also on the South Met. cars between West Croydon and Selby Road, neither of these two operators had their own stocks of this value and style of ticket printed, preferring to use those supplied and printed by the L.C.C. printing works at Effra Road, Brixton.

The London Passenger Transport Board

In the early days of the takeover of all London's tramways by the new Board on 1 July 1933, very little evidence of any upheaval was noticeable either in fares or tickets in the Croydon area. Indeed, the existing stocks of Corporation tickets were used up first, and it was not until they started to become exhausted that the first signs of the new regime became visible. As far as the former Corporation routes were concerned, no further tickets were ordered from the Bell Punch Company, but a new set of tickets produced by the Effra Road Printing Works in the former L.C.C. colours (1d. White; 2d. Pink and 3d. Blue) appeared on the scene. Separate sets for the Thornton Heath and Norwood routes now disappeared, and the new tickets carried the heading "CROYDON AREA" and the farestages for both routes appeared on the one ticket. The stages from "The Greyhound" to Purley were no longer shown as had been the case on the Corporation tickets. The 1d. to 3d. values were the only ones produced in this style, and they did not have a very long life, as the Penge route was withdrawn on 7 December 1933, and the Thornton Heath route was soon included in the schedules of the newly-extended Route 30 (about which more will be said later), and also in the schedule of Routes 16/18, and thus was embodied in the tickets of those routes. The separate set of tickets issued from Purley and Thornton Heath depôts on the former Croydon Corporation workings on Routes 16/18 were also soon withdrawn, and the same set of tickets as used by cars from Streatham depôt were now used from the former Croydon depôts.

Gradually, even almost un-noticed, other minor changes came about. Children's transfer facilities were withdrawn on 1 January 1934, and the standardised ruling that a child's fare should be half that of the corresponding adult fare, with the exclusion of fractions of a penny, came into force. In the Croydon area, where no odd halfpenny child's fares had existed previously, this ruling did not make any difference, except that, whereas until then the twopenny adult Cheap Mid-day Fare was restricted to adults only, there now came into force a penny Cheap Mid-day Fare for children in this area (it had existed in the L.C.C. area since the commencement of Cheap Mid-day Fares in 1922). All separate Child's tickets were now withdrawn, although these had only been carried previously on Corporation cars on Routes 16/18, also on both S.M.E.T. and Corporation cars for use in the South Met. area between Selby Road and Penge or Crystal Palace.

A new facility introduced at this time was that of a quarter-rate prepaid ticket issued in bulk to education authorities for re-issue to students up to the age of 18. These tickets, pink in colour, with a white centre stripe, bore numbers instead of names to indicate stage points and were universal for the whole of the L.P.T.B. area. They were accepted by Conductors and merely cancelled in the number of the stage to which they were available. At cost to the student of one halfpenny, they were available for a normal twopenny adult stage—to or from—school—and for journeys over the normal twopenny adult stage, two or more tickets could be used.

The withdrawal of the children's transfer facilities was not accepted meekly by the children and parents of Croydon, and as a result, they were reinstated fifteen days later, and for a long time, were the only children's transfer tickets available anywhere in the London area. Special tickets were not provided, and the transfer stages were included on the Ordinary Adult tickets.

In September 1937, a reversal of the colours of two values of tickets took place as a start towards standardisation of ticket colours between the tramway and bus sections of the Board. The twopenny value, formerly pink, became blue, and the threepenny which had hitherto been blue became pink, and now the values between 1d. and 4d. were the same colours on both buses and trams.

The first of what was destined to become a series of fare increases and adjustments came into operation on 11 June 1939. This did not affect the Croydon services to any great extent, except as regards the tickets carried by conductors on Routes 16 and 18 for use in the former L.C.C. area. The former fivepenny and sixpenny ordinary return tickets and fares were withdrawn, and the transfer facilities which had been available on them in the London area were transferred to the threepenny and fourpenny adult single tickets. The eightpenny return fare was increased to ninepence, but an additional facility was granted in that the return journey could be made by bus between common points, also bus returns could be used for return journeys on trams between common points. The twopenny Cheap Mid-day Fares between the London termini and Norbury and from Norbury to Purley were increased to threepence, and the Cheap Mid-day adult penny fare for three sections was withdrawn and replaced by a new twopenny fare which covered the same distance as a fourpenny Adult Single fare, which not only applied in the London area, but also on the Norbury— Purley section of routes 16/18. Children travelling at mid-day were now charged half of the new twopenny mid-day fare, and twopence for the threepenny all-the-way facility.

The second increase in July 1940 brought a change throughout the whole system with the introduction of a 1½d. minimum Adult Single fare, and the increase of the twopennny Workman Return fare to 2½d. The new 1½d. ticket took the colour (white) of its predecessor, and indeed for a while, the same ticket was used, but overprinted 1½d. To cover the penny value still required for Children's fares, a new ticket with salmon-tinted edges was brought into use. The 2½d. Workman Return had apple-green edges instead of the former blue, bringing it into line with the colour of the 2½d. Adult Single bus ticket used on certain East London routes at that time.

Soon after this change, the need for conserving paper owing to wartime restrictions became greater, and the hitherto long issues were reduced to not much more than half their size by the substitution of all printed stage names (except in the case of transfers) by stage numbers. Previously, both the names and numbers had appeared on the tickets, but the complexity of the routings meant that numbers were often repeated for different stages. As, in addition to routes 16/18 and 42, the tickets in the Croydon area also carried stages for Routes 2A/4A, 8, 10, 20 and 22/24, the using of numbers only enabled a good deal of space to be saved. The faretables carried in the cars showed both numbers and stage names, so that passengers could, if necessary, ascertain the length of their journey for the fare paid.

Even greater saving of ticket length was achieved a year or so later by the inclusion of some of the stage numbers on the reverse side of the ticket, always providing that they did not conflict in that punching position for punching purposes, with numbers on the front.

The 1/- All-Day ticket was finally withdrawn after 11 October 1942 as was the sixpenny Evening Tourist ticket and the 6d. Child All-day ticket. From 1 January 1934, the two sixpenny tickets had covered a very different area to the 1/- All-Day ticket. This was available in the County of London, East Ham, West Ham, Walthamstow, Croydon and from Merton to Wimbledon Station, whereas the two sixpenny tickets were two-zone issues, available on any tram or trolleybus either north or south of a line closely approximating to the River Thames. The fourpenny Scholar or Pupil ticket, which had been withdrawn at Easter 1935, was also a two-zone ticket. It was superseded by the issue of one penny and twopenny Scholar Return tickets, for which at a quarter rate (i.e. the penny return covered a normal Adult twopenny fare in each direction), pupils were able to travel to and from school. These tickets were only available up to 6 p.m. on Mondays to Fridays or 2 p.m. on Saturdays, after which times normal children's half fares applied. Genuine students over the age of 14 were able to obtain a registration card to enable them to get a Scholar Return ticket. These tickets, of course, also replaced the former twopenny prepaid (quarter-rate tickets) which were supplied to and issued by the Education Authorities.

It is interesting to note that, for a time, Sixpenny Evening Tourist and Sixpenny Child All-Day tickets were available over the Selby Road—Crystal Palace (High Level) and Mitcham and Sutton routes of the former South Metropolitan Electric Tramways, but the Shilling All-Day ticket issued to adults was not.

During the remainder of the war years, no further alterations in either fares or tickets took place, but on 9 February 1947, all twopenny Adult Single fares were increased to 2½d.; all fares above twopence Adult Single being increased by one penny, including the Cheap Mid-day fares. The Maximum Adult Single Fare in the former L.C.C. area, which had been raised from 5d. to 6d. in June 1939, now became 7d. The two lowest Children's Single fares were altered, the Child's penny fare now only covering the same distance as the Adult 1½d. fare, with a new 1½d. Child fare covering the same distance as the Adult 2½d. Single fare.

Adjustments were made to the Adult Cheap Mid-day fares as follows:— a threepenny Adult Cheap Mid-day fare covered the same distance as a 5d. Ordinary Single Fare, with fourpence any distance being charged in the former L.C.C., Croydon and Leyton areas, and, at this time, the minimum 2½d. Workman fare was increased to threepence, and all Workman Return fares above threepence were increased by one penny.

Once again the opportunity was taken to advance the unification of ticket colours, the trams again changing to colours formerly used by buses only. The old 5d. brown became orange; the primrose 6d. gave way to brown; the 7d. bright salmon changed to lilac, while the grey of the eightpenny became yellow. The dull green-blue 9d. changed to buff, but in the Croydon area, this colour only applied to a Workman Return ticket used on routes 16 and 18. The 9d. Ordinary Return ticket issued in the London area on these routes was increased to 11d., the colour for this ticket being a poor imitation of the sage-green used for the bus ticket of this value. The two new fares (2½d. Adult and 2d. Child) took each other's former colours, becoming blue and apple-green respectively. With the increase, the various transfers in the Croydon area still survived, although the latest changes meant they were 1½d. and 2½d. for adults and one penny and 1½d. for children.

The next increase was introduced on 1 October 1950, and then the 2½d. Adult fare was increased to threepence; all Transfer tickets and fares and Workman Return fares were withdrawn, but the Workman fares were replaced by a new facility entitled "Early Morning Single Fare" — a twopenny single ticket available for any journey completed up to 8 a.m. up to an equivalent ordinary fare of 1s. 1d. It was considered that the combination of an Ordinary Single Fare in the evening, plus the issue of an Early Morning Single in the morning would be the same as the replaced Workman Return Fare (plus its relative increase), whilst, at the same time, the simplification of the fare scale by the elimination of any fare covering more than one vehicle, would pave the war for mechanisation.

In this latest increase, the higher fares affected were the 6d., which was increased to 6½d. (3d. Child); 7d. to 9d. fares were increased by one penny; 10d. to 11½d., and 11d. to 1s. 1d., which was the fare for the through journey from Purley to London on routes 16 and 18. In the Croydon area itself, the highest ever maximum Single fare had been achieved, as the Norbury—Purley fare was now 6½d. The former threepenny and fourpenny Cheap Midday Fares were withdrawn and replaced by a new sixpenny fare available between London and Norbury and also from Norbury to Purley. A simplified ticket was now being used for the whole of the London tramways, with the exception of the Subway routes. Carrying the requisite stage numbers only, one printing block was used for the whole range, with the exception of the sixpenny midday ticket, only the colour and the overprint denoting the value. This range of tickets consisted of 1d., 1½d., 2d., 3d., 4d., 5d., 6½d., and 8d. values only, higher or intermediate values being made up by double issues, and as such were still in issue when the last tram ran in Croydon on the night of 7 April 1951.

THE SOUTH METROPOLITAN ELECTRIC TRAMWAYS AND LIGHTING COMPANY LIMITED

Sutton and Tooting Routes

The introduction of these two routes in 1906 occurred at a time when frequent minor changes in fares were taking place, but a set of single tickets for each route issued about twelve months later, together with a route map containing faretables and issued about the same time, have revealed the following fare structure:—

Sutton Route:

Croydon Terminus				
1	Waddon Bridge			
1	1	Croydon Boundary		
1½	1½	1	Sandy Lane	
2	1½	1	1	Woodcote Road
2½	2½	—	—	1	Park Lane
3	3	—	—	1	1	"Windsor Castle"
3½	3½	3½	2½	2	1½	1	Tramway Depot
4	3½	3½	3½	2	1½	1	1	Sutton Terminus

Tooting Route:

Croydon Terminus				
1	Canterbury Road			
1	1	Croydon Boundary		
2	1	1	Blue House Bridge	
2	2	1	1	Fair Green
3	2	2	1	1	Tooting Jct.

Both the tickets and the faretable for the Sutton route reveal several discrepancies. The route was divided into four penny farestages, but only two twopenny fares appear on both tickets and faretables, also only one threepenny fare. It will be observed that the journey from Croydon Boundary to Sutton Terminus can be made for threepence by purchasing a penny ticket to Woodcote Road and re-booking from there. This also applies to the fare from Croydon Boundary to "The Windsor Castle" (Carshalton), which can be made for twopence by re-booking. The stage named as Croydon Boundary was later renamed, The Chase on the Sutton route and Red House on the Tooting Route. On early tickets, the Sutton terminus was simply shown as "Grapes Hotel" with no mention of the locality.

The tickets of this period were of the fareboard type, being punched at the stage of boarding and available to the stage printed opposite. The colours to denote the various values were as follows:—1d. white; 1½d. green; 2d. lilac; 2½d. salmon; 3d. blue; 3½d. magenta and 4d. cerise. At this time, there was a return fare covering the full journey from Croydon to Sutton at a fare of sixpence, this ticket being cerise in colour (the same as the corresponding four-penny single). No Workman Single fares or Return fares have been seen for the Sutton route, but on the Tooting route, both one penny and 1½d. Workman Single Fares applied. The penny ticket (coloured yellow) bore the following fares:—

Croydon Terminus	—	Windmill Road.
Canterbury Road	—	Fair Green.
Croydon Boundary	—	Tooting Junction.

The 1½d. ticket (coloured sage-green) was available as follows:—

Croydon Terminus	—	Fair Green.
Canterbury Road	—	Tooting Junction.

The fares on the Tooting route had evidently been set at too low a level at the commencement of operation, and by 1909 had been revised as follows:—

Croydon Terminus								
1	Handcroft Road							
1	1	Canterbury Road						
1	1	1	Croydon Boundary					
2	2	2	1	Windmill Road				
2½	2	2	1	1	The Monument			
2½	2	2	2	2	1	Blue House Bridge		
2½	2½	2	2	2	1	1	Fair Green	
3½	3½	2½	2½	2	2	1	1	Tooting Junction.

172

It will be observed that the threepenny fare had now been completely eliminated from the new faretable, but when it is remembered that for a distance of 2¼ miles from Croydon Boundary to Mitcham (Fair Green) the tramway was running through the middle of Mitcham Common, which at that time was devoid of any habitation whatsoever, even along the now populated Commonside East it will be seen that the revenue on this route had to be gathered from the following three sources:—

(1) Through traffic from Tooting Junction and Mitcham to Croydon and in the reverse direction.

(2) From local traffic between Tooting Junction and Mitcham (Fair Green), a source which was badly eroded after 1912 by the introduction of L.G.O.C. bus routes from the direction of London which gave a through connection from Mitcham to the main Tooting shopping area.

(3) From local traffic in the built-up area along the Mitcham Road between Aurelia Road and West Croydon, which also was not so heavily built-up in those far-off days.

In addition, some of the local traffic between Tooting Junction and the Fair Green was also carried on the cars which shuttled back and forth to the Cricket Green (Mitcham) until they were withdrawn in the early days of the First World War. Incidentally, there was only one fare on this route, it being a penny all the way.

The increase of the single from Croydon to Tooting to 3½d. was somewhat alleviated by the issue of a sixpenny Return ticket covering the full journey. A blue ticket was used, having the letters A to G alphabetically down the left edge, these being used as a code to indicate the day of issue. Down the right edge the hours were printed, starting at 12 o'clock, then 1.0 p.m., 2.0 p.m., and so on to 11.0 p.m. These tickets were collected on the return journey, and an Exchange Ticket (yellow in colour) issued in place. This ticket carried the stages "Croydon" on the left side and "Tooting/Sutton" on the right.

Workman's Return Tickets were also issued, and these were of the two-coupon type, the top portion being retained by the conductor on the return journey. As this top coupon was serially numbered in conjunction with the bottom coupon, a ticket being presented to an inspector on the return journey could always be verified by reference to the stubs held by the conductor. These tickets also had the lettered coding for the day of issue down the left-hand side, but the right-hand side carried the stages for which the ticket was available, set out in full geographical style (i.e. with both boarding and alighting point in the same box).

The frequent small adjustments in fares at this time was a feature of the majority of tramways, and on 29 December 1909, a new system was adopted on most of those associated with the British Electric Traction Company. It was unique to them, and amongst the companies to bring it into operation was the South Metropolitan, which adopted it on the date stated above. Known as the "Fair-Fare" system, the idea was for a large number of short stages to be fixed on each route, of which three were given for a penny, fares then rising in farthing stages up to two-pence, and then halfpenny stages from there onwards. The Sutton route was divided into nineteen stages and the Tooting route into fifteen.

There is not room to quote all these fare stages here, but large discs bearing the stage numbers, were fixed high up on traction posts, and moved to other posts later when the system was changed.

The tickets used the stage numbers to represent the stages, but were printed in fareboard fashion, with the number of the stage boarded showing opposite the number of the stage to which the fare was available and in all cases, the numbers for odd-numbered stages being shown in negative block. On issue, these tickets were punched at the stage of boarding. The complete colour scheme was 1d. white; 1¼d. blue; 1½d. green; 1¾d. buff; 2d. pink; 2½d. brown; 3d. orange; 3½d. grey and 4d. sage green.

This system was patented by the B.E.T. under the number 552927, and lasted on the South Metropolitan until about 1913, when the frequent fare stages were retained, but the odd farthing fares deleted. The special tickets used with this system were also withdrawn, and again a reversion was made to the geographical form of layout. There was a peculiarity about the order the stages on the tickets however. Each route was divided into half and the stages of each half were then set out alternatively, first down the left side and then down the right. Thus the stages down the left-hand side of a ticket on the Tooting route would read:—"Croydon Terminus, Monument, Sumner Road, Blue House, Canterbury Road, Cold Blows, etc." When this was combined on the higher values of tickets into both routes, and at the same time stages to which the fares did not apply were omitted, it must have been difficult for the conductors to see at a glance the correct position for punching. This scheme was modified to some degree during the early stages of the war and then alternate stages were placed on alternate sides of the ticket, giving a more logical progression to the farestages themselves It also paved the way for a simplification of tickets by dispensing with the stage names and using numbers only. The first series of these numerical tickets had the odd numbers 1-19 down the left side, with even numbers 2-20 down the right, the letters A and B appearing at the foot of each respective column. Here again was the system adopted by London Transport in the days of the Second World War used by the South Metropolitan Electric Tramways during the first. With the large number of stages, and tickets universally adaptable, changes in the faretables could be made without much ado.

Turning now to fares, on both Sutton and Tooting routes, weekly tickets were issued conceding twelve 2½d. fares at a rate of 1½d. each or twelve fourpenny fares for 2¼d. (on the Tooting route this was twelve 3½d. fares for 2¼d. each). These tickets were introduced on 26 April 1915, and were followed on July 1 by the introduction of a halfpenny children's fare for a penny adult ordinary stage, the previous minimum child's fare having been one penny.

On 14 August 1916, some fares on both routes were adjusted. 1½d., 2½d. and 3½d. fares were eliminated on both routes, and on the Sutton route 1d., 2d. and 3d. fares were adjusted, with the effect of lengthening the average penny stage and shortening the twopenny and threepenny stages, also having a corresponding effect on Workman and Child fares. On the Tooting route, the effect of eleminating the 3½d. fare raised the through fare from Croydon to Tooting from 3½d. to 4d.

Fares then remained static on both routes until 1 January 1918, when the weekly tickets introduced in 1915 were withdrawn. At the same time, attention was given to the Workman farescales. The penny Workman Single farestages were shortened, and Workman Return Fares at 2d., 3d. and 4d. were introduced covering all single fares of like value. Another adjustment was made a few weeks later on March 17, when the 6d. Ordinary Return Fares from Croydon to Sutton and Tooting were withdrawn and all twopenny and threepenny farestages were shortened on both routes.

Things were not allowed to remain undisturbed for too long, as on 4 May 1918, twopenny and threepenny stages on the Sutton route were shortened once more, with a corresponding effect on Workman and Child Fares. The minimum Child fare was increased from a halfpenny to one penny once more, while on the Tooting route, twopenny ordinary single farestages were shortened and one 3d. stage was lengthened, both changes having an effect on Workman

South Metropolitan and S.M.E.T./Croydon Corporation Joint tickets.
(Omnibus Society Collection. Courtesy R. J. Durrant

175

Returns and Child fares. The penny Workman Single and 3d. Workman Return stages were lengthened, but two penny Workman stages were shortened. As with the Sutton route, the minimum Child fare was increased from a half-penny to one penny.

Apparently all these changes were insufficient to produce the necessary revenue to meet the increased operational costs being incurred at this time, and at the same time produce a reasonable profit, and as a result, completely revised faretables were introduced on both routes on 1 September 1918. A copy of these faretables is reproduced on p.176 and 177 and surprisingly enough, the frequent farestages introduced with the "Fair-Fare" system in 1909 were still being used in 1918, although why the opportunity was not taken at this time to revise the farestage system is a mystery.

These fares remained in operation until 12 September 1920, when rising costs again made it necessary to increase fares on both routes. The new faretables did away at last with the frequent stages which were introduced with the "Fair-Fair" system in 1909, and instead of twenty farestages on the Sutton route there were now only twelve, fairly evenly spaced out. On the Tooting route the number fell from sixteen to nine, and it will be observed that on both routes, the minimum Adult Ordinary Single had been increased from one penny to 1½d.

A slight revision to the Single fares on the above faretables was made on 1 December 1921 when the first stage of every 1½d. fare was reduced to one penny, and again on 9 March 1922, when Cheap Ordinary Return Tickets were introduced on both routes on weekdays only, except Christmas Day, Bank Holidays or Proclaimed National Holidays fell on weekdays. The tickets were available for the return journey on the day of issue only and also between the farestages travelled on the forward journey only. On the Sutton route, 7d. Return was charged for all 4d. Single stages; 8d. Return for 5d. Single and 10d. Return for the all-the-way fare of 6d. On the Tooting route, 7d. Return was charged for all 4d. Single fares and 8d. Return for the all-the-way fare of 5d. Workman Single Fares were withdrawn, but Return tickets were issued at Single fares, with a minimum fare of twopence. Children's fares were issued at half the ordinary Single fare (fractions of a penny counting as a penny) to children between the ages of 5 and 14. Prams, Mailcarts and Bicycles were carried on the front platform of the tramcars at the discretion of the Motorman and were charged for at a rate of 6d. for any distance, and luggage was charged for at twopence per package over 28 lbs. in weight.

In common with other operators, a standardisation of fares was made from 1 January 1923, and this revision formed the basis of the fares which lasted until the withdrawal of the trams.

Workman Return Tickets were available at the return journey for the Single fare with a minimum fare of twopence, and, of course, available on weekdays only (public holidays excepted) in common with all other workman tickets in the London area.

All tickets were of a numerical style, and were of the standard 2½ inch length and had 24 stage numbers, 1-12 on the left-hand side and 13-24 on the right-hand side, the latter facing up the ticket. This applied to the whole range, at first even to the 6d. all-the-way ticket and the corresponding tenpenny return, although later these had the name of one or other of the termini down either side. The colours used were:—1d. white; 2d. magenta; 3d. brown; 4d. orange; 5d. grey; and 6d. blue, the colours for the Ordinary Return Tickets in the higher values being:—7d. green; 8d. pink and 10d. yellow.

The return tickets had a large black "R" in skeleton type in the centre panel and the conditions of issue printed on the back. Workman Return Tickets

FARE LIST.

CROYDON & SUTTON ROUTE.

1d.

		Section Number
1 Croydon	and Factory	5
2 Waddon Bridge	and Plough Lane E.	6
3 „ Station and	„ W.	7
4 Coldharbour	and Sandy Lane	8
5 Factory	and Stafford Terrace	9
6 Plough Lane E.	and Woodcote-road	10
7 „ W.	and Boundary-road	11
8 Sandy Lane	and Park-lane Bridge	12
9 Stafford Terr. and	„ Corner	13
10 Woodcote-road	and Salisbury-road	14
11 Boundary-road	and Windsor Castle	15
12 Park lane Bdge	and Ringstead-rd. Top	16
13 „ Corner	and Depot	17
14 Salisbury-road	and Benhill-road	18
15 Windsor Castle and	„ Wood-road	19
16 Ringstead rd Top	and Sutton	20

2d.

Croydon	and Stafford Terrace
Waddon Bridge	and Woodcote-road
„ Station	and Boundary-road
Coldharbour	and Park Lane Bridge
Factory	and „ „ Corner
Plough Lane E.	and Salisbury-road
„ W.	and Windsor Castle
Sandy Lane	and Ringstead-road Top
Stafford Terrace	and Depot
Woodcote-road	and Benhill-road
Boundary-road	and „ Wood-road
PARK LaneBridge	and Sutton

3d.

Croydon	and Park Lane Corner
Waddon Bridge	and Salisbury-road
„ Station	and Windsor Castle
Coldharbour	and Ringstead-road Top
Factory	and Depot
Plough Lane E.	and Benhill-road
„ W.	and „ Wood-road
Sandy Lane	and Sutton

4d.

Croydon	and Depot
Waddon Bridge	and Benhill-road
„ Station and	„ Wood-road
Coldharbour	and Sutton

5d. All the way

CROYDON & TOOTING ROUTE.

1d.

		Section Number
1 Croydon	and Redhouse	5
2 Sumner-road	and Watney's-road	6
3 Canterbury-rd.	and Windmill-road S.	7
4 Depot	and „ N.	8
5 Redhouse	and Monument	9
6 Watney's-road	and Bluehouse	10
7 Windmill-rd. S.	and Cold Blows	11
8 „ N.	and Fair Green	12
9 Monument	and Holborn Schools	13
10 Bluehouse	and The Farm	14
11 Cold Blows	and Crusoe-road	15
12 Fair Green	and Tooting	16

2d.

Croydon	and Monument
Sumner-road	and Bluehouse
Canterbury-road	and Cold Blows
Depot	and Fair Green
Redhouse	and Holborn Schools
Watney's-road	and The Farm
Windmill Road S.	and Crusoe-road
„ N.	and Tooting

3d.

Croydon	and Holborn Schools
Sumner-road	and The Farm
Canterbury-road	and Crusoe-road
Depot	and Tooting

4d.

Croydon	and Tooting

Workpeople's Single Fares.

1d. Croydon to Redhouse.
Sumner-road to Monument.
Redhouse to Holborn Schools.
Windmill-road N. to Tooting Junction.

2d. Croydon to Holborn Schools.
Sumner-road to Tooting Junction.

3d. All the Way.

1d. Croydon to Sandy Lane.
Factory to Park Lane Corner.
Sandy Lane to Ringstead-road (top)
Park Lane Corner to Sutton.

2d. Croydon to Ringstead-road (top).
Factory to Sutton.

3d. All the Way.

WORKPEOPLE'S RETURN FARES.

Return Tickets are issued to any person who completes his or her journey by 8 a.m. Return any time on day of issue, on any car. Special Fare 1d. Return Croydon and its Borough Boundaries. Factory and Redhouse. Return at ordinary single fares of 2d., 3d., 4d. and 5d.

Single Journey Workpeople's Tickets are issued at reduced fares minimum fares of 1d. (no half-pennies) for travelling on cars before 8 a.m., and between the hours of 5 p.m. and 7 p.m. Saturdays noon and 2 p.m. A bonafide workman must be either an artizan, mechanic, or daily labourer (male or female) travelling to or from work, and must present an identification or munition card if demanded. Penalty for infringement 40/-.

CHILDREN 14 years or under. will be carried at Half Single Fares (Minimum Fare 1d.)

INFANTS only if under five years of age and sitting in the lap carried free.

PARCELS Personal Luggage. under 28lbs, free. providing no inconvenience is caused to other passengers. All other parcels and pushcarts are carried on the front platform at a charge of 2d. any distance.

PRAMS, MAILCARTS AND BICYCLES will be carried at the discretion of the Motorman at a charge of 6d. any distance.

SMALL DOGS carried free at the discretion of the Conductor on top decks only at owner's responsibility and risk.

NOTE—All articles carried on platforms are carried under special conditions and at owner's risk. These Regulations will be strictly enforced.

114, CHURCH STREET, CROYDON.   AUGUST 1918.   A. V. MASON, General Manager.

W. A. CLARKE & SONS, PRINTERS. 30. TAMWORTH ROAD, CROYDON   TELEPHONE 1928 CROYDON

S.M.E.T. narrow Fare Table.   (Courtesy R. F. Makewell

carried a large "X" overprint in red, the basic colour being that of the corresponding Ordinary Single ticket, and in the case of these tickets, the stage numbers all faced outwards. A peculiarity of these 24-stage tickets was in the conditions of issue printed vertically up the centre panel on the Ordinary Single issues. To avoid having a separate printing block for use on the Penge depot issues, where the cars worked over the Corporation tracks, these read as follows:—"Available for a through journey to and from the lines of the Company and Croydon Corporation Tramways, or for a journey on the Company's lines only to Fare Point number indicated by punch hole. Issued subject to Bye-Laws and to be shown or given up on demand".

Later the length of all tickets was reduced to 2¼ inches, and the number of farestages to twelve. On the Single tickets, these were inset either side of a central line, six on each side, with the Company's title and conditions of issue along the edges. The Ordinary Return tickets were considerably altered with this size reduction. The fivepenny Return, although only used for the Tooting—Mitcham (Fair Green) stage, nevertheless had the full 1-12 stage number arrangement, the stage numbers being set in ladder formation either side of a central column which contained the Company's title, the fare value set in large type, and underneath in capital letters, the words "ORDINARY RETURN TICKET". This causes one to wonder whether the Company had proposed to introduce the issue of fivepenny return fares on the Sutton route and also to other threepenny stages on the Tooting route, but decided against such a procedure, due to its affect on the revenue returns. The 7d. Return had the stage numbers 1-4 and 9-12 set in heavy type in ladder style left and right of the central column, and the 8d. value carried the stage numbers 1 and 2 on the left-hand side with 11 and 12 on the right-hand side, whilst the tenpenny now bore the stage name "WEST CROYDON (LONDON ROAD)" on the left and "SUTTON (HIGH STREET)" on the right. The stage layout occupied about one inch of the space on the ticket, underneath which was set the conditions of issue, over which was printed a small "R" on the 5d. value and a large "R" on the others. The same colours were retained as used in the 24-stage issues.

Sunday 28 October 1928 saw the introduction of a new facility on the Sutton route, when a penny transfer ticket was made available from Benhill Road to Sutton Station, Chaucer Road or "The Angel" (Sutton), changing to the LGOC buses at the tram terminus. A special salmon coloured ticket was provided for this transfer, which carried on the right-hand side, with the type set facing inwards, the titles of the two companies, as follows:—"S.M.E. TRAMWAYS LTD., & GENERAL OMNIBUS COMPANY LTD. & ASSOCIATED COMPANIES". Underneath the serial number of the ticket, the fare value plus the words "TRANSFER TICKET" in heavy type capitals were set, below which the availability of the ticket was set out in full:—"SUTTON, Benhill Road to SUTTON RAILWAY STATION (HIGH STREET), THE ANGEL or CHAUCER ROAD". Below the availability was set in smaller type the following instruction:—"Change at 'THE GRAPES' (Tram Terminus) to Omnibus —L.G.O.C. Ltd. & ASSOCIATED COYS". No exchange tickets were issued, either for the Transfer or for Return Tickets, a special perforating and non-registering punch making an identifiable number in small holes, being used as a cancelling machine.

The 2¼ inch form of ticket remained in issue to the end of trams on the Sutton route, except that from late in 1933 until their withdrawal in December 1935, a few values bore the title "LONDON PASSENGER TRANSPORT BOARD" in place of the former South Metropolitan title. On the Tooting route, things remained undisturned until 1 September 1926, when L.C.C. Route 8 (Victoria—Tooting Junction) was extended to Mitcham (Cricket Green) over the lines that had lain derelict since just after the First World War started, and the South Met. cars were withdrawn between Fair Green (Mitcham) and Tooting Junction. In order that local passengers in the Mitcham area should suffer no inconvenience through this withdrawal, the following transfer fares were introduced, passengers changing cars at Mitcham (Fair Green):—

"Blue House" and "The Swan", Mitcham ... 1d. Single
"Blue House" and Tooting Broadway... ... 2d. „

The introduction of the twopenny transfer to Tooting Broadway had the effect of cheapening the ride for tramway passengers. Hitherto, they had had to pay twopence from "Blue House" to Tooting Junction on a South Met. car, and another penny to Tooting Broadway on an L.C.C. car. No special transfer tickets were provided, as, on the Ordinary penny and twopenny single tickets issued on South Met. cars, four lettered sections at the base of the ticket, with A and B on the left and C and D on the right. A passenger boarding between "Blue House" and the Fair Green and asking for a transfer to "The Swan" would be issued with a penny ticket punched at "A". If he asked for Tooting Broadway, he would be issued with a 2d. ticket punched at "B". The L.C.C. method of dealing with the transfer was much simpler. On the reverse side of the penny and twopenny Ordinary Single tickets issued on cars from Clapham depot, a section was added on the top of the ticket on reverse side, reading:—"Change at Mitcham (Fair Green)—Blue House". As both organisations used non-registering cancelling punches for dealing with Ordinary and Workman Return tickets on the return journey, these were also used for cancelling Transfer Tickets, thus no Exchange Tickets were required.

In December 1933, the London Passenger Transport Board decided to withdraw the S.M.E.T. cars and extended the former L.C.C. route 30 from Tooting Junction to West Croydon. This should have meant the withdrawal of the transfer fares but, due to the fact that, in the late evenings cars after a certain time, reversed at Mitcham (Fair Green) from both Harrow Road and West Croydon, caused an extension rather than a dimunition of the transfer facility at Fair Green. The ex-L.C.C. style of ticket was used on the extended route and the transfer section carries the following farestages above the double line:—Tooting Broadway; Tooting Junction; Swan, Mitcham; Red House; Windmill Road and Blue House, on the 2d. Adult and 1d. Child Tickets, whilst the 1d. Ordinary Adult ticket simply carries the stages Swan (Mitcham) and "Blue House". Apparently the transfer fares were now as follows:—

"Swan", Mitcham and Blue House ... 1d.

2d. Adult Single; 1d. Child Single:—
Tooting Broadway and "Blue House"
Tooting Junction and Windmill Road
"Swan", Mitcham and "Red House".

As mentioned above, the extension of route 30 meant the withdrawal of the South Metropolitan type tickets and their replacement by the standard tickets of the ex-L.C.C. type. At first, a separate set for the extended route 30 was produced, and these tickets went back to the old style of using stage names as well as numbers; so as to obviate a complete renumbering of these stages over the original section of the route between Tooting Junction and Harrow Road, it was necessary to commence the stage numbers from West Croydon, giving that point the number "0" and thus retaining the number "8" for the former terminus at Tooting Junction. After a time, certain journeys on route 42 were combined for schedule purposes at Thornton Heath Depot, with journeys on route 30, and a joint ticket for these two routes remained in use until route 30 was replaced by trolleybuses.

PENGE AND CRYSTAL PALACE (HIGH LEVEL) ROUTES

These two routes, although the shortest of the through routes worked in Croydon, and in their turn, probably the routes with the least variation in fare structure, have without doubt, had the greatest variety of tickets in proportion to their length. This had come about, in the main, through the need for a close financial check on traffic across the boundary at Selby Road (Anerley).

When the line from the boundary at Selby Road to the "Pawleyne Arms" (Penge) was opened to the public on 10 February 1906, the Croydon tramways were being worked by the British Electric Traction Company, of which the South Met. itself was also a subsidiary. In these circumstances therefore, there was no real problem with ticket issue.

The Croydon Corporation terminated the B.E.T's lease of its tramway system on 31 May 1906, and from the following day, the cars from West Croydon terminated at Selby Road, and the South Met. operated two local services in its own area.

On the route to Selby Road, through bookings were introduced across the boundary into the Corporation area as follows:—

(a) Anerley Road, Croydon Road— Selhurst New Road   ...   1d.
(b) Crystal Palace (High Level)   —   West Croydon Station   2½d.

Fare (a) was covered by the issue of a special penny transfer ticket, printed on a white base and overprinted with light brown bars, and (b) by a 2½d. transfer ticket printed on a white base overprinted with grey bars.

The South Metropolitan tickets covering these transfers have been seen. They were headed "South Metropolitan Electric Tramways and Lighting Company & Croydon Corporation Tramways" (in capitals), and even longer title than the one used later on the tram-to-bus transfers at Sutton. In the absence of sight of the Corporation tickets covering these fares, but in view of the colours used on the through tickets issued when through running was resumed, it is safe to say the same colours were used, the only difference being that the Corporation name came first in the title.

On changing cars at Selby Road, the original ticket was handed to the conductor on the second car, who then issued an Exchange Ticket in replacement. There were two Exchange Tickets in use, as follows:—

(a) Selhurst New Road to Anerley Road, Croydon Road. Colour:—White base, overprinted with pink stripes.
(b) West Croydon—Crystal Palace (High Level). Colour:—White base, overprinted with green stripes.

Through running was resumed on 24 June 1907, two routes being introduced, as indicated in Chapter 4.

It might be thought that, in view of the facts stated in Chapter 4, each operator would retain all the takings collected on its own cars, but instead, it was decided that the receipts for fares collected for journeys wholly inside the Corporation area would pass to the Corporation, and those for journeys inside the South Metropolitan area would pass to the Company, and that all cross-boundary fares would be divided in proportion to the distance travelled in each area. A daily return was exchanged between the two organisations showing issues of tickets and the balance of receipts due to each operator, accounts being adjusted every 28 days. Any excess mileage operated by the South Metropolitan was paid for by the Corporation on the basis of the mean average operating costs per car mile. An interim payment of 9d. per car mile for excess mileage was included in the 28-day adjustment, final adjustment being made quarterly. The fares at this time on both routes were as follows:—

West Croydon
1	Selhurst New Road					
1	1	Station Road (Norwood)				
1	1	1	Selby Road (Croydon Boundary)			
2	1	1	1	Anerley Road, Croydon Road		
2	2	1	1	1	Beckenham Road, Croydon Road	
2	2	2	1	1	1	Penge, Crystal Palace entrance.

2	2	1	1	1	Anerley Station	
2	2	2	1	1	Thicket Road	
2½	2	2	1½	1	1	Crystal Palace, High Level.

There was also a Workman facility of one penny single between West Croydon and Anerley Road, Croydon Road and between Selhurst New Road and Penge or High Level. Presumably, these fares were divided in one-third and two-thirds proportions.

The penny fare from West Croydon to Selby Road was in the Corporation area and was covered by the issue of the standard Corporation white penny ticket on the cars of both operators, the South Met. being supplied with stocks of these tickets for use on their cars. The penny fare from Selby Road to Penge was entirely within the South Met. area and was covered by the issue of the standard South Met. penny ticket on Corporation cars, the Company supplying the tickets to the Corporation for this purpose. At first, this ticket was white with a pink centre stripe, but later, the colour was changed to salmon.

For the twopenny fare from West Croydon through to Penge, each operator was entitled to exactly half of each fare collected. This fare was met by the issue of a special twopenny ticket by the Corporation printed on white paper overprinted with purple bars and headed with the titles of the two operators as follows:—"Croydon Corporation Tramways and South Met. Electric Trams and Lighting Company Ltd." (in capitals). The twopenny fare from West Croydon to Thicket Road on the High Level route was met by the use of a ticket in the same colouring with the titles reversed, and as this ticket was only used on South Met. cars, was provided by the Company.

For the other twopenny fare from Selhurst New Road to Crystal Palace (High Level), the Company provided a lilac-coloured ticket bearing a pink central stripe. This leaves us with the penny through fares across the boundary at Selby Road, of which there are three:—

(a) Selhurst New Road—Anerley Road, Croydon Road (both routes).
(b) Station Road (Norwood)—Anerley Station (High Level route).
(c) Station Road (Norwood)—Beckenham Road, Croydon Road (Penge route).

Fare (a) was met by the issue of a ticket printed on white paper overprinted with brown bars on Corporation tickets, but one brown bar over the farestages on the Company issue. The ticket for fare (b) was issued by the Company only and bore a light blue bar printed over the farestages, whilst the ticket for fare (c) was a Corporation issue overprinted with two light blue bars.

The 2½d. through fare from West Croydon to Crystal Palace was handled by the issue of a joint Company/Corporation ticket on white paper with a grey overprint block covering the farestages. It was only issued on the Company cars, but a proportion of the fare was credited to the Corporation.

A significant feature of the farescale prevailing at that time was the absence of Children's fares. Despite the fact that other systems in London had adopted a reduced rate for children by 1915, and which the South Met. itself had introduced on the Sutton and Tooting routes, both Company and Corporation did not give any concessionary fares on these two routes until 1921, and when they were introduced, the following routes came into force at the same time:—

Tickets issued in respect of Children's fares on the Penge and Crystal Palace routes to be as follows:—

From West Croydon:—S.M.E.T. Ordinary Ticket (Single Adult) punched as for the limit of a Child's fare.
To West Croydon:— Croydon Corporation Ticket (Single Adult) punched as for the limit of a Child's fare.

It was mentioned earlier that, during the period between the withdrawal and resumption of through running, the Company ran a service between Penge and Crystal Palace (High Level). This was discontinued after a few weeks in favour of a more remunerative operation between Penge and Selby Road. In order not to inconvenience passengers who had used the through service, transfer tickets were introduced at one penny between Penge and Thicket Road and 1½d. between Penge and High Level respectively. The tickets were of a two-coupon variety, the lower coupon of which had letters on the left hand side to indicate the day of issue, and numbers on the right hand side to represent the hour of acceptance on the second car. The letters from A to G were used as a code to indicate the day of issue, whilst the figures were arranged in two-hourly intervals from 8 a.m. to 12 midnight, the letter "N" being used to distinguish 12 noon. On issue, it was punched in the date letter, and on the second car, it was punched in the section nearest the time at which it was accepted, the top coupon being retained on the second car to account for the punch registration. So as to distinguish between transfers issued from Penge and those issued from High Level or Thicket Road, those issued from Penge on Corporation cars were in plain colour, whilst those from High Level and Thicket Road issued on Company cars had a colour overprint block on the right-hand half of the lower coupon. Consequently, outward from Anerley Road (Croydon Road) only those throught tickets which were different from those being issued on the accepting car were valid for the second leg of the journey. The penny tickets were basically dull brown and the 1½d. value was in orange. The overprint on the lower coupon of the High Level and Thicket Road tickets were normally green. These transfer tickets were withdrawn during the fare increases of the first war, and although brought back again at a later date, were dealt with in a different manner.

Another transfer that was used on this section of the joint lines was brought into being in 1912 by the linking of control of the L.G.O.C. and South Met. Tramways through the UndergrounD group of companies. A special threepenny transfer was available between Penge or Selby Road and Brixton, changing from tram to bus at Crystal Palace (High Level). The ticket for this transfer was supplied by the L.G.O.C. Pink in colour (corresponding with the bus ticket of that value), it carried the title of both operators. An exchange ticket was issued on the second vehicle, the transfer ticket being retained. Although from Penge it would have meant a second change of vehicle, there does not seem to have been any provision made for a check across the change point at Anerley Road (Croydon Road). On journeys from Brixton to Penge or Selby Road, the bus transfer was collected by the tram conductor on the first car (from High Level), who issued an ordinary 1½d. transfer ticket to Penge (the bus transfer being retained to account for its issue). Should the ticket be issued to Selby Road, a normal exchange ticket was issued on the tram. Later tickets on the trams, when the fare to Croydon was increased to threepence, carried the bus transfer at the top of the ordinary ticket of that value. Underneath the transfer stage to Brixton was printed:—"When punched above, please change at High Level. Hand ticket complete to Bus Conductor and receive Exchange Ticket. Penge passengers should change also at "The Robin Hood".

The importance of Crystal Palace was always well-known as a place of entertainment, and in 1909, through fare and admission tickets were issued from any point en route for a combined fare of 1s. 3d. On the outbreak of war, of course, the Palace was closed to the public, the facility then being withdrawn, and it was not repeated on the re-opening of the Palace after the war.

Turning now to fares, changes were made to those charged in the South Met. area between Penge, Crystal Palace and Selby Road on 14 August 1916. The penny fares on this section were shortened, and the 1½d. fare from High Level to Selby Road was increased to twopence, resulting in the following faretable:—

West Croydon
1	Selhurst New Road					
1	1	Station Road (Norwood)				
1	1	1	Selby Road (Croydon Boundary)			
2	2	1	1	Anerley Road, Croydon Road		
2	2	2	1	1	Maple Road	
2	2	2	1	1	1	Thicket Road (Low Level)
3	3	3	2	2	1	1	Crystal Palace (High Level)

2	2	2	1	1	Beckenham Road, Croydon Road
3	3	2	2	1	1	Penge Terminus

The penny transfer fare from Thicket Road on the High Level route was now only available to Beckenham Road (Croydon Road) on the Penge route, whilst the 1½d. transfer from Crystal Palace (High Level) to Penge terminus was increased to twopence, but the tram-bus transfer fares to Brixton remained unchanged. A minor fare change took place on 13 January 1917, when a threepenny return fare was introduced between Selby Road and the termini at Penge and High Level respectively. This facility remained in issue until 1 May 1918, when it was withdrawn. On this date, new fares were introduced throughout both routes (including the Corporation area), these being as follows:—

West Croydon
1									The Gloster
1	1								Selhurst Station
2	1	1							Station Road (Norwood)
2	1	1	1						Portland Road
2	2	1	1	1					Selby Road (Croydon Boundary)
3	2	2	1	1	1				"The Robin Hood"
3	3	2	2	2	1	1			Maple Road
3	3	2	2	2	1	1	1		Thicket Road (Low Level)
4	4	3	3	3	2	2	1	1	Crystal Palace (High Level)
3	3	2	2	2	1	1			"The Pawleyne Arms"
4	3	3	2	2	2	1	1		Penge Terminus.

TRANSFER FARES:—
Change Cars at "The Robin Hood".

Penge (St. John's Road)	and	Anerley Station	1d.
Penge Terminus	and	Crystal Palace (High Level)	2d.

Change at "Robin Hood" (to another tram) and High Level (to bus)

Penge Terminus	and	Brixton Station	4d.

Change at Crystal Palace (High Level) to bus.

Selby Road (Croydon Boundary)	and	Brixton Station	4d.

Change at West Croydon Station.

"The Gloster"	and	Broad Green or "The Greyhound"	1d.
Portland Road	and	Croydon, "The Greyhound"	2d.

The only alterations to these fares was the withdrawal of the penny transfer stage from Penge (St. John's Road) to Anerley Station from 30 May 1918, and its replacement by the original penny transfer from Thicket Road (Low Level) to "The Pawleyne Arms", which was now the official definition for the former Beckenham Road (Croydon Road) farestage.

The May 1918 faretable remained in operation until 10 October 1920, when rising costs caused both the Corporation and the Company to increase fares, the following faretables being introduced at this time:—

Transfer Fares:—
Change car at "The Robin Hood" (Anerley).

High Level and "The Pawleyne Arms" ...	2d.
High Level and Penge Terminus	3d.

The tram-to-tram transfers (change at West Croydon) were also altered as follows:—"The Gloster"—"Greyhound" fare was increased from 1d. to 1½d., the former penny transfer from this point to Broad Green being withdrawn. The former twopenny transfer from Portland Road to "The Greyhound" was now available from Selhurst Station instead of Portland Road.

The tram-to-bus transfers to Brixton Station remained unchanged until the L.G.O.C. increased their fares on 14 November 1920, when a new scale was introduced, as follows:—Selby Road or "Pawleyne Arms" to Brixton Station, 6d.; Penge Terminus to Brixton Station, 7d.

A slight revision to the October 1920 faretable was made on 1 December 1921, when penny fares were reinstated in the South Metropolitan area.

It will be observed in these faretables that no farestage number was allotted to the Maple Road farestage, but, as it only applied to the 1½d. fare to and from Crystal Palace, tickets were punched at Stage 7 (the same number as used for the "Robin Hood" from the direction of Croydon). When the penny fares mentioned above came into operation, a special section was introduced on the penny ticket, as will be explained later.

The tram-to-bus transfer fares to Brixton Station were withdrawn on and from 14 June 1922.

By this time, the method of issue of through tickets across the boundary at Selby Road had been altered. The Corporation continued with the type of ticket they had always used, namely, printed on white paper with different coloured overprint blocks over the farestage spaces and titled with both the Corporation and Company names.

The South Metropolitan however, brought into issue a ticket bearing 24 numbered stages, Stages 1-12 being on the left side and 13-24 facing upwards on the right of a central column in which was printed the very abbreviated title "S.M.E.T. Ltd." followed by the conditions, which read:—"Available for a through journey to and from the lines of the Company and Croydon Corporation Tramways or for a journey on the Co.'s lines only, to Fare Point number indicated by punch hole. Issued subject to Bye-laws and to be shown or given up on demand". With the commencement of issue of this type of ticket, the Company gave up the issue of tickets printed on white paper with an overprint block in differing colours for cross-boundary issues, the 24-stage tickets being used, with the two stages for the fare in question printed at the foot of the tickets. The colours used for the various values were as follows:—

Fare:	Ticket Colour:	Farestages over which available:
1½d.	White/Blue Bars	"Robin Hood" and Station Road (Norwood)
2d.	Magenta	"Robin Hood" and Selhurst Station
2d.	Green	Thicket Road and Station Road (Norwood)
3d.	Yellow	"Robin Hood" and West Croydon
3d.	Pink	Thicket Road and "The Gloster"
3d.	Brown	Station Road (Norwood) and High Level
4d.	Green	Thicket Road and West Croydon
4d.	Flame	High Level and "The Gloster"
5d.	Grey	High Level and West Croydon.

There was also a threepenny Ordinary Single ticket coloured brown which carried the through transfer fare from High Level to Penge terminus, which also carried the 1-24 stage array, but which was only used for the transfer fare. Cancelling machines had now been introduced by both Croydon Corporation and the South Metropolitan Electric Tramways, these being used to cancel Workman Return tickets on the return journey, and also Transfer Tickets when tendered to the Conductor on the second car.

Fares on both Penge and Crystal Palace routes were standardised on 1 January 1923, there being reductions on both routes, the faretables being:—

Stage Nos.:									Additional Single Fare:	
1	West Croydon								High Level and Maple Road ... ... 1d.	
2	1	"The Gloster"								
3	1	1	Selhurst Station							
4	2	1	1	Station Road (Norwood)						
5	2	2	1	1	Portland Road					
6	2	2	1	1	1	Selby Road (Boundary)				
7	3	2	2	1	1	1	"The Robin Hood"			
8	3	3	2	2	2	1	1	"The Pawleyne Arms"		
9	4	3	3	2	2	2	1	1	Penge Terminus	
8	3	3	2	2	2	2	1		Thicket Road (Low Level)	
9	4	3	3	2	2	2	2	2	1	Crystal Pal. (High Level)

Transfer Fares:
Change cars at "The Robin Hood"
Thicket Road and Pawleyne Arms ... ... 1d.
High Level and Penge Terminus ... ... 2d.

As stated above, the transfer fares between the two routes had been revised with this fare standardisation, and, unlike the pre-war procedure of distinguishing marks on the tickets as to the route on which it was issued, the position of the punch-hole now sufficed to indicate to the conductor of the second car as to its availability. The penny transfer (Thicket Road—Pawleyne Arms) was dealt with by the issue of a penny Ordinary Single ticket punched as follows:— On issue on a Corporation car, the ticket would be punched in lettered section "A" indicating that it was available to Thicket Road. In the reverse direction, it would be punched in lettered section "B" indicating that it was available to "The Pawleyne Arms". The twopenny transfer from Penge to High Level was dealt with on the Corporation cars by the issue of a normal S.M.E.T. 2d. Ordinary Single punched in lettered section "C" indicating that it was available to Crystal Palace (High Level). In the opposite direction from Crystal Palace to Penge a special ticket was issued which will be described in a later paragraph.

It will be observed that no scale of Workman Return fares have been quoted in these later faretables, but there were only two fares in operation, these being:—2d. Return, West Croydon to Selby Road (Corporation area) and 2d. Return, Selby Road to Penge or High Level (S.M.E.T. area). These were covered by the issue of the Corporation 2d. ticket in their area on both authorities' cars, and the S.M.E.T. ticket in their area on both Company and Corporation cars. Probably due to the fact that it would be difficult to apportion the receipts between the two organisations, there were no cross-boundary Workman Return Fares, except for the through fare of 4d. from either Penge or High Level to West Croydon, these being covered by the issue of a Corporation 2d. ticket, plus a Company 2d. ticket, both being issued at the same time.

When the Croydon Corporation introduced their new ticket system in 1926, consequent upon the commencement of through running to London, two new issues were brought into use between West Croydon and Selby Road. These were a new penny single ticket on cedar-coloured paper and a twopenny on blue. Both carried the transfer stages that were required for changing cars at West Croydon, and, in addition, were headed with the fare value plus the word "NORWOOD" in heavy type. Below the transfer stages were printed the farestage names for the section between West Croydon and Selby Road. The threepenny and fourpenny fares from West Croydon on the Penge route were now covered on the Corporation 3d. and 4d. "LOCAL" tickets. This left a smaller number of overlap tickets to be provided by the Corporation, all of which were on a white base with a coloured overprint block on the right-hand side. Later, this was switched to the left side when the lay-out of the ticket was reversed, but in each case, it was always on the side of the ticket which carried the titles of the two companies, and not over the farestages as previously. The only stages shown on each value printed were the two specific stages for the overlap fare in question and these were printed for each direction. An interesting feature of these tickets, which were used until the time that London Transport took over, was that although in 1913, when the control of the South Metropolitan had been taken over by the UndergrounD Group from the B.E.T., Croydon Corporation still utilised the full title of its Company companion on these overlap tickets, although the Company used a shortened version.

A full list of the tickets in question was as follows:—

Fare:	Overlap Stages:			Overprint Colour:
1d.	Station Road (Norwood)	and	"The Robin Hood"	Yellow Bar
2d.	"The Gloster"	and	"The Robin Hood"	Red Bar
2d.	Selhurst Station	and	"The Pawleyne Arms" ...	Blue Bar
3d.	"The Gloster"	and	Penge Terminus	Green Bar

The equivalent tickets used by the South Metropolitan Tramways were in the style of their Ordinary Single tickets which had been reduced to 2¼ inches in length, and carried twelve stage numbers in similar style to those used on the Sutton and Tooting sections. They did have, however, the two salient stages for the overlap fare printed at the foot of the tickets, and, as these tickets were never punched in the stage numbers and could not be used for any other purpose, one wonders why the overlap farestages were not printed vertically up the ticket instead of the twelve stage numbers. Here again, a separate all-over colour was used for each individual overlap (with the exception of the ticket used for the penny overlap fare between "The Robin Hood" and Station Road (Norwood), which was printed on white paper with blue bars overprinted at the edges). The rest of the range was as follows:—

Fare:	Overlap Stages:			Colour of Paper:
2d.	"The Robin Hood" ... and	"The Gloster"		Magenta
2d.	Thicket Road (Anerley) and	Selhurst Station		Buff
2d.	Crystal Palace (High Level) and	Station Road (Norwood)...		Green
3d.	Crystal Palace (High Level) and	"The Gloster"		Salmon
3d.	Thicket Road (Anerley) and	West Croydon		Pink
4d.	Crystal Palace (High Level) and	West Croydon		Flame

Having dealt with the tickets used by both operators in the Corporation area, as well as the tickets used by them to cover the overlapping fares from one area to the other, we now come to the tickets used by both operators in the South Metropolitan Tramways area, which lay between the Croydon boundary at Selby Road and the termini at Crystal Palace and Penge. These were, naturally, supplied by the Company for both use on its own cars and those of the Corporation. They were all of the normal 2¼ inch size, and with the exception of one special ticket used on the High Level route, all carried the 1-12 farestage number array as used on the Sutton and Tooting routes, plus the four lettered sections "A-B-C-D" at the foot of the lower value tickets, whilst the penny Ordinary Single ticket carried the special geographical names used on the High Level route, of which more later.

As stated before, the Corporation cars worked the Penge route, and, between that point and Selby Road used four values of the S.M.E.T. tickets, these being:—1d. Adult Single, white; 1d. Child Single, sage; 2d. Adult Single, magenta and a twopenny Workman Return in the same colouring. On issue, the through fares from Selby Road and intermediate stages to Penge were dealt with by punching the stage number to which the ticket was available, these being as follows:—

6 — Selby Road.   8 — "Pawleyne Arms".
7 — "The Robin Hood".   9 — Penge Terminus.

There were two transfer fares in operation between the Penge route and that to High Level, passengers changing cars at "The Robin Hood". The fares consisted of a penny Adult Single from "The Pawleyne Arms" to Thicket Road (Anerley) and a twopenny Adult Single from Penge Terminus to Crystal Palace (High Level). The penny fare was dealt with on a Corporation car by the issue of an Ordinary 1d. Single S.M.E.T. ticket punched in lettered section "A" which represented the farestage at Thicket Road. On a S.M.E.T. car from Thicket Road, and Ordinary 1d. Single S.M.E.T. ticket would be issued punched at Stage "C", indicating to the conductor on the second car that it was available to "The Pawleyne Arms". In both cases, the conductor on the second car, after satisfying himself as to the availability of the ticket, would cancel it in his non-registering cancelling punch.

The twopenny transfer fare from Penge to Crystal Palace (High Level) was dealt with on the Corporation cars by the issue of the Ordinary 2d. value S.M.E.T. ticket punched in Stage "B", which represented the Crystal Palace (High Level) farestage. Like the penny ticket, this would be accepted by the S.M.E.T. conductor on the second car, and cancelled accordingly.

There is now the question of the twopenny Ordinary fare from Penge. This could be changed to Selby Road in the S.M.E.T. area or to Station Road (Norwood) in the Corporation area, and passengers boarding cars at Penge Terminus and asking for a twopenny fare, were asked by the Conductor for their destination. If they were travelling to any stop between "The Robin Hood" and Selby Road, a South Met. twopenny ticket was issued and punched at Stage 6, the whole fare being rendered by the Corporation to the Company. Should the answer be any stop between Selby Road and Station Road (Norwood), the appropriate overlap ticket would be issued, entitling the Corporation to a half-penny from the fare in question.

We now come to the Crystal Palace (High Level) route. Although throughout the London area, the normal farescale was two stages for one penny and four stages for twopence, with the scale going up two stages for every penny, there was exceptional treatment for the section of the S.M.E.T. between "The Robin Hood" (Anerley) and High Level, as the route rose in a constant and steep climb, requiring extra current to propel the cars up the steep hills. In consequence, although there were only two farestages between "The Robin Hood" and High Level, the fare between the two points was twopence, with penny stages from "The Robin Hood" to Thicket Road (one stage only) and from Maple Road to High Level (one stage plus a slight overlap). Maple Road, intermediate between "The Robin Hood and Thicket Road (Stages 7 and 8) was unnumbered, hence its presence as a special geographical stage at the foot of the S.M.E.T. ticket. Although the "Robin Hood" was numbered as Stage 7 on the faretables, it was also shown as a geographical stage at the foot of the penny ticket. The procedure for the issue of penny tickets over this section of the High Level route was as follows:—

On journeys to Crystal Palace:—

Selby Road—"Robin Hood" ... ... Punched at Stage No. 7.
"Robin Hood"—Thicket Road ... ... Punched at Stage No. 8.
Maple Road—High Level ... ... Punched at Stage No. 9.

On journeys to Croydon:—

High Level—Maple Road ... Punched at geographical stage (Maple Road).
Thicket Road—"Robin Hood" Punched at geographical stage ("Robin Hood").
"Robin Hood"—Selby Road ... Punched at Stage No. 6.

This brings us to the twopenny fares from High Level. Like those from Penge, a passenger boarding at High Level and asking for a twopenny fare would be asked to which point he was travelling. If the reply was any stop between Maple Road and Selby Road, the special 2d. ticket mentioned in the paragraph below would be used, the whole fare going to the South Met. If the reply was any stop up to Station Road (Norwood), the twopenny green overlap ticket would be used, entitling the Corporation to a halfpenny from the fare.

The special twopenny ticket, coloured magenta and mentioned in the last paragraph, was of the fareboard type, three fares being quoted, as follows:—

> (a) High Level—"Robin Hood"
> (b) High Level—Selby Road.

Transfer Fare

> Change at "Robin Hood".
> (c) High Level—Penge.

Section (a) was used when normal service cars were running from High Level to Penge depot (which was near "The Robin Hood") and also on the special peak hour cars between Crystal Palace (High Level) and "The Robin Hood".

Section (b) was used on cars proceeding to Croydon and was issued to passengers who were proceeding beyond "The Robin Hood" but not beyond Selby Road.

Section (c) is self-explanatory, being used for passengers who wished to transfer at "The Robin Hood" and proceed towards Penge on another car. It will be remembered that passengers from Penge and transferring at "The Robin Hood" were issued with an Ordinary South Met. twopenny ticket punched in lettered section "B" and only tickets punched thus would be accepted on High Level cars. Similarly, conductors on cars to Penge would only accept the twopenny fareboard type of ticket, thus avoiding misuse of transfer tickets.

The formation of London Transport removed the need for the various overlap tickets, and the different coloured tickets used by South Met. were used up on the ex-Company cars until they were exhausted, after which an L.P.T.B. issue appeared which was printed by the Bell Punch Company in the old South Met. standard colours of 1d. White; 2d. Magenta; 3d. Brown and 4d. Flame. These bore the code "PGE" in the centre column, indicating they were for use at Penge depot, and the twopenny issues carried the adult transfer fares issued via West Croydon in fareboard style at the foot of the ticket. From the copy of the ticket seen, it would seem that the High Level—Penge transfer fare had been withdrawn as it does not appear on thest tickets either.

The Effra Road issues on the ex-Corporation cars did not last for long, as the Penge route was withdrawn and the tracks abandoned from 7 December 1933, the former Thornton Heath—Greyhound stages for Route 42 being included on the reverse side of the tickets used on Route 30. The Bell Punch tickets used on the ex-South Met. cars remained in issue until the trolleybuses replaced the trams, when a set of standard named-stage tickets printed by the Effra Road Works was produced for use on Route 654. Incidentally, the penny transfer fare between Thicket Road and "The Pawleyne Arms" continued to be issued, passengers changing to buses on Routes 12, 75 and 78 (later 194) at "The Robin Hood".

The author of this section would like to thank the Omnibus Society for the use of tickets from their collection with which it is illustrated.

CROYDON POST AND TELEGRAPH OFFICE.

Money Order Office, Inland Revenue Stamp Office, Post Office, Savings Bank, and Insurance and Annuity Office.

HEAD OFFICE: HIGH STREET.   Postmaster—E. L. WISTEL.

Week-days—8 a.m.—8 p.m.
Sundays, Christmas Day and Good Friday.—9—10.30 a.m., 5—6 p.m.
Bank Holidays.—9—12 noon and 5—7 p.m.

TRAMCAR LETTER BOX CONNECTIONS.

For the convenience of residents in the Croydon Postal Area who may have urgent correspondence to post after the final general clearance from street letter boxes has been effected, posting receptacles are provided on tramcars leaving :—

	MONDAYS TO FRIDAYS.		
—		Car Returning from Outer Termini.	Due at West Croydon Station on Return.
WEST CROYDON STATION *for:*	p.m.	p.m.	p.m.
PURLEY	10.15	10.36	10.56
THORNTON HEATH	10.23	10.38	10.53
PENGE	10. 5	10.34	11. 0

	SUNDAYS.		
—		Car Returning from Outer Termini.	Due at West Croydon Station on Return.
WEST CROYDON STATION *for:*	p.m.	p.m.	p.m.
PURLEY	7.20 / 9.10	7.34 / 9.30	7.50 / 9.46
THORNTON HEATH	7.30 / 9.20	7.45 / 9.35	8. 0 / 9 50
PENGE	7.11 / 8.53	7.37 / 9.21	8. 3 / 9.47

Both on the outward and the inward journey, persons having letters to post **may hail the Motorman to stop the car at the stopping places.**
The tramcars that are used for the above purpose will be **distinguished by an illuminated SIGN** bearing the words "**POST CAR.**" This sign will be **fixed** against the window above the step to the front platform. **The Letter Box** will be found at the front of the car on the outward and the back on the inward journeys. The sign, "Post Car," is not shown on the cars to and from Purley.

The notice about postal services on Croydon trams, from Ward's Croydon Directory, circa 1925.
(Courtesy J. B. Gent

Appendix A

DESTINATION EQUIPMENT — CROYDON CORPORATION TRAMWAYS

When put into service, the first two batches of cars did not carry any destination equipment at all. Once more than one service was being provided, it became necessary to indicate on which any car was working and paper strips were printed to be stuck on the fronts of the canopies of the cars.

This temporary arrangement was soon replaced by boards against the wire screens, slotted into brackets at the top of the metal end screens. These showed:—

<table>
<tr><td>NORBURY & PURLEY
– via –
WEST & SOUTH CROYDON</td><td>THORNTON HEATH
PURLEY
– via –
WEST & SOUTH CROYDON</td></tr>
<tr><td>CROWN HILL &
ADDISCOMBE
via
EAST CROYDON STATION</td><td>WEST CROYDON &
NORWOOD
via
WHITEHORSE RD. & SELHURST</td></tr>
</table>

At the same time as these boards were fitted on the fronts of the cars, route boards were fixed on the side decency panels, reading:—

<table>
<tr><td>NORBURY and PURLEY</td><td>THORNTON HEATH and PURLEY</td></tr>
<tr><td>NORWOOD and WEST CROYDON</td><td>ADDISCOMBE and CROWN HILL</td></tr>
</table>

The boards in both positions were in white lettering on black or chocolate.

The bogie cars were delivered with roller blind destination boxes to show a destination in one line at a time. Before long, similar boxes were fitted to the older cars and subsequent cars were delivered already fitted with destination boxes, mounted on tall stanchions above the ends of the upper deck. These showed all the regular turning points on each of the routes, but "NORWOOD" had to be used for Selby Road and the blinds included "WOODSIDE" in case an extension to that place were ever constructed.

When through bookings commenced with the L.C.C. at Norbury, Croydon cars carried additional boards above the route boards on the upper deck, when working on the main line. These were inscribed:—

| Change cars AT Norbury for | STREATHAM BRIXTON KENNINGTON ELEPHANT & CASTLE WESTMINSTER WATERLOO & BLACKFRIARS BRIDGES EMBANKMENT 'SWAN' STOCKWELL VAUXHALL & VICTORIA STATION |

Some cars carried "Through Bookings, Croydon and London" on a small board just below the destination box.

The introduction of through running between L.C.C. and Croydon cars forced a number of L.C.C. practices onto Croydon Corporation Tramways. Like the standard L.C.C. cars, the new Croydon E/1 class cars carried two line destination boxes with L.C.C. type two line blinds in them. The return made to London Transport, just before they took over in 1933 gave the list for destination blinds as shown on p.190.

The E/1s also carried brackets under the saloon windows for standard L.C.C. route boards. Those occupying the position under the two centre windows normally showed:—

16	KENNINGTON STREATHAM	16
	EMBANKMENT CROYDON PURLEY	
18	BRIXTON NORBURY	18

SCHEDULE OF WORDING ON DESTINATION BLINDS

Service 16/18

SPECIAL CAR

BRIXTON STATION

ANGEL ROAD

BRIXTON

WATER LANE

BRIXTON HILL

KENNINGTON GATE

STREATHAM LIBRARY

WORKMEN'S CAR

(NORBURY
(via BLACKFRIARS

(NORBURY
(via WESTMINSTER

(EMBANKMENT
(via KENNINGTON & WESTMINSTER

(EMBANKMENT
(via ELEPHANT & BLACKFRIARS

WESTMINSTER

BLACKFRIARS

ELEPHANT & CASTLE

DEPOT

(CROYDON
(& PURLEY

CROYDON

THORNTON HEATH

GREYHOUND

(PURLEY
(DEPOT.

Local Services

(a) Thornton Heath & Greyhound
(b) West Croydon & Penge.

WEST CROYDON

NORWOOD

PENGE

THORNTON HEATH DEPOT

THORNTON HEATH

GREYHOUND

RED DEER

PURLEY DEPOT

PURLEY

NORBURY

SPECIAL CAR

The schedule of wording on the destination blinds, as submitted to London Transport, in answer to the questionnaire. (Courtesy R. F. Makewell

190

For use on weekday off-peak midday working, they were lettered on the backs:—

16 EMBANKMENT	**CROYDON 16**
CHEAP FARES	
18 BRIXTON	**PURLEY 18**

The wording "Cheap Fares" was in white on red, the rest of the lettering on both faces was black on white, but 16 and 18 appeared in white on black squares.

There were brackets for separate boards under the end windows and when the "Shilling All Day" and "Sixpenny Evening Ticket" arrangements of the L.C.C. were extended to include Croydon, these spaces were used for boards carrying the following information:— (black on white).

6d. Evening Tourist (from 6 p.m.) in L.C.C. and Croydon Corporation Tramways Area.	**1/- All Day in L.C.C. and Croydon Corporation Tramways Area.**

The two local routes continued to use single line route boards, often in white letters on black:—

THORNTON HEATH – WEST CROYDON – GREYHOUND (Croydon)

WEST CROYDON – SELHURST – SOUTH NORWOOD – PENGE

For special occasions (Bank Holidays, etc.) there was a board:—

THORNTON HEATH – WEST CROYDON – RED DEER – PURLEY

The cars used on the local services had brackets for a board near the top of the centre saloon window and when used on the Penge route, showed:—

To and from CRYSTAL PALACE (PENGE ENTRANCE)   in white on black.

On the reverse was,

Near SELHURST PARK FOOTBALL GROUND   also in white on black.

This board was also carried on Thornton Heath cars on Saturday, as the Football Ground lies just off Whitehorse Lane between the Penge and Thornton Heath routes (after it moved from opposite Selhurst Station in the 1920s).

Not long before the take over in 1933, Penge cars received two small end boards under the windows, reading:—

SELBY RD. (Cheap fare 2d.)–NORBURY   **SELBY RD. (Cheap fare 2d.)–PURLEY**

The only changes made when London Transport took over, was that the "Shilling All Day" boards became white on light blue and the "6d. Evening" white on red.

From the outset, South Metropolitan cars were equipped with single line destination boxes, with blinds lettered for each of the regular turning points on the route concerned. The ex-Gravesend cars had boxes suitable for two line blinds, but used single line blinds, with the destinations more widely spaced.

During the 1914-1918 War, some cars carried "CROYDON & SUTTON" or "CROYDON & TOOTING" on the blinds as an economy. Note that the Tamworth Road terminus was normally shown as "CROYDON", while the Corporation used "WEST CROYDON" for the terminus across the road.

No major changes seem to have been made to the information displayed on the blinds throughout the life of the Company and when the London United cars appeared, they were provided with sign-written boards giving the same information as the blinds for the Mitcham and Sutton routes.

From the early days, until the cars were sent to Hendon for overhaul, there were three boards attached to the wire netting on the upper deck sides, lettered in white on green. (At first Nos. 1-16 had positions for four boards, but they were soon altered to take three like the rest).

WEST CROYDON	ANERLEY	CRYSTAL PALACE
CROYDON	MITCHAM	TOOTING
CROYDON	WALLINGTON	SUTTON

They were not entirely consistent, some cars showing "West Croydon" and others just "Croydon". When the red livery was adopted, some cars had the boards repainted with black lettering on white.

When the cars were sent to Hendon, these boards were replaced by more accessible long narrow single line boards, under the saloon windows:—

5 CRYSTAL PALACE ANERLEY STATION ROBIN HOOD SELBY ROAD NORWOOD SELHURST WEST CROYDON 5

6 WEST CROYDON   MITCHAM ROAD   CANTERBURY ROAD   MITCHAM COMMON   FAIR GREEN 6

7 WEST CROYDON   WADDON STATION   AERODROME WALLINGTON   CARSHALTON   WESTMEAD ROAD SUTTON 7

There was also a board numbered 5A for the Crystal Palace—Robin Hood or Selby Road short workings, probably on the back of the Route 5 board. There do not appear to have been special boards for the various short workings on the Mitcham and Sutton routes. The route boards with numbers were always black on white.

No ex-South Metropolitan car survived long enough into London Transport days to receive L.T. route boards. When route 30 was extended to Croydon the cars carried standard L.C.C. type route boards

30	WEST CROYDON	MITCHAM TOOTING	WANDSWORTH PUTNEY	HAMMERSMITH SHEPHERDS BUSH	SCRUBS LANE	30

Ex-Croydon No. 385 (formerly 41) outside Purley Depôt in 1950.   (Photo W. J. Haynes

ADVERTISING ON CROYDON CORPORATION CARS

From 1901 to 1906, when the B.E.T. operated the Croydon system, the Corporation did not permit them to display commercial advertisements on the exteriors of the cars. However, very soon after the lease to the B.E.T. was terminated, the Corporation concluded an agreement with J. W. Courtenay Ltd., who arranged to pay the Corporation £30 per annum for every car which was decked out with a display of advertisement panels, provided by them. Only coloured enamelled iron plates were used, in eight positions round the decency panels of the upper deck, i.e. two main sides, four corners and two ends. The bogie cars had only two ends and longer sides. All positions were not always occupied and panels left uncovered were painted in the normal livery. Courtenays entered into agreements with national and local traders who wished to advertise on the cars. If enamelled iron plates were used, the contract would be for not less than three years and if for any reason a car were to be out of service for an extended period, the Corporation was expected to transfer its advertisements to another car.

There would appear to have been three distinct generations of advertising on Croydon Corporation trams, but they overlapped to some extent. As first built, most of the Croydon cars had patterned or frosted glass opening lights above the saloon windows, which precluded advertising on them during the first generation. One car, No. 26, had a feature usually associated with the B.E.T. Group, namely exclusive advertising—all eight positions on the upper deck were allocated to Bateman, the well known optician.

(a) 1906 to the 1914-1918 War.

Advertisements on the main side panels included—Heinz 57 Varieties (white shaded black on light blue, with green cucumber), Beecham Pills (black shaded blue on white), Penge Empire Theatre (blue on white), Dewar's Whisky (white on light blue), Lipton's Tea (white on green) and Bateman, Optician (white on light green on No. 26 only). The ends most commonly carried—Bovril (white shaded black on blue with yellow edge), Borwick's Baking Powder (white on dark blue), Military Pickle (white on yellow and red) or the similarly coloured Birds Custard. Corners usually carried a variety of local advertisements, whose colours are no longer recorded.

(b) 1918-1927.

During the 1914-1918 war, a number of main side plates, whose contracts had presumably run out, were covered with paper stickers, inscribed "Eat Less Bread" and other patriotic slogans.

Beecham's Pills, Dewar's Whisky, Bovril and Borwick's Baking Powder continued to be displayed as before, but the Bateman's advertisement on No. 26 gave way to a more striking Bateman's sign on the fronts of several other cars. It was in the form of a large pair of yellow spectacles on dark green, so at least the cars could see where they were going!

Double Royal size posters were carried on the dash corners, usually announcing forthcoming local events. Very occasionally two were placed side by side, or one near the front (size 30 x 20 in.).

The bogie cars usually carried slogans advertising "Croydon Corporation Electricity" in black on white, in various styles, but a number of new signs appeared on the four wheeled cars, such as Mann, Crossman's Stout (yellow on dark green with a red seal each end), Rawling & Oldfield, optician (blue on white, with pink round eye). The only distinctive new one on the ends, was Dunster's "Bon Ami" Cigars (brown on yellow) and some cars had "Punch" magazine (white and red on blue).

Opening Vents in Saloon.

As the cars were overhauled after the war, the patterned glass in the opening vents was replaced by plain glass, onto which "transparency" advertisements were usually fixed. They usually represented cleaning fluids and other household goods. These included:—

"Compo" (white on blue), "Gospo—Cats white homes bright" (white cats with black lettering on blue), "Carbosil" (white shaded black on yellow), "Hall's Wine" (white on dark red), "Glaxo" (white on blue), "Rinso" (white on blue and red). They sometimes overflowed onto the tops of the saloon windows.

(c) 1927-1933.

Although renumbered and painted in a new livery, the twenty single truck cars that were retained kept the enamelled iron plates already mentioned, while the ten old bogie cars retained "Croydon Corporation Electricity", Hammond & Hussey and Batchelars advertisements, but there were fewer advertisements on the ends of the bogie cars.

With the delivery of the 25 new bogie cars, advantage was taken of the fact that they worked outside the Borough boundaries and on their main side panels they advertised the large departmental stores in Brixton and Streatham, which they passed. They advertised local Croydon traders on the corners, but the end positions were occupied by ample destination boxes.

Main side panels carried Bourne Bros., Drapers (black shaded white on orange), Quin & Axten, Draper (white on red on some cars and red on white on others), Sharman's of Streatham (white on blue or blue on white), etc. The corners advertised such things as Southwell & Marriage fire places (white on red), A. Priddis (white on blue) and Waterman, Dyers (white on green).

At first the dash corners of these cars showed "This car has cushion seats and Pullman comfort" but later they carried official notices and theatre posters like the other cars. They also carried window transparencies like the other cars.

(d) 1933-1951.

The older cars did not have their advertising changed during their short stay with London Transport and the new bogie cars continued to carry them until about 1942, when the leases must have run out and the enamel plates were required for war salvage. From then on, they carried London Transport's standard range of paper displays. Nos. 383, 386 and 393 received "Oakey's Cabinet Glass Paper" (white on blue) on the corners, evidently transferred from L.C.C. cars. which had perhaps been scrapped.

London Transport continued to fix window transparencies on the cars, showing a slight preference for the windows themselves rather than the opening lights above them and evolved a system of displaying an oval sticker between two rectangular ones, all three advertising the same product. Of course this arrangement was only suitable for the saloon windows.

ADVERTISING ON SOUTH METROPOLITAN CARS

The British Electric Traction Company had a very active commercial advertising department, who on some of the provincial undertakings they controlled, sought to cover every possible flat surface on their tramcars with advertising material. In the case of the South Metropolitan company, although advertisements were carried as soon as possible after operation commenced, the policy was slightly more restrained. The eight usual positions on the upper deck received coloured enamelled iron plates and in the early days, many cars carried small advertising plates on the stair risers. At least one car carried one on the platform step riser and another (No. 42) had an additional plate fixed on the wire screen, above the usual end position, with "Festival of Empire".

Like the Corporation, the South Metropolitan advertising arrangements went through three distinct phases, which overlapped to a certain extent and the dates given below must be taken as only approximate.

194

(a) **1906 to 1920**

Many of the cars carried Mackintosh Tyres (white on light green), Claymore Whisky (white on light blue), Lipton's Tea (white on dark green) or Hammond & Hussey, Ironmonger (yellow on green) on either the main side or corner positions. On the corners there was also the colourful "Gossages Soap" (white on blue, yellow and red), Hudson's Super Soap (white on red) or Hudson's Soap with a lantern design (black lettering on white and red). Ends included Glaxo Baby Food (white on light blue) and Charles Baker, outfitter (white on red). The earlier Sunlight Soap advertisement was blue on yellow, but the later curved design was white on blue above and blue on yellow below. The Nubolic advertisement on the stair risers was white on blue.

During the war, as with Croydon Corporation, a number of advertisements whose contracts had run out, were covered over with "Eat Less Bread" paper bills.

(b) **1920 to 1927.**

In the meantime, the South Metropolitan Co. had changed hands from B.E.T. management to UndergrounD Group management. This had no immediate effect on advertising policy, but several of those enterprises who had advertised widely on the cars, did not renew their contracts after the war, in particular, "Mackintosh Tyres", "Claymore Whisky" and "Charles Baker". Walter Cobb at Sydenham was a little too far away and the places of those removed were taken by new advertisers, mainly more local to the area served. There were also paper "Transparency" advertisements pasted onto the inside of the saloon opening lights and along the tops of the windows. Some cars had an advertisement for "Empire Tobacco" low down on the door window. The Lipton's Tea plate was replaced by a paper display, which looked identical. There were also advertisement boards hung on the rear end of the dash. There was a plate across the top, lettered in red on white "S. Met. Electrics" so evidently this space was originally intended to advertise the Company's electric supply department.

The UndergrounD Group, by which the S.M.E.T. was now controlled, made a distinction between its "Publicity" and "Commercial Advertising" departments. "Publicity" was only concerned with the sale of the Company's own wares, i.e. pointing out places of interest served by their own and associated cars, special facilities, etc. On the other hand, Commercial Advertising was concerned with the sale of advertising space to other traders. Officially, each space on the car was allocated to one or the other, but they could use each other's spaces by mutual agreement. Thus, the dash corner and the bulkhead frames inside the car belonged to "Publicity", the latter being intended for fare tables and travel notices. Commercial Advertising sometimes used for dash corners and Publicity would provided "fill-ups" for any advertising spaces left unsold. It was very rare to see Company's cars with any empty advertising spaces.

Among the new advertisements carried on the main side panels, were Rawling—North End, Optician (blue on white as on Corporation cars). This and Hammond & Hussey also appeared later on three of the ex-L.U.T. cars loaned to the S.M.E.T. There was also Mazawattee Tea (white on blue) on some cars. Among the more colourful end positions, were Bryce Grant, Draper, Penge (white on blue, with red on white panels), Turtle for Cutlery (yellow shaded red on dark green), Swan Vestas Matches (yellow shaded black on red) and Stockwell & Oxford, Furnisher (white on dark blue).

The UndergrounD Group produced attractive coloured Double Royal size posters (30 x 20 in.) at approximately two monthly intervals. These were displayed on station platforms and entrances, bus rear corners and tram dash corners. Several were fixed in glass frames above the seats in the Crystal Palace shelter, together with a larger route map. They usually took the form of brightly coloured paintings by well known contemporary artists, depicting places of interest served by the Group, such as Hampton Court, Kingston Bridge, Virginia Water,

Exhibitions at the Crystal Palace, Flying at Hendon and at Waddon (Croydon Aerodrome).

Others were in the form of notices, such as announcing Mitcham Fair, Greyhound Racing at Wimbledon (blue on white with red jacket on hound). If not required by Publicity, the dash corners were often occupied by Bovril slogans (red and black on white), Morning Post (white on blue or black on white), Dalton's Weekly, etc. From 1926 when the L.C.C. took over the Tooting Mitcham section, one of the saloon bulkhead positions was usually occupied by a notice proclaiming transfer fares between the "Blue House" and the "Swan" at Mitcham. The fare table occupied the corresponding position at the other end of the car.

(c) **1927 to 1933**

By the time the South Metropolitan cars were sent to Hendon for major overhauls, most of the contracts for enamelled iron signs had run out and they were replaced by short term paper displays. Only a few metal signs remained on the ends of some cars. These were Bryce Grant, Hammond & Hussey, Turtle, Hudson's Soap (lantern), Sunlight Soap and Brymay. One or two cars retained Rawling on the main side panel. (Although the styles and colours were the same, the Rawling who advertised on South Metropolitan cars, was not the same as Rawling & Oldfield on the Corporation cars, but they were related).

The paper streamers were rather lacking in variety and the same advertisements seem to have been displayed in different combinations on every serviceable car in the fleet. The most common main sides were "Whitbread's Ale & Stout" (blue on white, sometimes with red first letters). "Black & White Whisky" (black on white or white on black). A few cars had "Mann, Crossman's Beers (yellow on dark green) or Mazawattee Tea (white on blue). Corners were usually occupied by "Whitbread's", "Maclean's Tooth Paste" (blue on white) or Boyd's Pianos (blue on yellow with red edge). Ends, where not still occupied by Bryce Grant's, or Turtle, usually carried "Whitbread's" or a "Batchelar's" paper display. There were also some Bovril displays.

Although moved to a new position above the dash, the dash corner material remained as before, plus "Sunday Graphic", "Daily Sketch" and "Heinz 57 Varieties"! The London United cars took a "dash corner" bill on the staircase landing, as well as on the dash.

When selling advertising space, the UndergrounD Group preferred to offer spaces of standard sizes. Standard ends and corners would fit most SouthmeT cars and the standard bus size "main side" panel fitted Nos. 36-51. There was a little bit left over each end on Nos. 1-16, but the old Milnes cars Nos. 17-26 had to have paper displays cut down slightly; this was noticeable with "Lipton's Tea" where there was no margin at the beginning and end of the lettering. The side panels of the bogie cars were so long that they could take a "main side" and a "corner" each side, but there was no corner position otherwise on the short canopied bogie cars.

The limited variety of paper displays and the few remaining iron plates stayed on the cars into London Transport days until they were scrapped. The London United cars and ex-Corporation cars were treated like the rest.

Window Transparencies.

Like Croydon Corporation cars, South Metropolitan cars carried paper transparency advertisements printed on thin paper in light colours facing inwards, so as to be legible to passengers riding inside the car. They were pasted onto the opening lights and the tops of the windows. Many firms advertised on both Corporation and SouthmeT cars. Those noted included:—

Brymay Matches (yellow on green), Gospo (as on Corporation cars), Abbey Road Building Society (lighthouse design—black on yellow), and Religious Tracts (white on blue).

THE ALL RED ROUTE RAILWAY

Apart from the electric tramways operated by the South Metropolitan Company and Croydon Corporation, there was an electric railway of tramway character, within the area served, for a short time.

In the summer of 1911, a Festival of Empire Exhibition was held at the Crystal Palace and in its extensive grounds, in which areas were set aside for the various Dominions and Colonies to set up buildings, pavilions and other features to represent the atmosphere of their own country. Naturally, the area the whole exhibition covered was quite extensive with several lakes and some heavy gradients.

There had been earlier experiments with railways in the grounds, including an atmospheric railway and it was decided that it might be a good idea to link the various pavilions by a circular railway, with a station at each. Thus a 3 ft. 6 in. gauge railway was built, not exactly circular, but more like two rectangles joined together. It served stations named "Pageant", "South Africa", "Newfoundland", "Canada", "India", "Australia" and "New Zealand". There was a tunnel between "Pageant" and "Newfoundland" stations, passing under the imposing flight of steps leading down from the main Crystal Palace building to the grounds, with gradients of 1 in 12 either side of it.

Thus, to use the language of the day, "The visitor gets a graphic idea in succession of a number of different countries over which the British flag flies in various parts of the world . . . At each one, there is a station bearing the name of the colony, so that playfully, the visitor may say that in a few minutes, he can make a tour of the world."

The All Red Railway was constructed by Messrs. Dick, Kerr & Co. Ltd. The permanent way was laid on twelve inches of ballast, with 60 lb. rails in 30 ft. lengths. As well as the tunnel, there was a cutting 100 yards long near Crystal Palace (Low Level) Station and "Canada" Station, also an embankment and a tressle bridge. Current was collected from outside third and fourth rails. The rolling stock consisted of nine motored cars and nine trailers. Both types were roofed crossbench cars, for 39 and 35 seats. The driving platforms were unvestibuled with an ordinary tramcar type dash and a vallance fixed to the canopy above to provide shade. The leading dimensions of the cars were:—

Bodies built by MILNES, VOSS & Co., of Birkenhead, in 1911.
Overall length 24 ft. 1 in. Width 7 ft. 6 in. (motor cars).
Seating 39 passengers on cross benches (5 bays and platforms).
B.T-H. k10D controllers.
Two GE/58 motors of 37½ horse power.
Mountain & Gibson 21EM truck. 31¾ in. wheels.
Braking—Hand and rheostatic.

The trailers had 23 ft. 4 in. long bodies and seated 35 passengers, otherwise, they were like the motor cars. They appear to have been painted in a plain red livery lined in yellow or gold. The cars were single ended.

After the exhibition was over, the cars were offered for sale and it was thought that having standard tramcar equipment, they would be of use to seaside or pier tramways of 3 ft. 6 in. gauge. In fact, one motor car and one trailer were sold to the Dublin & Lucan tramway in Ireland. The motor car was fitted with a short outside spring trolley mast and numbered 19. Later panelling and windows were fitted along one side and it was painted in the company's green and cream livery. It was scrapped in 1928. The others were cannibalized for spares.

Appendix B.—Acts of Parliament

Every tramway to be constructed on the streets of Great Britain and to carry passengers, whether by means of animal or mechanical traction required authorization through an Act of Parliament. This was prepared in the form of a Bill, by the undertaking's Parliamentary Agents and contained many details concerning the proposed methods of construction, operation and rules for passengers and staff. The actual lines to be constructed and routes followed, were set out as a number of numbered "Tramways". These numbers had nothing to do with service numbers adopted in later years, but were included for the ready identification of individual sections by parliamentarians. As the Bill passed through the House and various sub-committees, individual clauses to which exception was taken, could be deleted. This also applied to the numbered "Tramways". Each Bill would receive three readings before Parliament and passed or rejected. If too many clauses had been deleted, the Bill would almost certainly be rejected or passed in such a form as to be unworkable (The latter fate overtook the Croydon & District Bill of 1902.)

Around the turn of the century, a somewhat simplified system, known as "Light Railway Orders" was introduced and intended really for rural and agricultural minor railways, but was taken advantage of by a number of tramway authorities to construct ordinary street tramways. This applied in the case of Mitcham.

The lesser Acts of only two or three tramways are mentioned in passing in the text. The various "Tramways" in the more important Acts are set out here:—

The Croydon Tramways Act, 1878 (41-2 Vic., Cap. ccxxiv).

The preamble to this Act was surprisingly short and the following promotors were mentioned by name—Jabez Spencer Balfour, Francis Moses Coldwells, John Pelton, Joshua Allder and David Buck Miller.

Tramway No. 1—1 mile 41 chains commencing in London Road, Thornton Heath in the Parish of Croydon and terminating in North End also in the Parish of Croydon.

Tramway "a" —a short siding or passing place connected with and subsidiary to Tramway No. 1.

Tramway No. 2 —1 mile 20 chains and 69 links commencing in Brighton Road in the Parish of Croydon and terminating in High Street, Croydon.

Tramway "c" —a short siding or passing place connected with and subsidiary to Tramway No. 2.

Tramway No. 3 —24 chains and 60 links commencing in St. James' Road near its junction with Milton Road and terminating in Saint James' Road near its junction with Oakfield Road.

Tramway No. 4 —78 chains and 83 links commencing in South Norwood near Princes Road and terminating in Saint James' Road by a junction with Tramway No. 3.

Tramway No. 5 —26 chains and 20 links commencing at a junction with Tramway No. 3 and terminating by a junction with Tramway No. 1 in London Road.

Note how vague the descriptions of the "Tramways" are, compared with later Acts. Later clauses state that all was to be single track.

The Tramways Orders Confirmation (No. 1) Act, 1880 (43-4 Vic., cap. clxxii:—

(a) A junction line from the corner of Brigstock Road and London Road along Brigstock Road and Collier's Water Lane, High Street, New Thornton Heath and Whitehorse Road to the corner of Selhurst Road, 1 mile 5 furlongs 9 chains 20 links, single, except at sundry passing places.

(b) A line along St. James' Road East, Cherry Orchard Road, Addiscombe Road and George Street to North End, 1 mile 2 furlongs 2 chains 75 links, single.

The Norwood District Tramways Act, 1882 (45-6 Vic., cap. clvi), incorporated "The Norwood District Tramways Company", and authorised the following lines:—

(a) A line from High Street, New Thornton Heath, along Whitehorse Lane and Clifton Road to Selhurst Road, 3 furlongs 8 chains 70 links, single, with passing places.

(b) A line from the junction of Prince's Road with Selhurst Road to High Street, South Norwood, 5 furlongs 4 chains 40 links, single, with passing places.

(c) A continuation of the preceding along the Croydon or Penge Road, 3 furlongs 6 chains 75 links.

(d) A single line from High Street, South Norwood, along Portland Road to St. Luke's, Woodside, 6 furlongs 8 chains, single, with passing places.

(e) A continuation of the preceding to Lower Addiscombe Road terminus of the Croydon Line, 1 mile 1 furlong 9 chains, single, with passing places.

(f) A spur line from Lower Addiscombe Road along Stroud Green Road, 4 furlongs 5 chains 30 links, single, with passing places.

The Act gives power to use steam or other mechanical power under regulations and conditions.

The Croydon and Norwood Tramways Act, 1883 (46-7 Vic., cap. clxxiv.), amalgamated the two companies and their undertakings as before stated, and further authorised the construction of new lines about 3 miles in length, but all outside the County of London, and gave the new company power to use steam or other mechanical power, subject as usual to regulations.

Croydon Corporation Tramways Act 1900

Details of Tramways permitted to be constructed (the existing horse tramways are taken for granted):—

Tramway No. 1—2 chains single line wholly in George Street commencing at a junction with an existing tramway in Croydon High Street and terminating at a junction with another existing tramway.

Tramway No. 2—2.50 chains, double line, wholly in George Street, commencing at a junction with an existing tramway 28 yards east of Park Lane and terminating at a junction with an existing tramway.

Tramway No. 3—2.50 chains entirely double line on East Croydon Railway Bridge commencing 83 yards east of Dingwall Road and terminating at a junction with an existing tramway.

Tramway No. 4—2.75 chains entirely double line commencing in Upper Addiscombe Road at Altyre Road and terminating in Cherry Orchard Road 169 yards south-east of Oval Road.

Tramway No. 5—1 furlong 1.90 chains, single line, wholly in Cherry Orchard Road commencing at Oval Road and terminating at Cross Road, being joined to double line at each end.

Tramway No. 6—2.50 chains entirely double line wholly in Cherry Orchard Road commencing at termination of Tramway No. 5 and terminating 28 yards west of Leslie Park Road.

Tramway No. 7—3 chains double line wholly in Lower Addiscombe Road commencing 13 yards east of Leslie Park Road and terminating 53 yards west thereof.

Tramway No. 8—3 chains double line wholly in Lower Addiscombe Road commencing 66 yards south-east of Canning Road. Terminating at the commencement of an existing tramway.

Tramway No. 9—3 chains double line wholly in Lower Addiscombe Road commencing 33 yards south-west of Elgin Road and terminating 33 yards south-east thereof.

Tramway No.10—3 chains double line wholly in Lower Addiscombe Road commencing 33 yards south-west of Nicholson Road and terminating 33 yards north-east thereof.

Tramway No.11—3.41 chains of which 2.50 double line wholly in Lower Addiscombe Road commencing 8 yards south-west of Ashburton Road and terminating 75 yards north-east thereof.

Tramway No.12—3 chains single line wholly in Oakfield Road, West Croydon commencing 83 yards south-west of St. James' Road and terminating 17 yards south-west thereof.

Tramway No.13—3 chains double line wholly in Whitehorse Road commencing 33 yards south-west of Cromwell Road and terminating 33 yards north-east thereof.

Tramway No.14—3 chains double line wholly in Northcote Road commencing 17 yards north-east of Burdett Road and terminating 83 yards north-east thereof.

Tramway No.15—3 chains double line wholly in Selhurst Road from 33 yards north-east of Selhurst New Road to 33 yards south-west thereof.

Tramway No.16—3 chains double line wholly in Selhurst Road commencing 67 yards south-west of the railway bridge and terminating 1 yard south-west thereof.

Tramway No.17—3 chains double line wholly in Selhurst Road commencing 33 yards south-west of Clifton Road and terminating 33 yards north-east thereof.

Tramway No.18—3 chains double line wholly in Selhurst Road commencing 187 yards north-east of Clifton Road and terminating 253 yards north-east thereof.

Tramway No.19—3 chains double line wholly in Selhurst Road commencing 90 yards south-west of Whitworth Road and terminating 23 yards south-west thereof.

Tramway No.20—3 chains double line commencing in Selhurst Road commencing 13 yards north-east of Oliver Grove and terminating 53 yards north-east of Oliver Grove, in High Street, South Norwood.

Tramway No.21—3 chains double line wholly in Brigstock Road, Thornton Heath commencing 70 yards south-west, terminating 4 yards south-west of Frant Road.

Tramway No.22—3 chains double line wholly in Brigstock Road commencing 33 yards south-west and terminating 33 yards north-east on Bensham Lane.

Tramway No.23—3 chains double line wholly in Brigstock Road commencing 90 yards north-east of Quadrant Road and terminating 156 yards thereof.

Tramway No.24—6.1 chains double line wholly in Brigstock Road, commencing 13 yards north-east of Beulah Road and terminating 23 yards north-east of Bensham Manor Road.

Tramway No.25—3 chains double line commencing in Brigstock Road 7 yards south-west of Parchmore Road to High Street, Thornton Heath at Stuart Road.

Tramway No.26—1 mile 3 furlongs 1.05 chains of which 2 furlongs 7 chains double line commencing at Croydon's southern boundary in Brighton Road 66 yards north of Bynes Road.

Tramway No.27—5 furlongs 1.5 chains of which 9 chains double line in Brighton Road, commencing at the termination of Tramway No. 26 and terminating 28 yards south of Friends Road at the commencement of Tramway No. 30.

Tramway No.28—9.9 chains double line wholly in Brighton Road Commencing 70 yards south of Ledbury Road and terminating at Aberdeen Road.

Tramway No.29—2.5 chains double line wholly in High Street, Croydon commencing at Mason's Avenue and terminating 55 yards north thereof.

Tramway No.30—2.5 chains double line wholly in High Street, Croydon commencing 28 yards south of Friends Road and terminating 28 yards north thereof.

Tramway No.31—1 furlong 1.5 chains double line commencing 50 yards north of Whitgift Street and terminating at George Street.

Tramway No.32—2 chains double line wholly in North End commencing 22 yards south of gates of Whitgift Grammar School and terminating 22 yards north thereof.

Tramway No.33—1 mile 3 furlongs 1 chain double line commencing in North End 66 yards north of Drummond Road and terminating in London Road at the commencement of Tramway No. 34.

Tramway No.34—1 mile 3 furlongs 1.8 chains of which 2 furlongs 4 chains double line commencing at the termination of Tramway No. 33 in London Road near the junction with Brigstock Road and terminating in London Road at Croydon's northern boundary on Hermitage Bridge by a sign marked "Eight Miles to the Royal Exchange".

Tramway No.35—3 furlongs 2.94 chains single line (for use in one direction only) commencing in Whitehorse Road near West Croydon Baptist Chapel (Spurgeon's Tabernacle) at the junction with St. James' Road, continuing along Wellesley Road and Station Road to a junction with Tramway No. 33 in North End. (Tramway No. 12 was used in the opposite direction.)

The Croydon & District Electric Tramways Act—1902

Details of Tramways permitted to be constructed:—

Croydon, Sutton & Mitcham Section.

Tramway No. 1 —Not approved.

Tramway No. 2 —3 furlongs 7.40 chains of which 2 furlongs 5.40 chains to be single line and 1 furlong 2 chains double line.
Commencing in London Road, Mitcham as a junction with Mitcham Light Railway No. 2 and continuing along the Mitcham-Sutton Road to the Mitcham-Morden boundary.

Tramway No. 3 —1 mile 1 furlong 3.50 chains of which 2 furlongs 5.40 chains to be single line and 3 furlongs 5.60 chains double line.
Commencing at the Mitcham-Morden boundary as a junction with Tramway No. 2 and terminating at the Carlshalton-Sutton boundary.

Tramway No. 4 —1 mile 5 furlongs 7.30 chains of which 1 mile 0 furlongs 1.30 chains to be single line and 5 furlongs 6.0 chains double line.
Commencing at the Carlshalton-Sutton boundary as a junction with Tramway No. 3 and terminating in Brighton Road Sutton at its junction with Wellesley Road.

Tramway No. 5 —1 mile 0 furlongs 5.40 chains of which 6 furlongs 0.40 chains to be single line and 2 furlongs 5.0 chains double line.
Commencing in Brighton Road Sutton as a junction with Tramway No. 4 and terminating in Brighton Road Sutton at the boundary of the Sutton U.D.C. near Belmont Station.

Tramways Nos. 5A & 5B —Not approved.

Tramway No. 6 —4 furlongs 4.72 chains of which 2 furlongs 6.40 chains to be single line and 1 furlong 9.0 chains double line.
Commencing in Benhill Street Sutton 28 yards east of the junction with Sutton High Street and terminating in Westmead Road at the Sutton-Carlshalton boundary.

Tramway No. 6A —2 chains all single line.
A curve connecting Tramway No. 4 in Sutton High Street with Tramway No. 6 in Benhill Street.

Tramway No. 6B 2 chains all single line.
Another connecting curve between Tramway No. 4 in Sutton High Street and Tramway No. 6 in Benhill Street.

Tramway No. 7 —Not approved.

Tramway No. 8 —Not approved.

Tramway No. 9 —Not approved.

Tramway No.10 —1 mile 3 furlongs 3.0 chains of which 6 furlongs 7.60 chains to be single line and 4 furlongs 5.40 chains double line.
Commencing in Stafford Road at the Croydon—Beddington boundary and terminating at North End Croydon at a junction with the existing Croydon Corporation Tramway.

Tramway No.10A —2 chains all single line.
A connecting curve between Tramway No. 10 and the existing Croydon Corporation Tramway at North End, Croydon.

Tramway No.11 —1 mile 5 furlongs 5.0 chains of which 1 mile 3.0 chains to be single line and 5 furlongs 1.90 chains double line.
Commencing in Lower Church Street, Croydon and terminating in Mitcham Road as a junction with Mitcham Light Railway No. 3.

Tramway No.11A —1.50 chains all single line.
A connecting curve between Elis David Place and Lower Church Street, Croydon, joining Tramways Nos. 10 and 11.

Tramway No.11B —1.50 chains all single line.
A connecting curve between Tamworth Road and Lower Church Street, Croydon, also joining Tramways Nos. 10 and 11.

Tramway No.12 —Not approved.

Tramway No.13 —Not approved.

Tramway No.14 —Not approved.

Croydon and Penge Section

Tramway No.15 —1 mile 0 furlongs 6.60 chains of which 3 furlongs 0.50 chains to be single line and 5 furlongs 6.10 chains double line.
Commencing at the junction of Westow Hill and Church Street, Upper Norwood (Crystal Palace) and passing along Anerley Hill, Thicket Road and Beckenham Road to Crampton Road (Penge Station LBSCR).

Tramway No.16 —3 furlongs 5.40 chains of which 2 furlongs 3.40 chains to be single line and one furlong 2.0 chains double line.
Commencing in Beckenham Road Penge at the termination of Tramway No. 15 and terminating in Beckenham Road 20 yards north of Croydon Road.

Tramway No.17 —2.30 chains all single line.
Commencing in Beckenham Road Penge at the termination of Tramway No. 16 and terminating in Beckenham Road 30 yards south-east of the junction with Croydon Road.

Tramway No.17A —1.40 chains all single line.
Connecting curve between Beckenham Road and Green Lane Penge, joining Tramways Nos. 17 and 22.

Tramway No.17B —1.20 chains double line.
Connecting curve between Beckenham Road and Croydon Road, joining Tramways Nos. 16 and 22.

Tramway No.17C —1.20 chains all single line.
Connecting curve between Beckenham Road and Green Lane, joining Tramways Nos. 17 and 22.

Tramway No.17D —1.60 chains all single line.
Connecting curve between Beckenham Road and Croydon Road, joining Tramways Nos. 18 and 21 at their terminations.

Tramway No.18 —1 furlong 9.0 chains of which 1 furlong 2.40 chains to be single line and 6.60 chains double line.
Commencing in Beckenham Road at the termination of Tramway No. 17 and continuing in Beckenham Road as far as the Beckenham/Penge Boundary.

Tramway No.19 —Not approved.
(From correspondence, this would appear to have been a continuation of Tramway No. 18 through Beckenham as far as Manor Road.)

Tramway No.20 —3 furlongs 6.90 chains of which 2 furlongs 0.30 chains to be single line and 1 furlong 6.60 chains double line.
Commencing in High Street South Norwood at the termination of the existing Croydon Corporation tramway and terminating at a junction with Tramway No. 21 at the Penge U.D.C. Boundary at Croydon Road.

Tramway No.21 —7 furlongs 4.80 chains of which 4 furlongs 7.30 chains to be single line and 2 furlongs 7.50 chains double line.
Entirely in Croydon Road Penge commencing at the Croydon Boundary as a junction with Tramway No. 20 and terminating at a point 30 yards south of Beckenham Road at a junction with Tramway No. 22.

Tramway No.22 —1 furlong 6.40 chains of which 9.60 chains to be single line and 6.80 chains double line.
Commencing in Croydon Road at the termination of Tramway No. 21 and terminating in Green Lane Penge at the Penge/Beckenham boundary.

The Croydon & District Electric Tramways (Extensions) Act—1903

Carlshalton Section

Tramway No. 1 —1 mile 2 furlongs 8.50 chains of which 5 furlongs 5.10 chains to be single line and 5 furlongs 3.40 chains double line.
Commencing at a junction with Tramway No. 6 of the 1902 Act in Westmead Road Carlshalton and terminating in Park Lane Wallington at the Wallington/Carlshalton boundary.

Tramway No. 2 —7 furlongs 7.60 chains of which 3 furlongs 7.10 chains to be single line and 4 furlongs 0.50 chains double line.
Commencing in Park Lane Wallington at the termination of Tramway No. 1 and terminating in Stafford Road at the Wallington/Beddington boundary at Elgin Road.

Tramway No. 3 —1 mile 0 furlongs 6.8 chains of which 6 furlongs 2.80 chains to be single line and 2 furlongs 4.00 chains double line.

Commencing in Stafford Road Wallington at the termination of Tramway No. 2 and terminating in Stafford Road at the Croydon Borough boundary and making a junction with Tramway No. 10 of the 1902 Act.

Penge Section

Tramway No. 4 —5 furlongs 2.30 chains of which 1 furlong 7.80 chains to be single line and 3 furlongs 4.50 chains double line.

Commencing in Anerley Road at Thicket Road by a junction with Tramway No. 15 of the 1902 Act and terminating in Anerley Road 22 yards north-west of Croydon Road.

Tramway No. 4A —2.00 chains double line.

A connecting curve between Tramway No. 4 and No. 15 of the 1902 Act in Thicket Road.

Tramway No. 5 —1 furlong 6.60 chains of which 3.10 chains to be single line and 1 furlong 3.50 chains double line.

Commencing in Anerley Road at the termination of Tramway No. 4 and terminating in Elmers End Road at the Penge/ Beckenham boundary.

(This line would have crossed Tramway No. 21 of the 1902 Act at right angles.)

Tramway No. 5A —1.30 chains single line.

A connecting curve between Tramways Nos. 4 and 21 of the 1902 Act.

Tramway No. 5B —1.60 chains double line.

Another connecting curve between Tramways Nos. 4 and 21 (1902).

Trolleybus Powers

Just as one needed Parliamentary powers to operate tramways, so one also needed Powers to construct a trolleybus layout and operate vehicles thereon. The various sections into which a proposed line was divided, were not described as "Tramways", but to the same effect as "Routes".

Croydon Corporation presented a Bill to Parliament in 1924, seeking powers to undertake various municipal activities, but included in it, proposals for trolley vehicles to Addiscombe. These were:—

Route No. 1 —Commencing in George Street, Croydon at its junction with the High Street and proceeding along George Street, Addiscombe Road, Cherry Orchard Road, Lower Addiscombe Road, Spring Lane, to Portland Road at Woodside Green.

Route No. 1A—Commencing at the junction of George Street with High Street and proceeding along High Street, Katharine Street and Park Lane to George Street, making junctions with Route No. 1 at both ends.

Route No. 1B—Commencing at the junction of Morland Road with Cherry Orchard Road and proceeding along Morland Road to Woodside Green and Portland Road, again making junctions with Route No. 1 at both ends.

Plans of turning loops were to be submitted to the Ministry of Transport.

As predicted when London Transport came into being, it submitted a Bill to Parliament early in 1934, asking for very far reaching Trolleybus Powers. These too had to be submitted in the form of separate "Routes" even though some were of considerable length.

The Sutton-West Croydon-Crystal Palace section was set out as follows:—

Route No.14 —Commencing at a junction of the Crystal Palace Parade with Anerley Hill and following the existing tram route to a junction of Benhill Avenue with Benhill Street in Sutton.

Route No.14A —Commencing at the junction of Benhill Avenue and Benhill Street, and proceeding along Benhill Street and High Street, Sutton to a turning loop round a traffic island, by the Green at the junction of High Street and Bushey Road.

In subsequent correspondence between C. G. Page, the Secretary of London Transport and E. B. Hart of the Ministry of Transport, it was agreed that Workmen's fares would apply on trolleybuses and stated that the Minister insisted on a proper traffic roundabout at the top of Anerley Hill. Mr. Hart also had considerable misgivings about the section in Sutton High Street, but could suggest no alternative turning facilities there. Another roundabout had to be constructed where Stafford Road crossed Purley Way (Croydon Bypass).

Very little of what became trolleybus service 630 was covered by the above Act, The Lawn, Shepherds Bush Green, was Route 12A and Tamworth Road and Station Road, West Croydon were already covered by Route 14. The rest of this long route was all the subject of later legislation, mainly the London Transport Act 1936.

Appendix C — BIOGRAPHIES

A. V. MASON, A.M.I.E.E.—Manager & Engineer 1908-1918.
South Metropolitan Electric Tramways & Lighting Company Limited.

Archibald Victor Mason was educated at Sherborne School and became a pupil at the Brush Electrical Engineering Works in 1898. Brush was associated with the British Electric Traction Co., to which Mr. Mason transferred as Resident Engineer at Kidderminster. Later he was at West Hartlepool. In 1899 became Secretary to the Manager of Nelson Tramways, British Columbia, which he described as the smallest tramway system in the world. He supervised the track laying of Belfast Corporation Tramways and became Manager of Devonport & District Tramways, in 1903.

On the resignation of Mr. G. Ratcliffe Hulme in July 1908*, Mr. Mason became Manager and Engineer of the South Metropolitan tramways and lighting, and the company's former engineer C. W. Durnford took his place at Devonport. Mr. Mason remained in charge of the S.M.E.T. throughout the 1914-1918 war. Owing to wartime difficulties in placing trolley wheels on the wires in the blackout and the consequent danger to upper deck passengers, he had hoops fitted over the ends of the upper decks of all cars, starting in August 1916.

Late in 1918, C. J. Spencer was appointed Manager of the UndergrounD Group's other two tramway systems, with the intention that he should take over all three. Therefore an alternative post had to be found for Mr. Mason and on 18 December, he was appointed Assistant Manager and Engineer to all three companies§. The Electricity Department of the South Metropolitan Co., passed to other hands in 1932 and in July Mr. Mason received an annuity in compensation for severance. On the formation of the London Passenger Transport Board in 1933, Mr. Mason became Chief Engineer (Tramways). He retired from London Transport in July 1939, and died in 1948 aged 74.

---

* Gilbert Ratcliffe Hulme then became a Director of several other Companies in the B.E.T. Group.
§ A. V. Mason became Deputy General Manager and Engineer on 28 January 1921.

T. B. GOODYER O.B.E., A.I.E.E., M.Inst.T.—Tramways Manager—1902-1928
Croydon Corporation Tramways.

Thomas Boyce Goodyer was born in Edinburgh in 1865, where his father was Traffic Manager of the horse tramways. He was educated at the Royal High School and started work as a junior clerk in the Solicitor's Department of the Edinburgh Street Tramways Co. In 1884, he spent several months in the Traffic Office of the London Road Car. Co., which he left in 1885 to become Manager and Secretary of the Northampton Street Tramways Co. (in which Jabez Balfour had an interest). From here Mr. Goodyer transferred to the West Metropolitan Tramways Co. (later part of the London United Tramways) in 1887.

His stay there was short, as in October he was appointed Assistant Traffic Manager of the Birmingham Central Tramways and was promoted to Traffic Manager in 1894. Early in 1898, he was appointed General Traffic Superintendent to the British Electric Traction Co., evidently a roving commission, in which he visited various systems then under construction and also visited the United States of America and Canada. He was a member of the General Committee of the British Electrical Friendly Society.

Still with the B.E.T., he became General Manager at Croydon in February 1902 and supervised the development of the system. He was so well thought of in Croydon that in 1903, he was elected a member of the Council of the Croydon Chamber of Commerce. With the break up of the Corporation/B.E.T. Agreement on 1 June 1906, he was invited to remain with the Corporation as "Tramways Manager", which he accepted, bringing nearly all the staff with him.

He appears to have taken rather more interest in the well-being of his staff than many other tramway managers. He and his wife always supported all the Tramways' sporting events, concerts and annual dinners, at which he gave hair-raising accounts of events in the early days of electric traction. He became a Life Governor of Croydon Hospital in 1907, arranged a Sick Benefit scheme for C.C.T. employees in the same year. He had a recreation room laid out at Thornton Heath in 1909 and rifle ranges in both depôts.

For many years he was Secretary of the Municipal Tramways Association and was elected President in September 1918. In that capacity he advocated a "Traffic Board for Greater London", not to take over, but to regulate the activities of the less responsible operators. He was made a Member of the Order of the British Empire in the 1920 Honours List, for war work.

He retired from Croydon Corporation Tramways on 30 September 1928, aged 62, after piloting the system through a successful post-war reconstruction. He was retained by the Corporation as a Consultant at a fee of £500 per annum and took on a part time post as Municipal Sales Manager to Tilling—Stevens Ltd., the Maidstone manufacturer of petrol-electric buses. He underwent a serious operation in July 1931. He had an operation for cataract in July 1932 and gave up his business connections in February 1933. He died 23 July 1940, at South Croydon, aged 75, following a fall caused by failing eyesight.

"Tommy" Goodyer was described as one of the Great men among British tramways managers and was a genial dapper Scot with a pointed beard and waxed moustache. He proved a very astute and capable manager at Croydon. His son, Leonard B. Goodyer qualified as a Chartered Accountant in 1920 and during the war, was appointed Deputy Chief Censor, with the rank of Major in March 1940.

C. J. SPENCER O.B.E., M.I.E.E., M. Inst.T. General Manager—Tramways.
London & Suburban Traction Company Ltd.   1918-1933

Christopher John Spencer was born at Halifax in December 1875 and like Mr. Goodyer, he was the son of a tramway manager. He began work as a pupil on the Blackpool conduit tramways in 1889 and in 1892, became electrician to the South Staffordshire Tramways, where his father was resident Engineer. In 1898 at the early age of 22, he became General Manager of Bradford Corporation Tramways. During his twenty years at Bradford, he designed with the help of his father, the Spencer Slipper Brake, later to be found on any tramway in Great Britain which had any steep gradients. He also designed the Spencer-Dawson Oil Brake, an automatic colour light signal system for single track working and special cars which could change gauge for the Bradford-Leeds route, no mean achievement. He was shot at by a maniac, who fortunately missed, in December 1909. He was President of the Municipal Tramways Association in 1909/10.

Early in 1917, he was seconded to the Admiralty for the "Duration" to advise on staff control matters and no doubt while there must have come into contact with Sir Albert Stanley, (later Lord Ashfield), Chairman of the Board of Trade. Throughout 1918, Bradford Corporation continued to press for Mr. Spencer's release, to return and manage their tramways. Like Mr. Goodyer he became an O.B.E. in 1920, for war work.

Lord Ashfield returned to the UndergrounD Group in the capacity of Chairman and top management underwent a shake-up in the Autumn of 1918, following the resignation of Mr. Pott, Manager of the Metropolitan Electric Tramways. It appears that Mr. Spencer was invited in August to become Manager of the London & Suburban Traction Co. Ltd., that facet of the group that controlled the three tramway companies. His appointment dated from 1 November, at first only included the Metropolitan and London United Tramways, but on 18 December, his responsibilities were enlarged to include the South Metropolitan, their former manager, A. V. Mason, having accepted the post of Assistant Manager and Engineer to the three companies. On 28 January 1921, the importance of Mr. Spencer's post was increased and he was designated General Manager—Tramways.

When the London Passenger Transport Board was formed in 1933, the tramways department was divided into two areas "North & West" and "South & East". Mr. Spencer was appointed General Manager—North & West, with T. E. Thomas of the L.C.C. in charge of South & East. Mr. Spencer invented the Time Recording Charts, displayed in the foyer of 55 Broadway, showing the interval between underground trains at certain points and trams at Golders Green.

The North Metropolitan Electric Power Supply Co. Ltd. had to be separated from the other activities of the UndergrounD Group and did not pass to the LPTB. Mr. Spencer retired from the services of the LPTB in October 1933 and in November 1933, he was appointed Resident Director of the "NorthmeT", at Brimsdown near Enfield. He lived at Langley Park, Beckenham.

Before taking up his duties with them, he went on a tour of South Africa departing on 2 February 1934. He went specifically to advise Johannesburg and subsequently, their trams and trolleybuses showed many signs of his influence. While in Africa, he visited Bloemfontein and other places.

He retired from the "NorthmeT" in January 1941 and moved to Swansea. He died in 1950 aged 74.

G. V. STANLEY—Tramways Manager—Croydon Corporation—1928-1933.

Gordon Valentine Stanley was born in Croydon on 14 February 1889 and joined Croydon Corporation Tramways as an Engineering Assistant at the age of 17 in 1904. On the retirement of H. B. Harris, the Tramways Engineer in 1913, Gordon Stanley was appointed Assistant Engineer in charge of rolling stock and overhead lines. He reported to the Borough Engineer, who took direct charge of track maintenance.

On the retirement of Mr. Goodyer on 30 September 1928, Mr. Stanley was appointed Acting Manager. He was confirmed as Tramways Manager late in October.

When Croydon Corporation Tramways were taken over by the London Passenger Transport Board on 1 July 1933, Mr. Stanley received a letter of appreciation from the Mayor on his departure. He was allocated to an Engineering appointment at Chiswick Works, but in 1935, thanks to his experience in overhead wiring suspension, he was transferred to the Electrical Department and described as a Constructional Engineer, to supervise trolleybus overhead wiring in West London. "Transport World" for 2 May 1936, states "Mr. G. V. Stanley of London Transport has just recovered consciousness after sustaining a triple fractured skull in an accident and remained unconscious for ten days". While he had been carrying out a survey in Uxbridge Road, Southall, assisted by Mr. L. Marriott also ex-Croydon Corporation, both and others had been knocked down by a car that swerved onto the pavement to avoid a cyclist. Mr. Stanley who was aged 49 at the time, spent twelve months in hospital.

His long absence following this accident evidently put him out of the running for further promotion and on recovery he became Assistant Divisional Electrical Engineer at Camberwell, with the grade of Executive Assistant. He retired on 20 March 1954.

He died at Worthing in February 1979 aged 90. He had two daughters, the son of one of whom, now performs duties in the Public Relations Office of London Transport, similar to those undertaken by Mr. Morgan and the present writer in the 1950s.

G. D. MORGAN—Assistant Manager & Chief Clerk—Croydon Corporation Tramways 1922-1933

Graham Doran Morgan was a native of Swansea who served in the Royal Navy during the 1914-1918 war. He once mentioned that the whole of his service was in Taranto, Italy and Malta, both of which had British owned tramway systems at the time.

On demobilization, he joined Aberdare Corporation Tramways in a clerical capacity. On the sudden death of H. E. Smith in 1922, he was appointed Chief Clerk to Croydon Corporation Tramways and took up residence in Norbury. When Mr. Goodyer retired in September 1928, Mr. Stanley was appointed Tramways Manager, with Mr. Morgan as his deputy. He retained the duties of Chief Clerk and was directly responsible to the Borough Accountant for pay and other financial matters.

On the formation of the London Passenger Transport Board in July 1933, Mr. Morgan was allocated to a post in the Traffic Development Office at 55 Broadway. That was moved to Griffith House, Marylebone Road on the outbreak of war in 1939. Late in the war, he was promoted to an Executive post in the Public Relations Office at 55 Broadway and acted as one of the two deputy Public Relations Officers. The present writer worked directly under him from 1947 to 1955.

He retired in 1956 and died in December 1978, aged 84, He had one daughter, Gwyneth, who although a secretary at the Institution of Electrical Engineers, followed the Croydon Corporation tradition of entertainment and through her father took leading soprano parts for the London Transport Players in the 1950s*. Mr. Morgan is believed to have been accomplished on the church organ.

Morgan is a common Welsh name meaning "Sailor" and he is not thought to have been related to E. F. Morgan the original Borough Surveyor of Croydon or to W. P. Morgan who later became Operating Manager (Central Buses), but there were some embarassing incidents when they were mistaken for each other. Mr. Morgan had a great gift for making pronouncements in mixed metaphors. He once returned a letter to the writer and said "I want you to expand this, but be as brief as possible". He told a colleague "with his tongue in both cheeks" that he was "hanging his hat on a sheet anchor".

* There was a portrait of Gwyneth Morgan in "London Transport Magazine" for October 1951 on page 2.

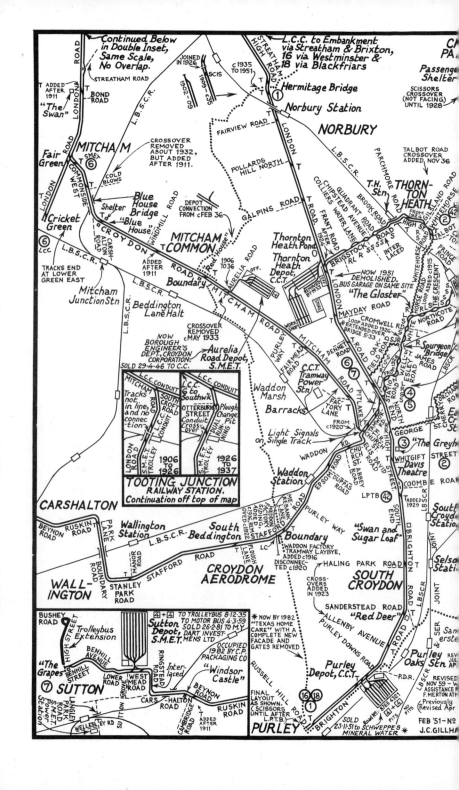